THE CASE OF THE MARRIED WOMAN

Also by Antonia Fraser

Non-Fiction

Fiction

THE CASE OF THE MARRIED WOMAN

*Caroline Norton and
Her Fight for Women's Justice*

Antonia Fraser

PEGASUS BOOKS

NEW YORK LONDON

THE CASE OF THE MARRIED WOMAN

Pegasus Books, Ltd.
148 West 37th Street, 13th Floor
New York, NY 10018

First Pegasus Books cloth edition May 2022

ISBN: 978-1-63936-157-1

10 9 8 7 6 5 4 3 2 1

Printed in the United States of America
Distributed by Simon & Schuster
www.pegasusbooks.com

To RONKE

my sister

and in memory of

KEVIN

CONTENTS

NOTE ON NAMES

In view of the profusion of similar names and surnames, as for example Caroline and Richard, Norton and Sheridan, I have taken certain decisions, intended to be helpful, listed below. These characters will be granted sole rights to these particular names; everyone else will have their name qualified in some way.

Caroline Caroline Norton, née Sheridan

Norton George Norton, husband of Caroline

Fletcher Fletcher Spencer Conyers Norton, first son of the above (referred to sometimes as Spencer, but Fletcher is used here)

Brin (Brinny) Thomas Brinsley Norton, second son

Willie William Charles Chapple Norton, third son

Richard Richard Norton, son of Brin, grandson of Caroline

Grantley Fletcher Norton, 3rd Lord Grantley, brother of George Norton

Mrs Sheridan Henrietta Caroline, mother of Caroline

Tom Sheridan Thomas Sheridan, father

Brinsley Sheridan Richard Brinsley Sheridan, brother of Caroline

Richard Brinsley Sheridan Playwright, grandfather of Caroline

Lady Caroline Lady Caroline Lamb, wife of William Lamb, later Lord Melbourne

FAMILY TREE I (simplified) of SHERIDANS and NORTONS
(Barons GRANTLEY) showing their connection

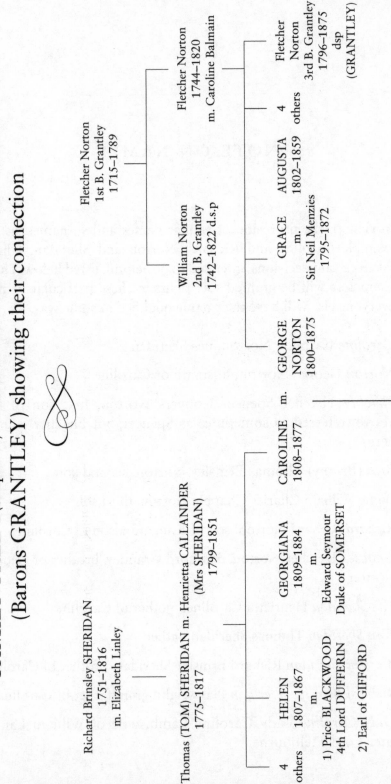

FAMILY TREE II (simplified)

CAROLINE m.1827 GEORGE
1808–1877   NORTON
                   1800–1875

William (WILLIE) Norton
1833–1842

FLETCHER Norton
1829–1859

Brinsley (BRIN) Norton
1831–1877
4th B. GRANTLEY m. 1854 MARIUCCA Federigo
                        1837–1892

CARLOTTA Norton
1854–1931

RICHARD Norton
1855–1943
5th B. GRANTLEY

→

BARONS GRANTLEY

NOTE ON MONEY

I have from time to time given rough estimates of the value of particular sums in our own day, using round figures for convenience. The website of the Bank of England provides a proper detailed guide.

AUTHOR'S NOTE

My interest in Caroline Norton springs from her role as an outstanding campaigner in an area of much-needed reform, that of a married woman's rights, not only in terms of property but specifically those of a mother. It follows my two previous studies of nineteenth-century reforms: parliamentary representation in *Perilous Question: The Drama of the Great Reform Bill 1832* and Catholic Emancipation in *The King and the Catholics: The Fight for Rights 1829*. *The Case of the Married Woman* is thus in a sense the third in a trilogy; although I hope it also stands independently as a biography of a remarkable person who was incidentally a woman.

Throughout I have tried to bear in mind the values of the mid-nineteenth century. Caroline's attitudes to several issues – notably the equality of women – are not those of our own day. But it is surely important to judge historical characters by the standards of their own time, while recognizing and applauding the changes that have taken place.

Antonia Fraser
10 October 2020

She Does Not Exist

'*She does not exist: her husband exists . . .*'

Caroline Norton, *English Laws for Women in the Nineteenth Century*, 1854

WHEN CAROLINE SHERIDAN, later known as Caroline Norton, was born in 1808, George III was on the throne. A married woman under the law had no rights at all. Caroline herself put it succinctly in one of her campaigning pamphlets printed in the mid-nineteenth century. In the case of a married woman: 'She does not exist: her husband exists.'[1]

Due to his encroaching madness, George III was succeeded by his eldest son as Prince Regent in 1811. Caroline grew up in the turbulent time of reformation and change which followed the ending of the Napoleonic Wars at Waterloo four years later. When she was in her early twenties, Catholic Emancipation in 1829 under the Regent, now George IV, resulted in the restoration of civil rights to Catholics. The parliamentary reform of 1832 under George's brother, William IV, changed the face of the House of Commons. Women, on the other hand – notably married women – remained without any effective rights and the pace of change, when it came, was slow and spasmodic, while change itself was strongly contested.

The process by which a man automatically extinguished the rights of a woman by wedding her began with the marriage service itself. It has been pointed out by feminists from the early nineteenth century onwards that there was indeed an 'extraordinary irony' here, by which the man promised to endow his wife with all his worldly goods during the very ceremony by which he actually received all *her* worldly goods without committing his own in any way.[2]

This was a patriarchal society. Although by 1790 women could carry on a separate business and hold and manage property, wives still needed their husband's permission. It would be relevant to the story of Caroline Norton that, although there were published married women writers, the copyright of their works – and thus their financial earnings – belonged legally to their husband.

There was a dangerous corollary – from the woman's point of view – to this lack of legal existence: mothers had no rights over their children. That is to say, married mothers had no rights, all of which were vested in the husband, who was the legal father. Bizarrely, from the point of view of the morality so often preached by lawmakers, unmarried mothers did have rights over their illegitimate children, who lacked a legal father.

As to the later preoccupation concerning women voting, not only did this play no part in the reforming Act of 1832, but there was further a backward step by which a widow's legal right to her dower (her money on her husband's death) was abolished; the loophole by which property-owning widows and spinsters sometimes voted in certain local elections was stopped by the Municipal Corporations Act of 1835. The opinion of a late-eighteenth-century radical has been quoted as summing up the prevalent attitude to female suffrage: parliamentary election was 'an essential part of dominion, and . . . the female is by a law of nature put under the dominion of the male'.[3]

It was part of the patriarchal picture of the late eighteenth century that Edmund Burke was able to write of the beauty of women being 'considerably owing to their weakness or delicacy and . . . even enhanced by their timidity'. Of course, there was wishful thinking here, as well as a narrow perspective. Women took part in riots even if they were not the same class of women whose delicacy Burke admired. Gallantry, publicly expressed, was the accompaniment to this perceived delicacy. In the words of *Fraser's Magazine*, a leading periodical, in 1831, printing a polite review of Caroline Norton's work: 'We think that a lady ought to be treated, even by Reviewers, with the utmost deference.'[4]

Gallantry apart, the harsh words addressed by a husband to his wife in one of Caroline Norton's novels, *Stuart of Dunleath*, published in 1851, were not in fact exaggerated: 'Everything that's yours is mine. The clothes you have on, the chain round your neck, the rings you have on, are mine. The law don't admit a married woman has a right to a farthing's worth of property.'[5]

The importance of any individual campaign – based, as in this case, on personal suffering – in bringing about change, versus the inexorable sweep of history, is eternally arguable. Caroline Norton herself was well aware of the composite nature of reform. As she put it in 1851: 'We are all ants moving our grains of sand to make a roadway – and by little and little the roadway will be seen – plain broad and direct – tho' the ants were swept away unnoticed.'[6]

This is the story of one individual worker on the roadway, whose whole life bore witness to the undeniable fact that a married woman did exist.

PART ONE

STARRY NIGHT

'I saw "Starry Night" yesterday'

Caroline Norton, described by Disraeli, 1833

CHAPTER ONE

Child in a Dark Wood

'This is not a child I would care to meet in a dark wood!'

Richard Brinsley Sheridan on his granddaughter Caroline, 1811

THE STORY OF Caroline Norton begins, appropriately, in an atmosphere of romance. This romance was provided by the elopement of her parents to Gretna Green in order to get married in 1805.

There was also, as it happens, an element of scandal. Caroline Elizabeth Sheridan was born on 22 March 1808. Her father Tom Sheridan was involved in a legal case of 'Criminal Conversation', or Crim. Con. (in other words, adultery) at the time of her conception and during the months of Mrs Sheridan's pregnancy. Finally, Tom Sheridan was found guilty and condemned to pay damages to the husband for his affair with a married woman three years earlier, before he himself was married.

Returning to the atmosphere of romance, everything about the Sheridan family was romantic – unless a stern line was taken about Irish blood, that is. There was no doubt that Irish blood frequently got a bad press during this period, and continued to do so throughout Caroline Sheridan's lifetime.

If the Irish themselves were commonly described as 'barbarous' or barbarian, from the Latin word *barbarus* for stranger (although it was actually the English who were the strangers in the land), Irish blood merited a more sophisticated judgement. A great deal of charm was involved – the writer Bulwer Lytton called it 'the Irish cordiality of manner' – and an element of frivolity was there too. On one occasion, apologizing for her own light-heartedness at some dire moment, Caroline turned aside criticism: 'Forgive my jesting . . . I feel sincerely anxious for your anxiety . . . but Irish blood *will* dance.'[1]

On the other hand, the light could be suffused with dark: Caroline was well aware of the tragic history of Erin, as the land of her ancestors was sometimes known. One of her own poems, 'A Dream of Erin', concerned a 'creature seen in thin air':

> 'Twas Erin's genius – well her voice I know
> Half wail – half music – sad but tender too
> England, I call thee from a land of slaves!
> Hear, tyrant sister!

Fortunately, the dream ends less tragically with the tyrant sister transformed: 'England and Erin mingling hearts and hands.'[2]

Certainly, where the blood of Sheridans of Caroline's generation was concerned, England and Ireland were mingled. An early biographer of Caroline's celebrated grandfather, the playwright Richard Brinsley Sheridan, speculated whether 'that singular compound of brilliancy, mercurial temper, carelessness, and solid and enduring hard work' was not due to the mixture of English and Irish blood.[3] Caroline's grandmother, his lovely actress wife Elizabeth Ann Linley, was English. And significantly, as we will see, Caroline's own mother – the wife of Tom Sheridan, the former Henrietta Callander – was actually Scottish. Despite being born in Dublin, she was brought up in Scotland among her relations, part of a Lowland Scottish family.

The result was that Caroline would grow up with a particular love of Scotland, which she came to know early on in her life. (Her first visit to Ireland came much later.) Over the years, she began to associate Scotland with tranquillity. As she wrote of Pitlochry in the Highlands late in life, after driving there in 'sweet chequered moonlight', there was still peace '*somewhere in the world*'. Yet Caroline still considered herself, like all the Sheridans, to be Irish, 'an Irish disembodied spirit', as she put it to an intimate friend at a low point in her dramatic story, when she confessed herself as feeling at a distance from her life, caring about nothing.[4]

Richard Brinsley Sheridan, author of *The School for Scandal* among other plays, manager and owner of the Drury Lane Theatre, Whig MP from 1780 onwards, friend of Charles James Fox and *bon viveur* beloved in the dissolute circle around the Prince of Wales, was born in Dublin in 1751. Although his last years had been harassed by debts once he lost his protective parliamentary seat, when he died in London in 1816 he was buried in Poets' Corner, Westminster Abbey – a measure of his celebrity.

Despite this fame, the strong dramatic connection meant that his descendants had a whiff of the stage about them, along with an impressive reputation for brilliance: 'the transmission of talent from generation to generation in the Sheridan family is really wonderful,' wrote William Maginn, the editor of *Fraser's Magazine*, who was not always so complimentary about others.[5] But the connection to the stage at this period was not considered to be totally respectable: George Canning, for example, the Tory politician who became Prime Minister in 1827, was sneered at for having an actress mother.

Richard Brinsley Sheridan's own marriage to Elizabeth Linley began with an elopement when he was twenty-one (which would turn out to be something of a Sheridan habit). Tom Sheridan, the father of Caroline, was their son. He fully shared the charm and talent to amuse for which the great playwright was famous in society. Disraeli's father, having known both Sheridans, told Caroline's sister Helen in 1833 that while her grandpapa was certainly a very amusing old gentleman, it was her father Tom that 'I have not forgotten'; his gaiety, like a fountain, was at the same time 'sparkling and ceaseless'.[6]

Richard Brinsley Sheridan also had a son, Charles, by a subsequent marriage following the death of Elizabeth Linley – Caroline's half-uncle. A man of great charm and a diplomat who was 'an enchanting companion', Charles Sheridan had a house in Mayfair and was thus able to help her at a vital moment in her life.

Another important aspect of Caroline's family was its writing tradition, which included the women as well as the celebrated playwright himself. Women writers were part of the literary landscape at this time: the bestselling writers of the period were in fact women such as Mrs Gaskell and George Eliot. The most famous example today, Jane Austen, published four novels in the first years of Caroline's life, including *Pride and Prejudice* in 1813, when Caroline would have been five. Richard Brinsley Sheridan's mother had been a writer. Her own mother, Mrs Sheridan, wrote poetry and several novels including *Carwell* (1830) and *Oonagh Lynch* (1833). Early on in her life it was natural for Caroline, in turn, to believe that she was a writer.

The younger Sheridans already had a two-year-old son, Brinsley, to whom the Prince of Wales was godfather, when Caroline was born. There would be two further boys, Frank and Charlie, born in 1815 and 1817 respectively, who lived to adulthood, Charlie being described by the actress Fanny Kemble admiringly in a general encomium on the Sheridan family as 'a sort of younger brother of Apollo Belvedere'.[7] Another brother, Tommy, died as a young midshipman in the Navy at the age of fifteen, inspiring lines in Caroline's later poems:[8]

He hath fallen asleep – that beautiful boy . . .
Blow, ye loud winds! roll on, thou restless main!
For he we loved will *never* sail again!

It was, however, Caroline's two sisters who were the vital elements in her family story, not only as a child but for the rest of her life. The closeness began with their births: all three girls were born within three years: Helen on 18 January 1807 and Georgiana, known as Georgia, on 5 November 1809, with Caroline, on 22 March 1808, in the middle.

The spectacle of three good-looking sisters – inevitably described as Graces – has always provoked an ecstatic reaction in observers: the Sheridans were no exception to this rule. In 1833, when they were in their twenties, the artist Benjamin Robert Haydon exclaimed in his Diary: 'I never saw three such beautiful women, so perfectly without the airs of Beauty – unaffected, witty, aimable [sic], bewitching, wickedly mischievous, and innocently wicked.' Charles Dickens, who knew them, described the three women as 'sights for the Gods, as they always have been'. Caroline herself was known to reflect complacently, looking round a drawing room 'resplendent with the light of Sheridan beauty male and female': 'Yes, we are rather a good-looking family.'[9]

In this case, the Irish blood added a piquancy to the contemporary picture of the Graces. They quickly earned a reputation for being amusing, not always in a respectable manner. As early as 1827, when the sisters were comparatively new to society, Lady Cowper, the lover and later wife of Lord Palmerston, reported that the Sheridans were much admired; but they were 'strange girls, [who] swear and say all sorts of things to make the men laugh'. She also expressed surprise that 'a woman as Mrs Sheridan should let them go on so'. The explanation was cynical, if not Sheridan-phobic: 'I suppose she cannot stop the old blood coming out.'[10]

What frequently followed was the rating of the individual women compared to each other. Georgia generally won on sheer looks, a judgement confirmed by a story that the Emperor of Russia asked her to sit still for two minutes so that he might just look at her: 'as he should never see anything so beautiful again'.[11]

Helen was generally awarded the prize for grace and gentle charm, in Haydon's words again, 'a most enchanting creature, great talent, and yet not masculine': a sincere compliment at that time which, as we shall see, her sister Caroline did not always receive. Yet even she was described as having 'a share of egotism like all the blood of Sheridan'. It was the young Benjamin Disraeli who was the recipient of Helen's mock-modest description of the three sisters: 'she told me she was nothing. "You see Georgy's the beauty, and Carry's the wit and I ought to be the good one and am not." [12]

What, then, of Caroline? There was from the first something strange, mysterious even, about Caroline Sheridan long before she was transformed into Caroline Norton. How much of it was based on her undeniably exotic appearance, is impossible to quantify; yet it must have played its part, since even in infancy it aroused startled reactions: 'a queer dark-looking little baby,' in the words of her own mother. As an adult, the unusual cast of her beauty would call forth admiring comments. In 1839, the distinguished American lawyer Charles Sumner wrote that there was something 'tropical' (his italics) in her look: 'it is so intensely bright and burning.' [13] But the enormous, heavy-lidded dark eyes, black brows and thick lustrous dark hair, which in an adult would arouse admiring comparisons to Greek, Italian, even biblical beauty, made her a strange-looking child where she had been an odd-looking baby.

Caroline actually resembled her father Tom strongly. Richard Brinsley Sheridan had what were described as 'fine eyes'. These looks may have been inherited from his mother, Frances Chamberlaine, whose eyes were 'remarkably fine and very dark, corresponding with the colour of her hair which was very black'. Frances would also have a 'high' complexion in later years, a quality her great-granddaughter inherited, while there was another similarity with 'the fairness and beauty of her bust, neck and arms [which] were allowed to have seldom been rivalled'. [14]

Whether he recognized the dark eyes of his own mother or not, Richard Brinsley Sheridan made a somewhat equivocal pronouncement when presented with his three-year-old grand-daughter towards the end of his life: 'This is not a child I would care to meet in a dark wood!' It is to be hoped he recognized a quality of strength, as well as an unexpected threat, in the tiny girl. In the dark woods which lay ahead for the future Caroline Norton, she would certainly need strength. [15]

The Sheridans as a family undoubtedly had glamour. But they did not have money. That is to say, as a generalization, Sheridans did not have a lucky touch with money. Richard Brinsley

Sheridan's debts, which have been mentioned, were a feature of his colourful life. There were no great landed estates, or indeed much land at all, where rents and produce would have provided for their way of life. Tom Sheridan was also plagued by debts.

Mrs Sheridan, the former Henrietta Callander, was delightful and talented according to all reports, if somewhat more reserved than her daughters; she was still 'very young and pretty' in her fifties, in the words of one observer, the youthful Disraeli.[16] Her elopement with Tom, however, had been for love, not money. Where Tom's daughters were concerned, this lack of substantial funding was one factor in their potential marriages. They were certainly not in that highly desirable marital category of heiresses; on the contrary, the dowries that would come with them were liable to be essentially modest. This made the other factors – beauty, grace and the unquantifiable element of sex appeal – of vital importance.

In Caroline's childhood, the first entry into the dark wood came as a result of her father's debts. His efforts to become an MP were unsuccessful. In 1806, Richard Brinsley Sheridan secured him a non-residential post connected to Ireland in the Whig ministry shortly before it fell. But the Sheridan finances tied up in the Drury Lane Theatre went from bad to worse. Tom Sheridan was also both extravagant and a gambler, a lethal combination, if all too frequently found. He was arrested for debt a few months after Caroline was born and sent to prison for a short period. The next year, the Drury Lane Theatre, which represented the major Sheridan asset, burnt down.

At the same time there was another hovering threat over Caroline's childhood of a very different nature. This was her father's health. Just as the fascinating Sheridans did not enjoy stable finances, they also did not benefit from hereditary good health. Too many deaths of close relations, including Tom's own mother, resulted from lung disease or consumption. The milder air of the Continent was the traditional remedy for this condition and Tom Sheridan began to make trips abroad for his health to places such as Spain and Madeira.

Finally, his condition worsened to the point when his father began to despair. 'He so reminds me of his mother,' wrote Richard Brinsley Sheridan, 'and his feeble way of speaking deprives me of all hope.'[17] Through the favour of the King's younger son, the Duke of York, Tom was given the post of Postmaster-General at the Cape of Good Hope. He left for the more salubrious climate of South Africa with his wife and Helen, their eldest daughter, in September 1813. He was not expected to return.

Tom himself shared this gloomy conviction. 'I shall have but twenty months to live,' he predicted to an old friend on the eve of his departure. In fact, Tom lived until September 1817. But the family banshee, in which an earlier Sheridan, Elizabeth, had believed so devoutly, if it wailed beneath the walls of his house, found him still in South Africa.[18]

This was a dark wood for any child. The last Caroline saw of her father was at the age of five and a half. The natural male protector of her youth vanished forever. With the other, younger children, she was despatched to Scotland to the unmarried Callander sisters of Mrs Sheridan. Here they would be cared for at her old home, Ardkinglas in Argyllshire on the edge of Loch Fyne, and later Craigforth near Stirling. Despite its tragic background, the sojourn gave Caroline a lifelong love of the country.[19]

Subsequently, Caroline's first lessons were given to her at a neighbouring house, Glenrossie, and shared with the young son of Lord Kinnaird. What must have been a boy's traditional education – far superior to that offered to girls – could certainly have caused no harm to a bright child like Caroline.

The next challenge was the children's return to London, escorted by their aunts. Now Brinsley, Caroline, Georgia and Tommy met their mother again after four years: their mother, a widow. Mrs Sheridan brought with her not only Helen, but also the two youngest boys who had actually been born out there, Charlie a few months before his father's death. It was Helen, of them all, who experienced an historic encounter on the journey. The boat stopped at a large island en route from the Cape of Good Hope. Helen, aged eleven, found herself staring at an immensely stout man in a straw hat. The island was St Helena and the man was Napoleon.[20]

The new life of the Sheridan family was to be a great deal more gracious than the deliberately remote exile of the Emperor. Through the influence once again of the benevolent Duke of York, who had been Tom's friend, Mrs Sheridan was granted a so-called grace-and-favour apartment in Hampton Court Palace, a few miles outside London.

Hampton Court Palace has been described as 'one of the world's most intriguing buildings' given that it is really two palaces, the sixteenth-century Tudor building constructed by Cardinal Wolsey and Henry VIII, and the Baroque palace commissioned by William and Mary at the end of the seventeenth century. The result for the Sheridans was a mixture of Tudor brick and huge, light windows designed by Christopher Wren.[21]

Mrs Sheridan took up residence in October 1820 when Caroline was twelve, in the apartments known as Suite XXXVI.* On the north side of the palace, with a view over Tennis Court Lane (as well as the German kitchen introduced by the first Hanoverian monarch, George I), it was spacious enough to satisfy the needs of a young, physically active family. The English Court had stopped using the palace in 1737, leaving it free for what Dickens in *Little Dorrit* described as 'the gypsies of gentility'; less romantically, the inhabitants were generally the widows of public men and other retired people like diplomats who wanted to be part of society yet, in a dignified fashion, apart from it. Children were, however, not unusual, given the young age of widowhood at the time.

Here at Hampton Court, Caroline, together with her brothers and sisters, would now enjoy a real family life – short of a father – for six years. The public were not yet admitted to gape at the palace and its wonderful grounds,† so that not only the palace

---

* Now known as Apartment 44, but with the layout of Mrs Sheridan's rooms well preserved.

† The public were first admitted in 1838, after which the numbers of visitors soon soared.

itself but its spacious surroundings of lawns, green fields, a lake and trees were available for the inhabitants to enjoy.

Under the sad circumstances, it was an ideal solution. The atmosphere of the child's wood had grown lighter. The Sheridans, boys and girls, certainly enjoyed rampaging through the palace, finding its layout an ideal mixture of high buildings and little courtyards for their high-spirited games to be played. And they could also continue the family tradition for theatricals. The other family tradition for writing was equally honoured. A year before their arrival at Hampton Court, Caroline and Helen together produced an illustrated book which they called *The Dandies' Rout*. It was an adaptation of an illustrated *Dandy Book* which had been a present from a family friend. The publisher of the *Dandy Book* offered to publish their own book and printed fifty copies for them.[22]

In the spring of 1825, when Helen was in her eighteenth year, Mrs Sheridan duly rented a house in Great George Street, Westminster, so that she could be introduced officially into society. The début was an undoubted success: in the high summer of that year, Helen, not yet eighteen, was married to a naval officer, Captain Price Blackwood. The Duke of York, continuing his tradition of philanthropy towards Tom Sheridan and his family, gave the bride away at her wedding at St George's, Hanover Square.

It was a good, solid match by the standards of the time, despite the fact that Blackwood's career was likely to take him on prolonged tours of the world away from his family. The bridegroom was from a prominent North Irish family, and eventual heir to the family title: he would become the 4th Lord Dufferin in 1839.

Mrs Sheridan spent most of her time in her London house, as did Caroline in turn. In the meantime, Caroline's education continued, not with a governess, as was usual among girls in her position in society, but at a proper school. Caroline was sent, in 1823, to the Academy at Wonersh, in Surrey. This was to have consequences which could never have been foreseen.

At the time it was probably a reflection of Caroline's quick intelligence; after all, it would be an agreed truth about the Sheridan girls that, for better or for worse, Caroline was the one who sparkled.[23] That lively spirit of repartee for which she would be celebrated was no doubt already showing itself in the home – where it may have aroused more irritation than admiration. The school concerned was close to Wonersh Park, the house of Lord Grantley and actually owned by him; Caroline's governess was the sister of Grantley's agent. A visit to Wonersh Park was therefore a natural social event.

Lord Grantley had been born Fletcher Norton and had succeeded to the title in 1822. He traced his title back to his grandfather, also Fletcher Norton, of Grantley in Yorkshire, who as a lawyer and an MP enjoyed a number of offices, including Attorney General. He ended up as Speaker of the House of Commons and was subsequently created Baron Grantley, of Markenfield in York, in 1782. The first Lord Grantley, as a lawyer, was known to display a certain briskness where money was concerned, to the extent that he was mocked by the name of 'Bullface Doublefees'. As the rhyme had it:[24]

> Careless of censure and no fool to fame . . .
> Sir Fletcher, standing without fear or shame,
> Pockets the cash and lets them laugh that please.

This was a hard-headedness which Grantley did not hand on to all his descendants – certainly not to George Norton.

The current owner of Wonersh Park was the 3rd Lord Grantley, who had inherited the title from his childless uncle. Unlike the original Fletcher Norton, who supported both Whig and Tory administrations at different times, this Lord Grantley was what was then called an Ultra and would now be known as a hard-line Tory.* Sitting in the House of Lords, he would be one of the twenty-two 'stalwarts' – peers who voted against the Great Reform Bill of 1832, despite the fact that the Tory leader, the

---

* It should, however, be made clear that political parties in the modern sense of organization and rigorous definition were not yet in existence although names like Whig and Tory, denoting social attitudes and alliances as well as political views, were in use.

Duke of Wellington, and the rest of the Tories had finally decided to abstain. There were eight children in this generation of the family: the next brother in line was George Norton, born on 31 August 1800.

It was in this way, during a school visit to Wonersh Park, that George Norton first caught sight of Caroline Sheridan. It seems that he decided more or less immediately to make her his wife. Something about her romantic, dark-eyed looks captivated this man, one of whose qualities, for better or for worse, would prove to be an astonishing obstinacy.

George Norton himself was certainly not a bad-looking fellow: tall and healthy-looking, with a ruddy complexion he maintained all his life. In the opinion of those anxious to marry off their daughters, there could be many worse. He was not a peer or even an eldest son, it was true. But he was obsessed by Caroline. That was made quite clear at the start. Time would show whether he had the three qualities of an ideal husband recommended in a guide to women's conduct published in 1843: 'the great requisite for one would be good Sense, good Nature and cheerfulness . . . surely that is the sort of Man with whom you may hope to pass your life happily.'[25]

Mrs Sheridan behaved correctly. Caroline was just a schoolgirl. Norton must wait for three years. In the meantime, George Norton was not the only admirer attracted to this alluring, dark-eyed young girl. Years later, Caroline reminisced about a certain Captain Fairfield who had fallen for her during a visit to Brighton, 'before London dawned on my senses!'. In Caroline's opinion he was 'clever, handsome and good-natured', but her mother took a different view and, to Caroline's fury, duly burnt his Valentine which alluded to his military profession:

> There came from the wars
> A man covered in scars. –
> Or let us suppose that he was.

Nor did Mrs Sheridan appreciate it when the gallant captain stood up in a boat at a Richmond water party, with the provocative words: 'Oh, Mrs. S., don't I look like *Apollo or something*?'[26]

It has been estimated that Caroline was about seventeen at this time. The formative romance of her youth took place the following year, when Caroline herself fell in love with someone quite different. Shortly after she left school in 1826, Caroline met a young man called Ralph Leveson Smith. He had been born in India, where his father made a fortune that enabled him to send his sons back to England, to school at Eton and later to university at Oxford. Ralph was a good scholar who practised law, a nephew of the fabulous, witty clergyman the Revd Sydney Smith. Inevitably his father wanted him to marry an heiress, therefore his engagement to Caroline was never official. Then suddenly, in 1827, he fell mortally ill with a fever.

We have Caroline's word for what happened next. In 1843, she confided in Benjamin Robert Haydon as he was painting her (appropriately enough, as Cassandra), and in turn he passed on to Elizabeth Barrett Browning that his beautiful subject was to be pitied: 'She loved Vernon Smith's Brother who died of a fever, and she then married an Ass, to get rid of her pang!' Eight years later, in a letter to her sister Georgia following the death of their mother, Caroline herself put it more poignantly: 'I begin life by the death of the person I wished to marry, and who loved *me* . . . when he was dying it was only of *me* he spoke – only to *me* he sent little tokens – only *me* he pitied, for the grief he said it wd. [*sic*] be to me.' In this letter Caroline reviews her life, lamenting its unhappy course, and incidentally rebuts claims that Leveson Smith had loved anyone else, 'for it is vain that others have the vanity to cling to his vanished preference'.[27]

Whatever the truth of her relationship with Leveson Smith, so sadly and mistily remembered, even to the end of her life, it is clear that something did happen to her at the very beginning of adulthood. As a result, Caroline Sheridan regarded herself as having been romantically blighted by fate. It is quite possible that the unexpected death of Leveson Smith influenced her decision to accept the proposal of George Norton. It certainly occurred to her as an explanation for their marriage much later, when one was needed: this letter to her sister goes on to detail what she regarded by 1851 as the many horrors of her life.

If it was not blighted romance, what was it that induced Caroline to take that fatal step into the state of married woman? The marriage of her elder sister Helen in July 1825 may have played a part, given the closeness – part love, part rivalry – of the sisters. In any case marriage was the obvious, indeed the natural solution at the time for a young woman without financial prospects. There do not appear to have been other obvious suitors following the death of Leveson Smith. The prospect of George Norton as a worldly match, quite apart from his declared passion for Caroline, which had evidently lasted over three years, was not a bad one.

The story told afterwards of the bridegroom being unavoidably late for his own wedding (trouble with the cabriolet) and Caroline observing on his arrival that he had come at last and looked handsomer than she expected, belongs to the tradition of the lively Caroline; ever covering an awkward situation with an amusing, slightly outrageous remark.[28] Mrs Sheridan would not have endorsed the marriage, nor Caroline herself tolerated it, if there had been genuine active distaste at this point.

At the same time, the match was not brilliant. Younger sons were, in principle, not well provided for. By the English aristocratic tradition of (male) primogeniture, everything went to the eldest son, in order to preserve the precious family estate. Thus, the younger sons were expected to find a suitable profession – notably the Army or the Anglican Church – to support themselves.

It is true that there was always the prospect of an eldest son dying without heirs, and the younger son being happily promoted. In the case of the Nortons and the Grantley title, George Norton was actually the heir presumptive (next heir) to his brother Fletcher, who had succeeded their uncle in 1822 and, although married in 1825, had as yet no children. If this state of affairs persisted, the possible future inheritance of the Grantley title and estate one day might feature in the lives of George Norton and his sons.

This younger son had already followed the traditional career path of his family: that is to say, he combined the law – he was a barrister – with politics. In 1825, he canvassed the borough of Guildford, where his brother at nearby Wonersh Park now had an electoral interest, and was elected unopposed in 1826. There was, however, now no question of the shifting political allegiance of his clever grandfather, Sir Fletcher 'Doublefees'. George Norton was a Tory. This was the age of reforming campaigns in the House of Commons. By the time of his wedding, George Norton had already voted against relief for the Dissenters, as proposed in the repeal of the Test Acts, and against Catholic Emancipation (although he finally voted for it, following the Tory Prime Minister Wellington). This was hardly the Whig tradition of the Sheridans in which Caroline had been nurtured, but then what business was it of hers? The traditional answer at the time was that politics was no business at all of women, who had other important domestic and maternal duties. On the other hand, not all women agreed with this; there were those who made and would make their concerns felt whether by word or deed.

Later Mrs Sheridan, according to one of her daughter's campaigning pamphlets, would take the line that she had been deceived about George Norton's financial prospects.[29] Certainly, Norton did not inherit much from his father at his death in 1820 – one-seventh of the residue of his estate, just under £7,500. Members of Parliament were unpaid at this date,* and Norton was thus dependent on patronage to receive paid positions, with some kind of judicial connection, to maintain himself (and his family, when he had one).

Mrs Sheridan declared that she had believed in the 'fidelity' of the statement of the trustees regarding the property destined for the younger brothers and sisters of Lord Grantley. Property, specified as 'to be land', to the value of £30,000 was mentioned. Otherwise, 'I should never have suffered you to marry N.' At the time a settlement was made, according to the usual practice, in the shape of a trust fund. This was to be handled by the trustees.

---

* MPs first received an annual salary, of £400, in 1911.

Caroline, as the bride, and later the married woman, could take no legal or executive decisions concerning the trust which was held for her. In short, she had no power over it at all.

That was the case for and against George Norton as a bride-groom. When we look at Caroline's prospects in turn, neither could they be described as brilliant. The Nortons resented – and continued to resent – her lack of fortune. In fact, she was granted an annual income of about £50 a year from her late father's pension (just under £1,000 a year in today's values).[30] It was the man's obsession which brought about the union.

On 30 July 1827, George Norton married Caroline Sheridan at St George's, Hanover Square. The new Mrs George Norton was nineteen years old and her husband just short of his twenty-seventh birthday. Their material prospects were not brilliant and would have to be addressed. It was hoped that the romantic con-nection, which would atone for this lack of material prosperity, was stronger.

CHAPTER TWO

'Here She Comes!'

'Nelly's vanity is to have all the room exclaim: "What a pretty woman!" Mine is that two or three persons I care about should turn round and cry: "Here she comes!"'

Caroline Norton to Richard Monckton Milnes

THE HONEYMOON OF the newly wed couple took place in Caroline's beloved Scotland. Here she encountered some of George Norton's relations with rather less enthusiasm than she felt for the country in general. This lack of affection was, in fact, felt from the beginning on both sides. One of George's sisters in particular, Grace, married to Sir Neil Menzies, took against Caroline either because her husband clearly admired her, or possibly because of a family prejudice against a bride who had arrived notably under-endowed.

After that, the Nortons did not begin their married life proper in particularly agreeable circumstances. Their first home was the cramped quarters of George Norton's legal chambers in Garden Court in the Temple. Then things improved outwardly. George Norton rented a house at No. 2 Storey's Gate, Westminster.* This

---

* This particular house is no longer in existence.

was a congenial neighbourhood for Caroline, since her mother's house in Great George Street was nearby.

In other ways, the particular situation of this house was to be of enormous importance in the story of the Nortons' marriage. That is to say, Storey's Gate was to be found in the geographical heart of London political society. This was an age when propinquity was an especially attractive feature of social life, since it was an age of walking and also riding in the park – ladies elegantly seated side-saddle to accommodate their long skirts. George Norton was also, at the time, a sitting MP, and from his new home it was a brief journey on foot to the House of Commons. Downing Street itself, the residence of the Prime Minister since the early eighteenth century, was only a short distance from Storey's Gate, with St James's Park adjacent. A balcony of Storey's Gate looked out on Birdcage Walk, and there was a back entrance consisting of a glass door which was convenient for the park.

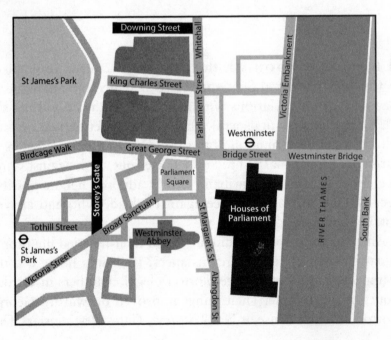

Of course, all this also meant that other Members of both Houses of Parliament could easily and pleasantly make the journey in reverse. They could use whichever entrance to the house was most convenient. Thus, politicians of all parties could call upon the fascinating young married woman at Storey's Gate. Brought up in the Whig tradition as she was, Caroline was also married to a Tory MP, so that Tories obviously had their place: an interesting, amusing, ambitious young Tory was surely as good, to her, as an older, staider Whig. A powerful, attractive Tory, with power at his elbow, was possibly better than both. It was natural that Caroline, with all her energy and charm, should swiftly find herself presiding over a salon.

Looking back on her own beginnings late in her life, Caroline wrote a significant letter of condolence to Lady Palmerston on the death of her husband. Stressing the influence that the former Emily Cowper, wife of the erstwhile Prime Minister, had exerted, she wrote: 'It was my dream when I thought to marry and live among the men who influenced their time, to be what I think you were, in this, the only reasonable ambition of woman.' Allowing for a certain polite exaggeration under the circumstances, Caroline certainly had this generous, yet ambitious, aspect of her character.[1]

Caroline now created the home which was evidently so important to her. Always present, according to the conventional standards of the time, were the servants of both sexes: maids to tend to her at every stage of the day, men to admit the guests and escort them away, among other duties. In the manner of attendants at all times, they served – and they observed.

White muslin curtains and an enormous blue sofa dominated the room in which she received her guests, the blue of the sofa chosen to set off the remarkable colouring which gave that special quality to her beauty. Guests declared themselves dazzled by her enormous black eyes under their heavy brows: the graceful modesty with which she lowered them became famous – or was it notorious? As Caroline's contemporary, the writer Lady Eastlake, observed: 'She uses her eyes so ably and so wickedly.' Perhaps this lowering of the 'downy eyelids' with their 'sweeping silken fringes' before the male gaze was a deliberate act of enchantment.[2]

In her dress, Caroline tended to play up to her 'Eastern' or 'biblical' appearance. Fanny Kemble first caught sight of her in rich gold-coloured silk, her head, neck and arms adorned with magnificently simple Etruscan gold ornaments. The painter Benjamin Robert Haydon declared, among other expressions of ecstasy, that everybody else looked pale and delicate by Caroline's side. She was like a Greek statue breaking into life.[3]

This statue, far from silent, was also endowed with a seductive power of speech; as one observer put it, she had 'a most peculiar, deep, soft contralto voice which was like her beautiful dark face set to music'. Then there was the question of what the voice was actually saying. The tone was 'dulcet and low', but the conversation which came forth was the opposite: sharp, sardonic, and from time to time outrageous. Here, there was unquestionably a remarkable contrast. As Disraeli observed on his introduction into London society: 'She had an exquisite way of telling free [that is, daring] stories, modestly,' and he, too, commented on the lowering of the eyes, fringed with their long, thick eyelashes. And she was never averse to public attention: the politician and diarist John Hobhouse reported a party given to celebrate the marriage of Georgia to Lord Seymour at which 'her sister, Mrs Norton, sang and acted a story of her own.'[4]

It became customary to say of Caroline Norton's wit that her ability to say 'stinging things' was 'mannish', in short the very reverse of her appearance. 'Mannish' was far from being a word of praise for women in the nineteenth century.

Thomas Hardy's beautiful heiress Bathsheba Everdene in *Far from the Madding Crowd*, inheriting a farm and choosing to do the masculine job of running it herself, enquired anxiously: 'I hope I am not a bold sort of maid – mannish.' 'Oh no, not mannish,' her female companion replied, 'but so almighty womanish that 'tis going on that way sometimes.' The same explanation might have been applied by her contemporaries to Caroline. Certainly, masculinity or mannishness of behaviour (rather than appearance) was a charge which would persist and be used against her in other connections.

Then there was that prudish criticism, deriving originally from her Sheridan blood, given its most notorious expression by Harriet, Countess Granville, a generation older, daughter of the famous Whig hostess Georgiana Duchess of Devonshire: 'Mrs Norton is so nice, it is a pity she is not quite nice, for if she were quite nice, she would be so very nice.' The Duchess of Wellington, born Kitty Pakenham, an Anglo-Irish aristocrat, suggested that Caroline had been misled by her Sheridan name 'with which *wit* is generally coupled'. In society the Duchess found her 'pert, flippant, *odd*' although admittedly 'wonderfully handsome'.[5]

It is true that very early in her career as a hostess – by the time she was just twenty – saucy stories were being told about her. Lord Wriothesley Russell, a son of the 6th Duke of Bedford, who was later to become a Canon of Windsor, described the 'airs of eccentricity' on which she prided herself, adding that she was 'much admired in London for them'. On one occasion it seems that when a certain John Talbot came up to speak to her for the second time in his life, she exclaimed: 'Jack, Jack, for shame! We must not be too familiar in public.' It was, of course, a joke. But such jokes from an essentially vulnerable young woman – for all her vivacity – made in a highly gossipy society, might prove dangerous. It does not seem that Caroline herself was of the temperament to appreciate the danger. She once told the writer and politician Richard Monckton Milnes that while her sister Helen's vanity was to have all the room exclaim: 'What a pretty woman!' Her own was that 'two or three persons I care about turn round and cry: "Here she comes!"'.[6]

When it came to appearances, Caroline's figure was full as well as graceful, 'fleshly' that is, voluptuous in the language of her time; among other things she prided herself on her beautiful bosom. On one occasion she referred to another girl with the most '*pleading* brown eyes', adding waspishly: 'but your eyes plead in vain if your chest is too narrow.' However, it is impossible to be sure exactly how naturally 'fleshly' she was, since it is a feature of Caroline's early married life that she was pregnant almost continuously: on one occasion, when six months gone, she was described as looking like 'a Sybil in repose'.[7]

She gave birth to her first child, Fletcher Spencer Conyers, in July 1829 (fifteen months after her marriage). Thomas Brinsley, known as Brin or Brinny, followed in November 1831 and William Charles Chapple, or Willie, in late August 1833. The fact that she had given birth to three children in five years left her admirer Haydon saying happily in 1834 that Mrs Norton was more beautiful than ever as she sat for him, because she was (at last) not pregnant.

The elegant phrase to denote pregnancy at the time was to refer to the lady concerned as being 'on a sofa'. Being on a sofa was obviously a familiar condition in the nineteenth century. 'What a horrid piece of work a lying-in is,' exclaimed the sharp-witted Emily Eden in 1826, who as a spinster had not actually experienced it. It was true that this was twenty years before anaesthetics were introduced. Nevertheless, it was the common fate of women: the average birth rate of the population (including, of course, those of the other class, whose pregnancy was spent in manual labour, not on a sofa) has been estimated at 5.5.[8]

Certainly, the chronology of her births makes it clear that Caroline Norton spent a great deal of the time during these crucial years at Storey's Gate being on a sofa – that beautiful lavish blue sofa on which she received her guests in her beguiling fashion – both as a hostess and a future mother. These births, and Caroline's consequent physical state, have to be borne in mind in considering the contemporary events in her story.

The salon itself was very much in the tradition of the times. This was the age of Lady Blessington, for example, the exotic Irish woman who kept a French count as her lover – if that was what he was. Caroline herself was nicknamed 'Starry Night' by Disraeli, four years older than her, a young politician (and novelist) just entering society. 'I saw "Starry Night" yesterday,' he said with satisfaction to her sister Helen – whom he nicknamed 'Sunny Day'.[9]

The existence of 'Starry Night' was not all glamour. There was another important feature of Caroline's early married life, equally significant, but frightening instead of gratifying. At some point, shortly after their wedding, for some reason George Norton became enraged with his young wife and attacked her physically. Thus, Caroline made the unpleasant discovery that her husband's obstinate passion for her did not preclude painful assaults. Or was it all part of the same twisted obsession?

That was less important at the time than the effect it had on her own feelings – one might legitimately say her respect – for him. Anthony Trollope raised the topic in his mid-Victorian novel *Can You Forgive Her?*. When one character, George Vavasour, deliberately caused his sister Kate to fall and break her arm, Trollope as narrator commented: 'I do not think that a woman can forget a blow. And as for forgiveness – it is not the blow that she cannot forgive, but the meanness of spirit that makes it possible.'[10]

In any event, from time to time Norton took to kicking his wife, pushing and shoving her, when she displeased him in some way. These attacks would be accompanied by an admonishment generally referring to her lack of respect for her husband. Some of them have a peculiarly modern resonance, as in Caroline's dislike of Norton smoking his cigars in her presence.

Many years later, contemplating the difficulties in her son Brin's character, Caroline looked back unhappily to those months when she had been pregnant with him. His troubles even now perpetually reminded her 'of those days of terror *while he was yet in the womb* [her italics] which have sent their miserable echo through the mystery of his blighted life'. Certainly, George Norton's anger was apparently never stayed by his wife's physical condition. He threatened to throw her downstairs when she was pregnant with her third child, as a result of which Caroline temporarily refused to sleep in the marital bedroom. There was an incident of putting a hot tea kettle on her hand, and on one occasion at least he was thought to have caused a miscarriage by a vicious blow.[11]

It is worth noting, perhaps, that there was no hint of collusion in these episodes, no suggestion that the wife actually rather enjoyed being turned into her husband's physical slave. At the time, Caroline's helpless anger, in the face of what Norton said were demands for respect, spoke for itself. Long afterwards, she reflected on the subject of physical punishment generally: 'I can recollect no single instance in which I was subdued by harshness.'[12]

Odious, therefore, as such attacks might be, it should be stressed they were not necessarily against the law at this period in the nineteenth century. There was a feeling that if a married woman was her husband's property – 'she does not exist', in Caroline Norton's words – then a man had a right to treat his own property as he wished.* Once again, a married woman was singularly unprotected. It was popularly supposed to be legal for a man to beat his wife so long as the stick was no thicker than his thumb. Bodily harm, as such, was of course punishable by law, but marital violence was considered to be a somewhat grey area in that respect. Cases that came up before the magistrates tended to be from the 'fetid, steamy atmosphere' of poor districts, where housing conditions meant that there was no privacy for marital wrongdoing. This did not mean that wife-beating was confined to the lower classes. Regrettably, Norton was far from alone in his behaviour: Bulwer Lytton, for example, later to be numbered among Caroline's admirers, was famously witnessed by a maid attacking his wife and biting her cheek. Gilbert Imlay, lover of Mary Wollstonecraft, was on occasion violent – as indeed Wollstonecraft's father had been towards her mother.[13]

The judgment of Lord Stowell on the subject of cruelty in the case of *Evans* v. *Evans* of 1790 was widely quoted in the following century. 'The causes must be grave and weighty, what merely wounds the mental feelings is in few cases to be admitted . . . Mere austerity of temper, petulance of manners, rudeness of language . . . even occasional sallies of passion . . . do not amount to legal cruelty.' He also made the vital connection between the behaviour of the victim and the treatment she received, suggesting that 'the suffering party must bear in some degree the consequences' of anything injudicious.[14] Perhaps Lord

* Nowadays such happenings are described as Domestic Violence or Abuse: such official terms were not in use in the early nineteenth century.

Stowell might have regarded the fights Caroline had with her husband over the subject of his smoking cigars in her presence as in some way provocative; it is difficult to see what else in Caroline's conduct at this stage was in any way 'injudicious' in order to justify legally what was morally unjustifiable.

One writer in 1844 defined a wife's role as follows: '*Her* business is to love! suffer!! and obey!!! the three articles of a woman's creed.' Certainly, Caroline obeyed at least one of the three commandments at this stage: she suffered. One assault that took place in the cramped environment of Norton's chambers was not actually physical, but it was in its way symbolic. There was a trivial argument about Caroline writing a letter to her mother, Norton grabbed it, Caroline proceeded to take another piece of paper and write again – at which Norton set the whole thing ablaze.[15] Norton's pointless destruction of a piece of writing paper seems to stand for a general resentment of Caroline's literary career – while at the same time being happy to live off the proceeds.

Caroline continued to write after her marriage as she had always done. Now, however, the financial profits of publication became crucial to their shared way of life. Mary Wollstonecraft, in one of her bold discussions of a woman's lot published forty years earlier, *Thoughts on the Education of Daughters*, had considered the question of female employment and reached the conclusion: 'few are the methods of earning a substance, and those very humiliating.' Companion, schoolteacher and governess were mentioned as possible jobs, as well as others which were 'gradually falling into the hands of men, and are certainly not very respectable'.[16] The fact was that authorship constituted, as it had always done, and perhaps always will do, the ideal job for a married woman – especially one with children. Without regular hours, and without the necessity of assistance from the male partner, it threw up other eternal problems such as publication, reviews and sales. But it was not humiliating. And it might produce much-needed money.

There was an additional advantage, although that would only appear with time and was not among Caroline's primary motives in writing: that is, the wider audience it would bring her for her enthusiasms – or her troubles. As she herself would put it: 'my one gift of writing gives me friends among strangers, I appeal to the opinion of strangers as well as that of friends.'[17]

Caroline was now involved in literary pursuits in two ways. The first was evidently her creative work, a well which never seemed to dry up entirely throughout her life: whether through talent, inclination, convenience, family tradition or all of these, Caroline Norton was always to be defined as a writer. Much later she would modestly term herself to Bulwer Lytton as very ill-read, because she married straight from school and 'scribbled' instead of improving herself. This necessity to write can be seen at first hand in her irrepressible generosity as a correspondent; letters were often accompanied by sketches which illustrated the wit and charm of the writer in another way.

But Caroline Norton also saw herself as what would now be termed a professional writer. Her work included poetry as well as novels. *The Sorrows of Rosalie: with Other Poems* was written when she was seventeen and, along with other shorter poems, it was printed, anonymously, in 1829. There was a dedication to the Whig grandee Lord Holland ('Taught in the dawning of life's joyous years / To love, admire and reverence thy name'.)[18] Caroline had evidently sent him a manuscript in advance and met with better luck on this occasion than when, in later years, she approached the great Duke of Wellington offering the dedication of a song. The latter responded coolly that he had been obliged to make a rule of refusing dedications, because in his situation as Chancellor of the University of Oxford he had been *'much exposed to authors'*. On the work itself, Lady Holland, the celebrated hostess of Holland House, commented to her son: 'Mrs Norton's poems are beautiful, the songs and short things. The Poem [*The Sorrows of Rosalie*] is too melancholy, so I shall never be able to judge of its merits.'[19] The poem certainly begins on a melancholy note:

> Oh, ye for whom this tale of woe is told
> Too weak for virtue, yet in vice not bold

and continues with a story of a maiden betrayed by a Lord Arthur in various stages:

> In evil hour (for me unfortunate)
> Did the deceiver come . . .
> But he was all to *me* – a single day
> Spent without *him* was a year of pain

At first, Rosalie nobly declines to leave her aged father. A baby son appears, but Lord Arthur avoids marriage, 'half playful, half displeased'. His visits become less frequent, and when Rosalie takes the baby in her arms to his house she is turned away by a servant. Things go from bad to worse: Lord Arthur marries and Rosalie ends up a beggar. She is eventually put in prison after stealing a cross from a rich lady, hoping to sell it for food. Her baby dies, leaving 'the grassy mound' which is his grave her only earthly consolation. The poem concludes with Rosalie sitting by the fire reading the Bible: 'And grant *her* peace in Heaven who not on earth may rest.'

Another melancholy poem was entitled 'Farewell', with a prophetic last line: '*All* love thee *now*, but I will love thee *then*'. *The Times* liked the volume but shared Lady Holland's view that the subject matter was too gloomy.[20] It concludes, in fact, with a light verse characteristic of the witty Caroline, entitled 'I Do not Love Thee!'. The last lines make the message clear:

> I *know* I do not love thee! yet, alas!
> Others will scarcely trust my candid heart
> And oft I catch them smiling as they pass
> Because they see me gazing where thou art

The other poems included the memorial to her dead sailor brother Thomas Sheridan, quoted earlier, as well as a poem in which a Crusader seduces and abandons a Moorish maid. She dies, then appears to him in a dream:

Madly fought he on the morrow,
Rage and love alternate burn;
Quickly death relieves his sorrow
Faithless hearts may read and learn!

The poem received a somewhat mixed review from *The Times*. There was condescending approval: this was 'an extraordinary effort for so young a person', some passages were 'beautiful and full of true poetical feeling' – combined with righteous disapproval of the events related therein – 'nothing could be less useful than the moral which would be drawn from them.' Fortunately, this controversial plot proved to be no bar to success: *The Sorrows of Rosalie* sold well. In fact, the sales enabled Caroline to pay for her first confinement, a solution to the problem that George Norton thought highly appropriate.[21]

Another collection of poems was published in 1830 under the title *The Undying One*.[22] This volume was dedicated to Adelaide (the future Queen), at that stage Duchess of Clarence, wife of the heir presumptive to the throne. Caroline had met her at Hampton Court since the Duke and Duchess lived nearby at Bushy Park. The title poem centred on the story of Isbal, the Wandering Jew, who is excluded from society:

They shrank from me, I say, as gaunt and wild,
I wander'd on through the long summer's day;
And every mother snatch'd her cowering child
With horror from my solitary way!

Thus, Isbal is robbed of his Linda when her brother marries her off to Carlos. Death plays a prominent part in the poem: Linda dies, and a series of girls die, but even when the death of Linda makes his own death desirable, Isbal the Wandering Jew cannot die. In vain he hurls himself into the ocean: the mighty waves reject him. The last line of the poem reads: 'And "the Undying One" is left *alone*.'

Although it was turned down by John Murray, a friend of Byron and the most desirable publisher of the time, *The Undying*

One was accepted by Colburn and Bentley, Caroline's previous publishers, negotiations being, of course, conducted by her legal representative – her husband. The satiric *John Bull* denounced it, but other reviewers, for example in the more distinguished *Athenaeum*, gave it praise along generous lines, referring to its 'rich profusion of imagery and dignity of sentiment'. Although Caroline herself would come to denounce her use of the story as hackneyed, the poem does in fact have great sweep, as well as the imagery to which *The Athenaeum* refers: all characteristic of the work of her early twenties.[23]

There was another side to Caroline's professional life: in the world of magazines. This time, the need to earn money was very much to the fore since contemporary magazines were for both the editor and the contributors a useful source of income. By 1820 a fashionable women's magazine, *La Belle Assemblée*, was exclaiming on the subject: 'every hour we find something new issuing from the Press . . . the daily teeming is like the explosion of Mount Vesuvius.' Trollope's penniless Irish political hero Phineas Finn, making his way in London, boasted, for example: 'I have already done a little for the magazines.' Here Caroline's position in society was helpful. In March 1831, *Fraser's Magazine* described her as a leader of 'the female band', that is, of writers. Her credentials consisted not only of writing long poems, but also of being 'a sprig of the nobility' and a granddaughter of Richard Brinsley Sheridan.[24]

Fraser's Magazine was founded in 1830 by Hugh Fraser, a Scottish 'briefless barrister' with family funds available, and edited by William Maginn, who described himself as a 'rollicking jug of an Irishman':[25]

Drink to me only from a jug, and I will pledge with mine
So fill my glass, with whiskey-punch and I'll not ask for wine

Maginn certainly had a disreputable personal side and, like many of his contemporaries, had trouble with debt. But he was clever. He published the early work of both Thackeray and Thomas Carlyle: the 'Fraserians' who met and dined together also included Coleridge, Harrison Ainsworth and Robert Southey. Born in Cork – described as having a rich rolling voice, with its 'gay Cork twang' – he was both a Protestant and a Tory; more important perhaps than either, he combined being a keen observer of the political and literary scene with being an equally merciless satirist: someone whose works Bulwer Lytton would denounce as 'journalism of the most dishonourable kind'. He would find a colourful character like Caroline Norton irresistible in the future; but when she started out in his world, he published Caroline's articles.

Of a different nature were the magazines that Caroline Norton actually came to edit, such as *Fisher's Drawing Room Scrapbook*, *The Book of Beauty*, *The Court Journal* and *The Keepsake*. Such magazines were desirable objects in themselves. The last-mentioned luxurious production flourished for thirty years, costing two and a half guineas and bound in tooled morocco and crimson silk; it was essentially an adornment, a perfect gift. Serious writers such as Scott, Tom Moore and Coleridge contributed, and there were illustrations by Turner (Caroline included many of her own poems when she first edited it in December 1835).

In their heyday, such magazines fulfilled a genuine need; De Quincey called them 'vehicles of liberal amusement'. Naturally they also incurred a certain amount of mockery as well. The cover of *The Book of Beauty* was described as looking like one of Lord Palmerston's cast-off waistcoats; a kinder and more appropriate comment was that of the writer Letitia Elizabeth Landon, known as L. E. L., who called the annuals 'butterflies of literature'.[26] The 'butterflies' enjoyed a readership not only in Britain but also abroad, in India and the Colonies and in America. What would now be known as celebrities, either as editors or contributors, were employed – Lady Blessington was another example of an editor – in the knowledge that this was a combination that would thoroughly satisfy the public at which they aimed. Nor were the payments meagre: Scott, for example, received £500 for contributing to *The Keepsake* and Tom Moore £600 for 120 lines of prose and verse. Lady

Blessington has been estimated as receiving £200 to £300 a year (£100 at this date has been estimated at just under £9,000).[27]

It is clear that Caroline Norton, in her early years in society, had a happy life – much of it of her own energetic making – rather than a happy marriage. And yet, as with many marriages, it was complicated. Caroline was happy with her life and with her children. One aspect of the Nortons' marriage which actually went well led to a crucial development in their lives. From the beginning, Caroline took her role as the promoter of her husband's career seriously. To bring about fortunate connections was, after all, part of a Whig hostess's picture of herself, quite apart from a wife's. It was in this way that Caroline happily acceded to a request by George Norton.

Having lost his seat in Parliament in the 1830 election, which according to custom at the time followed the death of the monarch, George IV, he needed a job. Privately Caroline allowed herself to indulge in a sarcastic description of Norton's candidature to her sister Georgia, which she said was typical of his mixture of sanguine hope, credulity and vanity: 'he assures me, that although thrown out, he was the most popular candidate; that his opponents are hated, and that all those who voted against him did it with tears.'[28]

Publicly she showed the correct loyalty of a wife. A magistracy would provide much-needed income. A Whig government had come into power in the course of the ructions of the Reform Bill, in November 1830, under the premiership of Earl Grey. This was after long years of Tory government, in which, in the words of Lord Byron:[29]

> Naught's permanent among the human race
> Except the Whigs not getting into place

It was thus at the suggestion of her husband, rather than on her own initiative, that Caroline agreed to talk to the Home Secretary. Why should she not use her own Whig background, her growing celebrity as 'Starry Night', her sheer charm, to lobby the minister in charge of such things as magistracies? In this way Lord Melbourne, Home Secretary in the new government, recently widowed, first called on Caroline Norton at Storey's Gate.

CHAPTER THREE

Melbourne's Hat

'I met Mrs Norton at the French Ambassador's. She talked in a most extraordinary manner and kicked Lord Melbourne's hat over her head. The whole corps diplomatique were amazed.'

Lord Malmesbury, *Memoirs*

THE MAN WHO CALLED AT Storey's Gate was in his early fifties, that is to say, nearly thirty years older than Caroline. But Melbourne was still an attractive man by any standards; the dark, Byronic looks of his youth – thick, waving hair, large eyes beneath heavy eyebrows – had matured into something more silvery but still handsome with his sensual curling mouth and fine aquiline nose. The painter Benjamin Robert Haydon referred to his 'personal beauty, his noble upright figure, prime in maturity, when manhood is beginning to end'. Fanny Kemble also described him as 'exceedingly handsome, with a fine person', even if it was verging on the portly.[1]

Melbourne was a widower, his fascinating, troubled and troublesome wife, Lady Caroline Lamb, having died in January 1828.* Their only son, Augustus, born in 1807, was mentally backward,

---

* Six months before William Lamb, as he was originally known, succeeded his father as 2nd Viscount Melbourne.

hyperactive and a perpetual problem. It was, incidentally, characteristic of the maternal Caroline that, despite these disadvantages,
she herself felt genuine affection for 'William's boy', of whom she
once wrote in a poem: 'I call this darling mine.'[2]

Melbourne had lived in the grandest and most entertaining
circles from birth. But such circles were, as ever, no strangers
to scandal. It was the subject of gossip that he was, in fact, the
natural son of Lord Egremont, his mother Elizabeth Milbanke
being, in Melbourne's own words, 'not chaste, not chaste but
remarkable'.[3] This rumour, if that was what it was, did not prevent him from inheriting the Melbourne title.

Melbourne's manner was genial and courtly. Perhaps it helped
the aristocratic and chivalrous impression he gave that he spoke
with the inimitable Whig accent of his forebears in which, for
example, 'gold' became 'goold' and Rome 'Room'.

His geniality was such that according to Lord Holland even
his rage ended with a laugh. Perceived indolence also went with
the aristocratic impression he gave. It was Disraeli – from a very
different background, a self-creation – who wrote of Melbourne
'sauntering over the destiny of a nation, and lounging away the
glory of an empire'. Haydon summed it up: here was a delightful
man of fashion.[4]

Melbourne himself was not blind to his own weaknesses. To
Emily Eden, sometimes suggested as a second wife for the widowed Melbourne, he acknowledged one weakness in particular:
'My Mother always used to say that I was very selfish, both Boy
and Man, and I believe she was right – at least I know that I am
always anxious to escape from anything of a painful nature, and
find every excuse for doing so.'[5] This was perhaps understandable
in view of his experiences with his wife, the openly ardent lover of
Lord Byron. Yet this anxiety did not extend to strictness regarding
his own conduct. In May 1828 (shortly before he inherited the
title) the future Melbourne was sued for adultery by the husband
of Lady Branden, who was in fact a clergyman as well as a peer.

There were warnings here for the future in Melbourne's
attitude to the whole imbroglio. He advised the lively, flirtatious Lady Branden to return to her husband, whom she had

abandoned, but in the meantime gave her financial support. In general, Melbourne, born in the eighteenth century, expressed himself against women's independence: a wife should adopt the country and politics of her husband, he declared in 1835, when Caroline praised Mary Wollstonecraft's *A Vindication of the Rights of Woman*. All this was in line with his dislike of public change: railways were inimical to him and he did not believe in compulsory public education. Charles Greville put it more simply: 'All his notions were aristocratic. He had no particle of sympathy for what he called progressive reform.' In the end, in keeping with his philosophy of avoiding the painful, Melbourne actually bought off Lord Branden, the man described as 'the noble and reverend cuckold'.[6]

Despite Melbourne's professed rejection of women's independence, paradoxically, he had, and continued to have, a preference for what might today be called strong women. (Better still if they were both strong and amusing.) His wife Lady Caroline – described by Lord Lytton as the 'Daughter of Feeling' and 'Queen of Love' – had been crazy, obsessional, frenzied, all these things, but she had been no modest cipher who would accept the idea that 'the wife is always in the wrong,' as Melbourne would write to Queen Victoria in 1839.[7]

Avoiding boredom at all costs was known to be another of his social characteristics. So from the very first, the odds were in favour of Melbourne and Caroline establishing some kind of friendship. After all, here was a vivacious and attractive young woman whose marriage to a boorish husband was troubled, encountering a charming and attractive older man looking for diversion. She was also, from the first, endearingly solicitous for his welfare, as demonstrated by the ending of an early letter: 'I do trust they will not work you too hard in the House as they seem to have every inclination to do.' Melbourne would undoubtedly have agreed with Disraeli's remark in his novel published about the same time, *Henrietta Temple*, that a female friend was more valuable than parks and palaces.[8]

When it came to Caroline Norton, the exact nature of the relationship which developed is one of the key questions of her dramatic story. But what is clear from the beginning is that a gentle rallying, teasing friendship was part of it. For example, early in their relationship Caroline twitted Melbourne with a flirtatious boast about her eyebrows, both of them having markedly heavy eyebrows as a physical characteristic. 'I admire your saying one should not be conceited,' she began, 'and then talking of your eyebrows in rivalry with mine. Fie!', wrote Caroline, 'yours were only made to shadow your eyes that mine might not dazzle you too much.'[9]

This is the same tone as the letter which teases Melbourne about his request for lavish accommodation during a Royal visit: 'I laughed for an hour at your conduct . . . you must have grown much more "lusty" (as the maids call it) if you thought yourself entitled to a "room for two".'[10]

One letter, in August 1831, which would have particular significance in the future, is clearly part of Caroline's merry mischief. Six months pregnant at the time, she wrote: 'I am exceedingly offended at your quotation: "See a long race" and your irony on the subject of my future family. I beg leave to mention to your Lordship that whom you so kindly promise to take for a wife will be born early in the ensuing November.'[11] Evidently a joke had developed by which the widowed Melbourne would take little Miss Norton as his second wife. It was a light joke between good friends, easily forgotten when a son was born in November.

With hindsight, this was perhaps one of the happiest – if not *the* happiest – time in Caroline's personal life. She had the theoretical protection of marriage, she was pregnant with another child, and she had the very public admiration of a leading politician who was also a glamorous older man. Her jokes were popular, her conversation was desired, and another child was on the way to join Fletcher, born two years earlier and 'conceived in love', as she wrote later. Even if the new baby was not conceived in quite so much love, the rest of her rich life made up for it.

The very first letter that survives from Caroline to Melbourne is dated July 1831, from Maiden Bradley in Wiltshire, the home of her sister Georgia Seymour.[12] It starts: 'Dearest Lord, I am very dull – how are you? Allow me to give you a description of the way in which we pass our days . . . We eat our breakfast in solemn silence as is meet and fit in the hall of Seymour's ancestors. After breakfast, we two females do a little needlework . . . many times do we inspect our watches.'

The day marches uneventfully on until Caroline manages to sit up late with her brother-in-law, and even then Georgia complains. 'She says it *fidgets* her to know that Seymour and I are sitting together down stairs.' So, Caroline goes to her own room and 'remains yawning and scribbling' until two or three o'clock in the morning. She ends by recommending, tongue in cheek, the 'day at Bradley' as a model for Brocket Hall, Melbourne's country house.

The ending of her next letter, written two days later, is more to the point: 'Write to me and tell me about yourself and public affairs.' As Caroline would tell Lady Palmerston, her ambition to be a Whig hostess – although it was too late for the great era of such celebrities as Georgiana, Duchess of Devonshire – found much gratification in the sheer importance of her admirer's position.

Melbourne took over as Home Secretary in the Grey ministry in 1830. Four years later, Lord Melbourne became Prime Minister. He was now resident in 10 Downing Street, a convenient stroll from Storey's Gate for his long, loping legs, with a short interval in 1834, before returning to office. Throughout all this period, Melbourne was a frequent caller, either joining the salon and gilding it by his presence, or making personal calls. Caroline's salon was, of course, not the only place where they met. It became quickly known that the presence of Mrs Norton put the great man in a good humour, with a consequent increase in Caroline's social prestige.

Part of the charm of Storey's Gate was the mixture which the guests presented, a mixture natural to a Sheridan who had grown up knowing writers and painters as well as politicians. It has been suggested that there was 'something *fin-de-siècle*' about the reign of William IV and that only 'inexorable chronological fact' prevents the use of the term. Bulwer Lytton (as he would later be known) described it as an age of visible transition in *England*

and the English, published in 1833, 'an age of disquietude and doubt'.[13]

The Great Fire, which consumed the House of Commons in October 1834, was seen by many as a welcome cleansing element to sweep away the old order, as symbolized by the inadequate ancient buildings, which had long been considered a danger by thoughtful observers like Sir John Soane. If it is true that certain grand old traditions were coming to an end, who knew what the next reign, presumably with an unknown young girl at its head, would bring?*

Into these circles, Caroline Norton, still in her early twenties, arrived as a fresh and lively presence and it was not only Melbourne who thought so. Caroline was a flirt, certainly, seeing this as part of her role as a hostess, and furthermore she laughed at everything, as Richard Monckton Milnes pointed out. The evidence for her flirtatiousness is incontrovertible: the Journal of Lord Holland went so far as to record it as being 'dangerous and indecent in so young a woman'. Yet, in these early years of Caroline's London life, there were plenty of admirers but no indication that she actually had lovers. When the disapproving Emily Eden observed, 'I suppose she is very amusing to people who have not much principle,' she added a sour comment regarding her 'wonderful anecdotes' about 'her husband' and 'her lovers'. But it is clear that her disapproval was earned by this distasteful joking, not by actual immorality. As she admitted grudgingly: 'after all Mrs. Norton is very young.'[14]

These years in English political history were both traumatic and thrilling. The Great Reform Bill was finally passed in the summer of 1832, under a Whig government. Therefore, the years from the accession of William IV in July 1830 until his signing of the Bill, just over two years later, were an exciting time for any political hostess, particularly one with a Whig background,

---

* William IV had no legitimate children; the heir presumptive was therefore his niece, Princess Victoria of Kent, only eleven when he came to the throne.

Whig sympathies – and a Tory husband with his own Tory connections.

Caroline did not let her husband's family traditions deter her: she electioneered for the Bill in true Whig fashion. This was to lobby the MPs she knew to vote in the right way: for a Bill which has been estimated as increasing the franchise to 18 per cent of the adult male population. The Bill finally received Royal Assent on Derby Day in 1832 – a coincidence which enabled certain conservative-minded critics to absent themselves plausibly from the actual occasion in the House of Lords, including King William IV himself.

The visitors to her salon included young politicians who were not Whigs but were ambitious, such as Benjamin Disraeli, twenty-two years old when Caroline introduced him into the Sheridan circle. Here he encountered Lord Melbourne, who asked him the friendly question: 'Well now, tell me what you want to be.' 'I want to be Prime Minister,' replied Disraeli. Melbourne was startled into replying: 'No chance of that. Nobody can compete with Stanley [the future Lord Derby],' before offering more kindly advice to put those foolish notions out of his head if he intended to enter politics. It was Caroline, not Melbourne, who made the correct political prophecy – even if it was half in jest – when she predicted in 1833: 'I'm afraid you will not turn into a Whig but a *nasty Tory*.'* At the time Disraeli told his sister that he had got into the habit of going to the theatre with Mrs Norton. 'Public amusements are tedious,' he told her, 'but in a private box with a fair companion, less so.'[15]

Disraeli pointed to one aspect of Caroline's salon, in those days at little Storey's Gate, when he reminisced years later to a friend about 'the wit and humour that then flowed more copiously by far than the claret'. In a famous ironic exchange with George Norton, the subject of the wine at Storey's Gate also came up. Norton chose to boast about the wines he had in his cellar, in reference to the wine he was actually serving: 'I have got wine twenty times as good in my cellar.' 'No doubt, no doubt,' replied

---

* Disraeli did in fact enter the House of Commons as a Tory in 1837.

Disraeli coolly, 'but my dear fellow, this is quite good enough for such *canaille* as you have got here today.'[16]

Unfortunately, George Norton did not fare well anecdotally either as a host or a guest. In the latter capacity, Caroline was seen as the dominant one, leading him reluctantly about. One observer of London society wrote: 'her poor husband is constantly brought in, in a very ridiculous manner.'[17] It was for amusement, much of it provided (occasionally outrageously) by the hostess herself, not lavish hospitality, that the guests flocked to the house of Caroline Norton. The extremely busy life she led with her own salon, and frequent visits to the salons of others, did not prevent the development of a social conscience.

As Caroline said of herself: 'I make it a rule to look about me in this world.' This was conspicuous when she demonstrated, in the modern phrase, in favour of the Tolpuddle Martyrs. A march was held on 21 April 1834, organized by the social reformer Robert Owen, of around 30,000 members of the Grand National Consolidated Trades Union.[18] The intention was to submit a petition, signed by a quarter of a million people, to the Home Office (where Melbourne, of course, held sway) in protest against the sentence of seven years' transportation of six agricultural workers from Tolpuddle in Dorset. Their offence was to have taken a secret oath to join the Union in the ceremony of admission, such oaths being forbidden by law at the time of the Nore Mutiny.

It was, in fact, Melbourne who ordered the magistrates to use this excuse for severe penalties: 'Perhaps you will be able to make an example by such means,' he wrote.[19] The march trailed from Islington to the Home Office; but Melbourne refused to receive representatives of the hostile and indignant crowd.

Nine years later, Caroline reflected on her experience marching down Whitehall: 'I pique myself on being the only "lady of fashion" who walked with the famous "Trades Unions procession" when cannon were planted on the Admiralty and the government was quaking with fear.'[20]

Throughout this time, Caroline's relationship with the Home Secretary grew warmer, despite her own liberal sympathies and Melbourne's views on society which were, in so many ways, more Tory than Whig. Given Caroline's high spirits and sense of mischief, there were some incidents when this apparent intimacy caused astonishment, if not worse. Lord Malmesbury in his Memoirs noted one such occasion: 'I met Mrs Norton at the French Ambassador's. She talked in a most extraordinary manner and kicked Lord Melbourne's hat over her head. The whole *corps diplomatique* were amazed.' Such an episode pointed at first sight to Caroline's lack of discretion – or was it her public fearlessness? – something which she evidently cultivated as she became famous for it. Melbourne himself was certainly equal to such situations. Benjamin Robert Haydon told a story in which Caroline, at a party of the Duke of Devonshire's, began by taking Melbourne's hand before begging a favour with the words: 'Lord Melbourne, *do*.' At which Lord Melbourne looked round and, at least according to Haydon, who was probably jealous, said: '*Do let go of my hand*. I want to scratch my nose.'[21]

By nature, the social world was inclined to assume the worst, with Caroline's ostentatiously free way with Lord Melbourne's hat standing for a host of more private liberties. After all, Melbourne himself did not have an untarnished reputation, at any rate where satirists were concerned. 'The Paw Paw Premier' was one merry nickname, along with a scurrilous poem about garter-groping.[22]

Meanwhile, the mission on which George Norton had sent his wife was successful. He duly became a Metropolitan City Magistrate, a paid position of £1,000 a year to judge cases in Lambeth Police Court (just under £90,000 in modern values). This helped give some economic stability, and made up for the loss of his parliamentary seat. Although Norton had his detractors, who spoke of his laziness, there were other stories of his charitable behaviour as a magistrate, to put against complaints of non-attendance. It should be borne in mind that when he finally came to retire, he was listed among the friends of the poor, including poor criminals, as 'one who was ever ready to stretch forth a helping hand for those in distress'.[23]

The magistracy was not the only kind of advancement that Melbourne, by his influence, secured for George Norton. There was another very different distinction for which Norton pined: the courtesy title of 'Honourable', which meant nothing in law but granted him the additional social status which he craved.* Melbourne helped secure a Letter Patent to this effect, which the King signed in November 1831. 'Thus was he made honourable,' was Caroline's double-edged comment; although she now used the description of 'The Honble [sic] Mrs Norton' on the title page of her books.

Throughout all this time, Caroline continued to write – to write for a living. As she whimsically described herself to Richard Monckton Milnes, she was 'a poor mercenary servant of the Muses'.[24] That the money she earned was her husband's legal property was something she, like other married writers, took for granted at the time.

Caroline would, however, become eloquent about the life of a working mother. To Frances Trollope in August 1832, she referred to her boys and 'a mother's love that toiled for them' (Caroline had two sons at this point; Willie was born a year later). In one of her campaigning pamphlets which followed, she would describe herself: 'I have sat up all night – even at times when I have had a young infant to nurse – to finish tasks for some publisher.'[25] It is clear that, even at this point, Caroline regarded herself as working for her children, not her husband, despite Norton's legal status as owner of her works.

A play, *The Gypsy Father*, produced at the Covent Garden Theatre (with its Sheridan connections) in 1831, was derided by Fanny Kemble, although she conceded: 'But after all, she is in the right – she has given the public what they deserve,' adding: 'Of course it made one cry horribly.' *The Wife and Woman's Reward* was published in 1835: two separate stories as a single publication. Caroline received a £300 payment for two editions

---

* In theory this courtesy title indicated that Norton was the son of a Lord. Actually he was the nephew of the previous Lord Grantley; the present Lord Grantley was his elder brother, with George in line to inherit the title if his brother remained childless.

(approximately £26,000 in modern values). This was a decent, even handsome reward for the time in which Caroline lived.

In February 1835, an American writer-cum-journalist, Nathaniel Parker Willis, visited another writer-cum-*salonnière*, Lady Blessington, and commented afterwards that her novels sold for more than any other writer except Bulwer Lytton, who got £1,500 to Lady Blessington's £400, with the Honourable Mrs Norton at £250 and Lady Charlotte Bury at £200, and most authors below that. 'D'Israeli cannot sell a book *at all, I hear*,' he ended, inaccurately.[26] This was a time when the price of books was rapidly declining in England in response to the tremendous rise in the numbers of the literate in the middle class with money to spend on them.

The story of *The Wife* has a particular interest, because it marks the conspicuous compassion Caroline would show in future for those in some way blighted at birth.[27] Its focus is a young girl, Catherine Dalrymple, who would now be called disabled, but was then described (by herself as well as others) as 'born crooked', to indicate that her spine was twisted.

Catherine's sister, Susan Dalrymple, was surely a self-portrait of Caroline: 'The most Grecian of heads [Grecian was a description often applied to her] . . . dark eyes, black silken hair', with her 'most lovely feature', her mouth. 'She herself is not so proud of her beauty as of her conversational powers and she herself admits that she has the reputation of being capable of giving up my dearest friend for a bon mot,' while 'those who laugh do not always approve.' 'Don't you see I'm crooked?' asks poor Catherine in contrast. A little boy takes her hand and says gently: 'People are not so pretty when they are crooked but they are just as much loved.' In short, little Frederick Haslingden, son of the snobbish Lady John, does not care: 'Catherine was the most loveable person he ever saw except his own father.'

Lady John Haslingden's behaviour remains conventionally disdainful, so that in the end poor Catherine loses control and asks: does Lady John never dream that God may turn her own child into a twisted thing? Despite the goodness of old Mr Brooksly, who decides to leave Catherine money in order that someone will marry her – money enough to make people think her 'straight as an arrow' – Catherine feels despair, as expressed in her poem:

> I know the startled glance is painful
> Which meets my twisted form,
> I've seen the stranger shrink away
> And shook with passion's storm.

It is Susan who comes to the rescue, out of sheer goodness of heart. In order to provide Catherine with a home, she decides to marry Lord Glenalton, although in love with someone else.

Naturally there are fearful troubles in such a marriage, but at least Catherine finds peace in 'the beautiful solitude of Loch-Lyne', on the Glenalton estate, with the rough deerhound and little shaggy pony, visiting the sick in the hamlet while the Glenaltons themselves depart for London. What Benjamin Richard Haydon described as 'a sad Picture of High Life within a certain class' follows.[28] The eventual marriage of Susan's daughter, whom she has protected until the unusually late age of twenty-three, does eventually give her a kind of happy ending.

Another of Caroline's prominent works, the poem 'The Creole Girl', published in the collection headed *The Dream, and Other Poems* in 1840, also features an innocent child victim – although in this case the disability is her mixed race (the meaning of Creole at the time), not physical deformity.[29] But it similarly illustrates Caroline's compassionate interest in the subject of such youthful victims, guilty of nothing yet condemned:

> She was the child of Passion, and of Shame,
> English her father, and of noble birth;
> Though too obscure for good or evil fame
> Her unknown mother faded from the earth.

'That fair West Indian' sends the child to her white father with what is termed 'a poison in its looks'. There may be poison in her racial heritage, but she is also beautiful. The child finds 'Curiosity's set frozen stare' fixing on her, thus making her understand 'her loveliness'. But this she shrinks from, and her loneliness increases. She is 'A flower transplanted to too cold a land'. One man does fall in love with her, but rejects his own passion: 'He *could* have loved her – fervently and well,' but the cold world, 'with its false allure', held him back. Yet he could not forget 'the Creole orphan' even when courting some more suitable heiress among her father's friends:

> The very glory of her features' play
> Seem'd like the language of a foreign land . . .
> And left us dreaming of the sunny south.

The ending is sad – in temporal terms. The Creole girl falls sick, becomes thin and wasted and finally dies. But the author encourages the reader to see this fate as finally a happy one:

> There (in Heaven) shall thy soul its chains of slavery burst
> There, meekly standing before God's high throne
> Thou'lt find the judgments of our earth reversed
> And answer for no errors but thy own.

Woman's Reward, the novel published together with *The Wife*, contains reflections of the Nortons' own situation, although the sacrifices are made by a sister for her brother, not a wife for her husband.[30] It is a long and often tragic journey, with Mary Dupré as a charming heroine. She gives up the love of her life, William Clavering, at the request of her handsome wastrel of a brother: he believes this will enable him to marry Lady Clarice Lyell. Clarice is flighty and spoilt: she will eventually abandon him. Lionel Dupré, the wastrel brother, 'ruins' a young girl who has a baby by him, Frank, who dies. Fortunately, Clavering by the end is a widower, and is able to offer 'the dregs of a heart' to Mary. Lionel has some of George Norton's characteristics: he is violent, for example, whereas William Clavering has those of Melbourne: he has a habit of putting down his book while reading and gazing long and hard at Mary – but never declaring his love. Interestingly, Melbourne himself thought she had made the wastrel Lionel 'too d----d [sic] a beast', while Mary Dupré sacrificed altogether too much for him. Nevertheless he admitted: 'It is not unnatural. Many people have acted as amiably, as romantically and as foolishly.'[31]

Alongside books published, and many more to follow, social success was being established. Caroline was presented at Court to King William and Queen Adelaide a few years after her marriage in 1831, a ritual indicating acceptance, which highly gratified that side of her nature which was extremely keen on such things. There were also social problems. It was true that, domestically, the two families of Sheridan and Norton had little in common. Just as Caroline found George Norton's sisters disagreeable and managerial, he in turn protested against the frequent visits Caroline chose to make, with the children, to the famously charming Helen Blackwood and the famously beautiful Georgia Seymour. The latter's home, Maiden Bradley, provided a convenient refuge from London life. In turn George's brother, Lord Grantley of Wonersh Park, had never shown any particular sympathy for Caroline.

A prolonged visit from George's sister Augusta in 1832 had done nothing to improve matters. Augusta Norton was aged thirty, a spinster who presented the most eccentric appearance. Her hair was cut severely short and she dressed in the style which would come to be associated with the American feminist Amelia Jenks Bloomer: a short dress and trousers gathered in at the ankle. None of this commended her to her sister-in-law. The need to take Augusta with her on social occasions became the subject of another dispute with George Norton.

Yet these were minor domestic difficulties compared to the glittering nature of Caroline Norton's public life. Surely 'Starry Night' would continue to shine forth in the particular sky she had chosen? It was not to be.

CHAPTER FOUR

What Mr Norton Liked

'They appeared better friends than I should have liked if I
had been Mr Norton'

James Stuart Wortley at Lord Melbourne's dinner, 8 December
1835

CHRISTMAS 1835 FOUND CAROLINE AND the three
boys with the Seymours at Maiden Bradley. In January 1836,
she described herself cantering on the downs on 'a pretty little
fat black mare'.[1] George Norton was with his own family in
Scotland. It marked the end of a year of strife in which Norton's
treatment of his wife degenerated horribly.

Looking at the situation from his point of view, it was the sub-
ordinate role in which he found himself that riled him. Norton
dreaded humiliation. He was haunted by the impression that
Caroline did not think he was quite good enough for her and
her friends, Whig or otherwise. He was unaware that the sharp
Lady Granville had pronounced on a rather different issue: 'the
great thing against him [Norton] is that he swallows the lovers
or not according to their rank and position. Lord Melbourne yes.
Captain Trelawny no.'[2] Nevertheless, he sensed the contemptu-
ous feeling in the world around him. After all, in a measure, it
was true.

Lady Granville was alluding to a new man in Caroline's life: Edward Trelawny. This was another romantic teasing friendship which began around the middle of 1835. Trelawny, then in his forties, had begun life in the Navy. He was the celebrated surviving friend of the Romantic poets Shelley and Byron, the latter having once described him as the 'personification of my Corsair'. It was Trelawny who arranged for Shelley's funeral after his tragic death at sea and Trelawny again who looked after the obsequies of Byron, having joined him in 1823 in supporting the Greek fight for independence.

Trelawny's personal life was equally adventurous: he has been described as attempting 'to live out in reality the life of a Byronic hero'.[3] His looks were certainly what is traditionally known as Byronic: a mass of thick, dark, curling hair, and a passionate gaze beneath his dark, overhanging brows. His hands, however, were 'brown as a labourer's' after a rough life of toil at sea and elsewhere. For Fanny Kemble, Trelawny resembled the hero of a wild-life adventure, very tall and powerfully made – Herculean was another word used – in contrast to which his deep voice was 'indolently gentle'.[4]

By the time Trelawny became close to Caroline Norton, he had already had two failed marriages, the second of which was to the sister of a Greek warlord. In 1827, he divorced her and returned to England; four years later he published *Adventures of a Younger Son*, which described the life he imagined he had led, rather than the reality. (The rank of Captain did not represent his actual naval career, either.) Trelawny also associated with the Philosophical Radicals, with their advanced political views, which included supporting rights for women.

Edward Trelawny was sufficiently besotted with Caroline to hold forth to another woman, Mary Shelley, on the subject. She was the daughter of Mary Wollstonecraft and William Godwin, now in her late thirties, who as a teenager had run away with Percy Bysshe Shelley and married him after the suicide of his first wife; she was famous as the author of *Frankenstein*, published in 1818. William Godwin had described his own daughter as 'singularly bold, somewhat imperious and active of mind. Her desire for knowledge is great, and her perseverance in everything she undertakes is invincible.'[5]

Mary Shelley also had her own physical glamour: a contemporary author, Mary Cowden Clarke, recalled her well-shaped, golden-haired head, almost always a little bent and drooping, her marble-white shoulders and arms, statuesquely visible in the perfectly plain black velvet dress which the customs of the time allowed to be cut low. Then there were her thoughtful, earnest eyes and her 'intellectually curved mouth, with a certain close compressed and decisive expression while she listened'.[6]

In September 1835, Mary Shelley listened to Edward Trelawny on the subject of Caroline Norton and responded in generous terms: 'I do not wonder at your not being able to deny yourself the pleasure of Mrs Norton's company. I never saw a woman I thought so fascinating. Had I been a man I should certainly have fallen in love with her, as a woman, ten years ago, I should have been spellbound, and, had she taken the trouble, she might have wrapped me round her finger.' This was a time, Mary explained, when she was frightened of men and apt to go 'tousy-mousy' (sic) for women. She proceeded to dwell at length on the pretty way Mrs Norton's witticisms glided from her lips, and her 'eloquent colour which ebbed and flowed', not to speak of her fine eyes and open brow, in a way which certainly sounded quite tousy-mousy, as it were. But Mary Shelley concluded by forbidding Trelawny to pass on these compliments. As a London lady, Caroline might 'quiz her' on them.[7]

Where Trelawny was the 'Pirate' to some, to Caroline he was her 'Tame Wolf' (just occasionally, 'Wolf! not tame, but most wild, strange and unmanageable'). He was actually Caroline's senior by sixteen years – but Caroline took the line that she was the older one: unconsciously echoing Mary Shelley, she was his 'much-valued Lady of London'. After that she gave Trelawny a political lecture on 'your hatred of *Lordlings* or rather the hatred you *imagine* you feel for them'. It began in her typically mocking style. Personally, she felt that 'considering the idleness, luxury and temptation of their lives it is marvellous how they turn out – many of them much *better* [underlined three times] and *none* of them worse, than the *multitude*.' Then she became more serious: 'It is not *contempt* for that class [aristocrats] which you feel or you would not be so eternally thinking and talking of them.' Was it curiosity, or perhaps 'an unconscious and involuntary envy, of men who enter life with all the advantages others spend a life struggling to *obtain*' which was the real secret of 'you *Levellers*', she concluded, making her own point of view clear. 'To be "a *Liberal*" is to be the best sort of man, to be a thorough "Democrat" is to be the worst sort of *boy*.'[8]

Caroline's own relationship with Mary Shelley was in fact endorsed by one of her acts of patronage, in which she made use of her influence with Melbourne. It was a question of the pension of William Godwin's second wife and widow. Godwin himself had been granted £300 a year from the Royal Bounty by the Prime Minister, but that ceased with his death. Caroline was a regular visitor to the Godwins' house at New Palace Yard, Westminster.

At Mary Shelley's request, Caroline went to Melbourne, something she prided herself on being able to do, and asked her 'Dearest Lord' to help the poor woman. Melbourne duly agreed to give £300 *ex gratia* (roughly £26,000 in modern values).[9] Caroline's accord with Mary Shelley contrasted with the hostile feelings which she evidently aroused in many women. The Whig ladies, for example, also allowed a kind of female misogyny to prevail in their judgements: it was as though it was really too much for one woman to be beautiful, talented – and extremely attractive to men.

Caroline's social antics in privileged circles naturally did nothing to soothe these feelings. Even Mary Shelley, contemplating Caroline's friendship with Trelawny – he had succumbed to her 'voluptuous charms and witty tongue' – reflected that 'she was said to have a stony heart withal'. She added: 'So I hope she will make him pay for numerous coquetries with our sex.'[10]

For her part, Caroline responded in kind. Referring to the undue sensitivity of Teresa Guiccioli, the last love of Byron, she described her as 'a little fool . . . the touchiness of *women* is insupportable, and it is the *real* reason why their companionship is not so pleasant as that of men, to men who have neither time nor inclination to go through a series of petty disputes.'[11]Although Caroline admitted that, along with the rest of the world, she had rushed to meet Byron's mistress . . .

Meanwhile, there was a renewed drama in the Sheridan family. In May 1835, Brinsley Sheridan, Caroline's handsome, dissolute brother, eloped with the heiress Marcia Grant, to the horror of the latter's father, General Sir Colquhoun Grant, of Frampton Court in Dorset, a veteran of Waterloo. It was generally felt that the Sheridan family (in whose history, after all, elopements featured strongly) had encouraged the match, and helped to obfuscate the escape route of the young couple so that they could get married at Gretna Green; after which it was too late to apprehend them.

Grant challenged Georgia's husband to a duel, and George Norton was similarly accused (although he was probably unaware of the plotting).[12] On the one hand, the whole business underlined the raffish nature of the Sheridan family; on the other it led to a long and happy marriage. Sir Colquhoun accepted his son-in-law, died not long after, and thus the happy couple lived at Frampton Court and enjoyed Marcia's substantial inheritance.

Gracious Frampton Court, built at the beginning of the eighteenth century and later enlarged, became a place of refuge for Caroline and her children under the sway of Marcia and Brinsley Sheridan. There were delights inside and out: a magnificent library and a park laid out by Capability Brown in 1790.

For Caroline at home in Storey's Gate, things were not turning out so happily. Norton's conduct had become so dangerous that Caroline, made additionally vulnerable by pregnancy, left him and took refuge with her sister Georgia in the summer of 1835. Negotiations followed for her return, in which this time brother Brinsley Sheridan acted for her. Promises of amendment were of course made, although Norton declined to improve their financial arrangements despite suggestions that Caroline should have greater control.[13]

She did then return. In the future, this voluntary return, which was a matter of record, was to be of considerable legal consequence. There was another ominous aspect to the whole episode: the attitude of Melbourne. He strongly discouraged her from leaving George – just as he would have discouraged any woman from leaving her husband, making his strong views on the subject clear.

In August 1835, it seems that Caroline had a miscarriage. It is not clear that this was directly caused by a physical assault by Norton. Caroline herself blamed 'the agitation and misery to which she had been exposed'. News of the miscarriage was considered interesting enough for *The Times* to report on 3 August: 'Mrs Norton has been dangerously ill but we are happy to say is now convalescent.'[14]

Subsequently, Caroline took the children to lodgings in Bushy Park, conveniently close to Hampton Court, so that they could all visit her mother. By this time, life with her children surrounded by her own family was beginning to offer a special domestic happiness, revealing a very different character from that other, public Caroline with her witty sallies and her ability to sing and recite a poem to fascinate society. Furthermore, at this point she prided herself on having no favourites out of the three children: 'But in the Mother's Heart found room for ALL', as she wrote in a poem published five years later.[15]

Now at Bushy Park, Caroline wrote lyrically about the deer: 'so tame that they join us while drinking tea in the open air and eat out of the children's hands. We call the King of the Herd "Hugh": he answers to it when Brin feeds him.' Brin refused to stop until the arrival of Captain Blackwood, Helen's husband, caused the deer to retreat. Even then Brin did not give up: 'Don't be startlesome, Hugh,' he said, 'this is a kind gentleman, Aunt Nelly's [Helen's] husband – if you is afraid, I'll send him away.'[16]

There were other country visits which did not include George Norton. For example, Caroline went to Brighton and from there went sailing with Edward Trelawny. The Pirate proved an admirable companion, notably kind to the children, and gentle altogether. She reassured her mother ('Dearest Muddles') in true Caroline style: 'He is *not* handsome: the hunchiest man that ever looked like a gentleman; and the *growliest*.' But she had 'sailed all over the seas in an open boat with him, and have neither been drowned, ravished, or sold on the coast of Barbary'.[17]

All of this fun contrasted with the atmosphere at home. Caroline complained that on one occasion, George Norton announced he was going out just as she arrived back. There was no dinner and no welcome. Her husband was 'sullen'. Caroline particularly disliked that; she announced to her mother that she'd '*much* rather be beat, even by *him*' than endure that kind of treatment.[18] This was a joke in slightly bad taste, given the horror of Norton's abuse, but at the same time it was characteristic of Caroline at this point that she still attempted to laugh off adversity.

After that, she spent an increasing amount of time at Maiden Bradley with the Seymours as well as at Frampton Court, while Norton developed a relationship with a rich cousin, Miss Margaret Vaughan, hoping that he might become her heir. (Naturally this middle-aged spinster thoroughly disliked Caroline.) He also went to his own relations in Scotland.

All this time, she had two other lives: one was as a writer, the mercenary servant, as she had described herself. Following the two novels, *The Wife and Woman's Reward*, a book of short pieces, *The Coquette, and Other Tales and Sketches*, was also published in 1835. In the main story it is tempting, once again, to detect elements of self-portrait in Bessie, the eponymous coquette – although not very flattering ones (just as the title was bait for her critics).[19]

A young man reproaches Bessie with 'that spirit of coquetry which is the curse of your existence', prompting her to encourage everyone around her 'to traffic for compliments – to barter looks for words, and words for feelings', thus making miserable everyone around her. But there are considerable differences: Bessie has no children, no lapdogs, no sisters-in-law, 'none of the torments of married life', and above all she is rich as Croesus. It all ends in tragedy, followed by repentance: Bessie insists on taking Lucy, a frail young lady, to a ball, indulging in the 'selfishness of a good deed' – 'Oh! madman! fool! *to let her dance.*' Lucy dies as a result. Bessie, overcome with remorse, resolves to stop being a coquette. 'The Traitor' has a similarly tragic ending, when Ida protects her lover Bertram, who has betrayed his chief, Count Isinger, for high-minded reasons, and dies with his name on her lips.

'The Spirit of the Hurricane', on the other hand, represents that persistent interest Caroline showed in 'looking around her': the principal character is a sailor, Charles Louvel, who witnesses a Barbade (*sic*) hurricane and goes to the rescue of his beloved half-sister Pauline. His father's illegitimate daughter, 'a person of colour', is starving and faces going back into slavery with all its horrors, on her mother's death. Louvel steals money from his stern captain to feed her, is discovered and receives 150 lashes, which kills him. Pauline dies too, embracing his corpse.

Caroline's third life as the enchantress who was known to have cast her spell over the Prime Minister continued. In this connection, the politics of the period were engrossing in themselves. Melbourne, having been appointed to succeed Lord Grey at the head of a Whig government in July 1834, was dismissed as Prime Minister in November; the King, impatient with the Whigs' ardour for reforms (Catholic Emancipation being followed closely by the Great Reform Bill), hoped to replace them with a Tory ministry. Unfortunately for him, the General Election which by contemporary custom followed in January 1835, did not provide the desired Tory majority; their leader, Sir Robert Peel, was thus unable to form a government.

Melbourne returned as Prime Minister in April 1835. At the same time as relations between the Nortons worsened publicly as well as privately, Melbourne was once more in the extremely exposed position of Prime Minister of the country. What was more, this was a man who had already featured in one suit alleging adultery – and was known to have dealt with it by throwing money at the problem. At this moment, the warmth of his relationship with Caroline Norton remained a matter of general comment.

In early December 1835, a certain James Stuart Wortley was asked by Melbourne to a dinner party explicitly to meet Mrs Norton. He described it all to Lady Wharncliffe: 'a more jolly party, or anything like a Prime Minister, I never saw. There was nothing improper said or done, *of course*, but they appeared better friends than I should have liked if I had been Mr Norton.'[20] That seemed to go to the heart of the matter: Norton knew perfectly well what the verdict of the world was. At the same time, there was another aspect to the whole matter which Mr Wortley did not mention: Norton himself was, in purely worldly terms, benefiting from his wife's relationship with the Prime Minister.

As for Caroline herself, it seems clear from her correspondence that if she was not in love with Melbourne at this point, he was at the least her love object, to use a later phrase, the focus of her sentimental feelings (apart from her children). Which did not necessarily mean that they were lovers. Caroline had many admirers; she flirted with many people, that was her nature. She even joked about her addiction to older men with George Norton and he found it fun. He responded by describing Miss Vaughan's passion for him, which had been expressed in 'a thorough love letter'. It is high time, wrote Norton, that he should sanction 'to a remarking world' her 'penchant for old men' by suffering 'this antique faux pas', as he unchivalrously termed Miss Vaughan, in his own life.[21]

Nevertheless, the tenor of Caroline's letters to Melbourne grows indisputably ever more tender as she makes it clear how much he has become the focus of her life. The frequency of his visits, however innocuous, could not fail to be remarked upon by the servants of various types, who admitted him downstairs, or ministered to their mistress upstairs.

Throughout her life Caroline made it clear that what she expected from men was protection: she was happy to accept – in theory at least – that 'the natural position of woman is inferiority to man', but in return men were expected to play their part and protect women. It was a bargain. A man who did not protect a woman was breaking his side of it.

Mrs Ellis, in her esteemed work *The Women of England*, published in 1839, summed it up: men must treat women as friends even if public schools have educated them to hold women in contempt. Women, on the other hand, must maintain a different attitude: 'in women's love is mingled the trusty dependence of a child, for she ever looks up to a man as her protector, and her guide.' It was, after all, a concept which was enunciated by Sir William Blackstone in his seminal eighteenth-century guide to English laws: she, the wife, performs everything under the 'wing, protection and cover' of the husband, since by marriage her very legal existence has been consolidated into his.[22]

The role of a man as protector was a theme to which Caroline would return again and again in hard times. It is significant in this connection that her father, Tom Sheridan, vanished from her life when she was three, came back briefly eighteen months later and left forever when she was five. The natural protection of a father was something she never really remembered – and perhaps craved in consequence.

The need for protection – as prescribed by Mrs Ellis and the conventions of the time – was also a note of positive entitlement which she struck from the beginning with George Norton, as when she was troubled by 'horrid dreams' and wrote to him: 'I *cannot bear sleeping alone; ahem!* You ought to come down and protect me.'[23] Clearly, George Norton's attacks on her betrayed this fundamental need in a fearful way. Melbourne, on the other hand, the distinguished older man with a worldly position that enabled him to help other people, incarnated Caroline's idea of a protector.

Just before Easter 1836, which fell on 3 April, things came to a head in a terrible way. Caroline had been invited to take the children to the Sheridans at Frampton Court. As she told the story much later, relations with Norton were perfectly friendly at this point, but all the same, the Sheridans declined to invite him. Shortly after Christmas, Norton had still been asking for her intervention with Melbourne to get an appointment for a friend.

A tender little anecdote sent by the mother to the father about this time shows how close they could still be. 'I was showing the opera-glass you gave me to the boys and Brin said: "What do you see?" "I see your dear little dirty face" quoth I.' She then handed him the glasses and asked Brin what *he* saw. '"I see your dear *big* dirty face" quoth he. Wasn't it quick and funny?' Another anecdote concerned Fletcher, suggesting they should 'resign', meaning go outside. It turned out that he had picked up the political term from the grown-ups' chat above his head. 'So much for living with Ministers,' commented the mother to the father.[24] Now George Norton urged her, since 'we were friends', to overrule her brother's objections to receiving him and get him invited to Frampton. She did not succeed. Then they began to quarrel again. Caroline announced that she was going to persist in her plan and head there with the children: Fletcher in particular needed a change of air after a bout of scarlatina. She also ordered her servants not to admit the egregious Miss Margaret Vaughan, who always made mischief, to the house.

The Nortons parted angrily, George's last words on her visit to Frampton with the boys being: 'Well, the children shall not; that I have determined,' and he ordered the carriage, which had been got ready for departure, to be unpacked. Upstairs in the nursery, he gave the same orders. In Caroline's account, when the nurse queried these orders, she simply told her to obey Mr Norton's orders.

The next morning Caroline made what would later seem to be a major mistake, probably still underestimating the seriousness of the situation. She left the house very early and went to her sister's house at Spring Gardens, near Trafalgar Square. It was while she was there that the dreadful message came: her own manservant arrived and told her that the children had been bundled into a hackney coach and taken away.

It transpired that they had been taken to Margaret Vaughan's house. Caroline followed them and confronted Miss Vaughan. She was met, in her own words, by 'bitter insolence'. The boys were subsequently taken down to Wonersh Park, where Norton's brother Lord Grantley was equally hostile to Caroline. On 2 April 1836, Easter Saturday, Caroline wrote an appalled letter to Melbourne: 'He has taken all my children from me!' She added: 'I could hear their little feet running merrily over my head while I sat sobbing below – only the ceiling between us, and I am not able to get at them! my little Briney! and poor Spencer [Fletcher] who has been so ill.' She told him: 'I have done nothing but cry since I saw you.'[25]

A few days later, Caroline wrote to Melbourne telling him that she intended to go back to her husband 'unconditionally'.[26] What she outlined was not exactly unconditional. Her first reason was the need to prevent others, who were her enemies, from guiding George Norton. She also needed to pave the way for a final departure, which, even though 'utterly unendurable', she might need to make. Thirdly, this way she could be with her children without a struggle. If, on the other hand, Norton forced her to sue for alimony and kept the children from her, she might see if there would be a refuge for her abroad, in Belgium (where she thought Queen Louise of the Belgians might 'countenance' her at Brussels since her husband, King Leopold, had shown himself favourable to Caroline), failing that Italy or Germany.

Caroline reflected bitterly about her husband: 'Here is a man, who was mad to marry me at 18, who turns me out of his house 9 years afterwards and inflicts vengeance as bitterly as he can, by taking away the children,' the children 'who were the offspring of that long desired union', thus 'cursing me *thro' them* . . . I cannot write any more – write to *me* – there is more comfort in a word of yours or in a look than in all that other people can do.'

There was a further addition: 'I have just had a letter from *my footman*', who gave her details of where they had been taken. She then added with a confidence that might have been misplaced when the power of money was added into the equation: 'Thank God everyone in the house hates him, so they will tell me what is done.'

Wild threats began to be exchanged on both sides. George Norton talked of marrying again – this would assume a divorce – and having further children. A clergyman, the Revd Barlow, was brought in to negotiate, as opposed to George's lawyer, Sir William Follett. Caroline responded by saying to Barlow on the subject of Norton's putative second marriage: 'I would rather starve as Norton's wife all my life, than leave him free to give a stepmother to my children.'[27]

In the meantime, Melbourne's response to her appeal was not exactly encouraging: 'I hardly know what to write to you, or what comfort to offer you. You know as well as I do, that the best course is to keep yourself tranquil, and not to give way to feelings of passion, which God knows, are too natural to be easily resisted . . . You know that I have always counselled you to bear everything and remain to the last.' Although even Melbourne admitted that it might no longer be possible.[28]

It was the question of the children which drove Caroline to madness – or was it the reasonable response of a devoted mother? On the other hand, it was the question of adultery which seemed to be driving George Norton to equal madness. Mr Norton had stopped liking the situation. But was it purely adultery or were there, in fact, other motives behind his conduct?

The man who had written earlier in the year asking his wife to use her influence with Melbourne, was now about to take an action against the Whig Prime Minister of enormous danger to the latter. He proposed to sue him for adultery with his wife, and ask for a prodigious sum in damages.

PART TWO

SUMMER'S GONE

Hour after hour I wander
By men unseen –
And sadly my wrung thoughts ponder
On what hath been.
Summer's gone!

Caroline Norton, *The Coquette, and Other Tales and Sketches*

CHAPTER FIVE

Helpless

*'Well – a woman is made a helpless wretch by these laws of
men, – or she would be allowed a defence, a counsel, in such
an hour.'*

Caroline Norton to Mary Shelley, 25 June 1836

CAROLINE NORTON WAS NOT A co-defendant in the action
that her husband, the Hon. George Norton, proposed to bring
against William Lamb, 2nd Viscount Lord Melbourne. Her name
was, however, central to the case: it was for Crim. Con. with
Caroline, his lawfully wedded wife, that George Norton was
suing the Prime Minister. Damages to this, his legal property in
human form, were estimated at the vast amount of £10,000.* But
since Caroline had no legal existence outside marriage, she was
not represented in court.

During the trial, her words and deeds would be widely cited
in the sworn testimonies of witnesses, but, unlike Melbourne,
she would have no one to speak on her behalf about the truth
or otherwise of this evidence. As Caroline would write bitterly
to her friend Mary Shelley: 'Well, – a woman is made a helpless

---

* Just under £900,000 in modern values.

wretch by these laws of men – or she would be allowed a defence, a counsel, in such an hour.'[1]

The history of Crim. Con. actions was a chequered one. Vitally, this was a completely separate process from divorce, which was illegal as such at the time.*[2] Up to this date, for those determined to secure a divorce, with permission to remarry, the only route was an Act of Parliament. That was an extremely expensive business – so expensive that divorce was in effect limited to a tiny minority in the shape of the rich. Legal separation, heavily penalizing the wife according to the property rules of the time, was a more common route; although, obviously, that did not encompass remarriage. That left the poor with their own pragmatic method of divorce, which was to separate with the possibility of marrying again illegally, relying on obscurity to get away with it.[3]

Crim. Con., as opposed to divorce, concentrated on damage to property rather than any kind of legal separation of the couple involved. Not only was it separate, but a successful action for Crim. Con. did not automatically entitle a husband to ask for a divorce under the rules of that time; if there was any hint of collusion, it might even tell against him. A report by a Franco-American visitor to England who arrived in 1810, L. Simond, made clear what a strictly commercial process it was: 'This criminal conversation is not prosecuted *criminally*, but produces only a civil suit for the recovery of damages, estimated in money.'[4] Simond also placed significant emphasis on what might destroy the husband's case. The degree of happiness in the marriage at the time of the alleged Crim. Con. was to be influential in deciding the amount of damages. Crudely put, if the property – that is the wife – was no longer particularly valued by its owner, the damages would be less. 'The smallest appearance of negligence or connivance on the part of the husband deprives him of all

---

* Divorce in England was first legalized by an Act of Parliament in 1857, as we shall see. The rules were different in Scotland, where divorce had been allowed since the mid-sixteenth century for adultery or desertion, with remarriage possible for the innocent party.

remedy against the seducer.' The latter would owe the husband nothing if he, the seducer, only took what was of no value to him, and which the husband 'guarded so ill'.

The case of *Worseley* v. *Bisset* had been a notorious example of this in 1782. It began with Sir Richard Worseley marrying a seventeen-year-old girl. She was dissatisfied with the match, to put it mildly: the new Lady Worseley was said to have had twenty-seven lovers before running off with a certain George Bisset. It was against Bisset that Worseley brought his action for Crim. Con., at which point Lady Worseley turned things in her favour by making scandalous revelations about Worseley's own behaviour; these included displaying his wife, naked, to Bisset in a bath house. As a result, Worseley did get damages – but only one shilling.[5]

There was a considerable rise in the numbers of cases of Crim. Con. around the turn of the nineteenth century. Such actions were certainly not unknown in the circles in which Melbourne and the Nortons moved at this time. Close to home had been the suit brought against Caroline's father, Tom Sheridan, in 1807, regarding a married woman when he was a bachelor. The development of the concept of Crim. Con. took place as a result of the decline of the Church courts. The days of public punishments for adultery and fornication – exposure in the stocks, public whipping, standing in front of the congregation or in the marketplace in white holding a candle – were over. Yet some kind of guardianship of public morals was thought necessary. The idea of trespass was extended, in the sense that the seducer of a wife trespassed on the rights of her husband. Two superior courts of common law, the King's Bench and Common Pleas, began to hear such actions. There would be judge, jury and counsels for the plaintiff and the defendant, who would neither of them be present. Once damages had been assessed, payment was enforced as with any other debt.

In the meantime, Caroline Norton's troubles continued and grew deeper. She had long had problems with the press. There were editors like Theodore Hook of *John Bull*, whose loud voice and red face were dreaded by Caroline. He had a coarse after-dinner wit, in the words of Fanny Kemble. 'Witty!' exclaimed Caroline indignantly on the subject of Hook: 'One may well be witty when one fears neither God nor the devil.'[6]

In the world of gossip, most prominent was the magazine which correctly styled itself *The Satirist*. The Hon. Mrs Norton was such an obvious target, beginning with her beauty and social connections, continuing with her legendary ability to attract admirers to her salon, and ending with the enjoyably flagrant (from the gossip writers' point of view) relationship with the Prime Minister himself. Quotations from Caroline's own published works also came in handy.

Publication of *The Wife and Woman's Reward* the previous year had elicited a parody.[7] Melbourne questioned how long 'fair Caroline' would be occupied with her book, and received this reply:

> 'Within a week or two, I hope,' she quietly repeats,
> 'You'll see me free of Proof and press, revised and
>   bound in sheets.'

There were inevitable innuendoes about the parentage of Caroline's children. About the time she had a miscarriage, there was an amusing – to outsiders – story that her new work was to be dedicated to Melbourne: it was said to be 'now lieing in [lying-in] sheets awaiting only the leisure of the publishers to present it to the world'.[8] The fact that Melbourne's family name was Lamb did not detract from the fun. There was a 'LAMB-POON' and verses headed 'THE WOLF IN LAMB'S CLOTHING', warning Norton: 'Take care the Lamb prove not the Wolf to your domestic peace.'

Melbourne was not the only admirer featured in the press. There was the Duke of Devonshire (dukes were always good copy), a Whig, son of the glamorous Georgiana, Duchess of Devonshire, and periodically Lord Chamberlain to the King. But Hart, as he had been known for years from his courtesy title of Marquess of Hartington, was unmarried and remained so;

his association with Caroline was not a serious contender for press attention.

Then there was the highly intelligent lawyer Abraham Hayward, in his thirties, whom Caroline, in her teasing mode, nicknamed 'A' for Avocat because he disliked the name Abraham, signing herself 'C. Client'.[9] Hayward founded *The Law Magazine*, which he edited in 1828; furthermore, he was famous for his dinner parties. Hayward's great intelligence, not his physical appearance, was his attraction: he was very short, and his face verged on the ugly with a big nose and a prominent bulging lower lip. His attitude to the ladies, wittily flirtatious, friendly, helpful, was exactly suited to Caroline's own taste. This was an important friendship, increasingly so as time went on, but clearly not a romance in any torrid sense on which the press could build.

Her friendship with Samuel Rogers, the poet, sage and distinguished host to writers and artists for fifty years at his house at 22 St James's Place, came into the same category. In this case, here was a clever, amusing older man (he was in his seventies and would live long enough to turn down the post of Poet Laureate in the next reign), but not a romantic connection.

Melbourne remained the focus of the press's attention, especially since references to Caroline seeking his influence to benefit her family could be added to the salacious innuendoes. Unfortunately, there was no comfort to be got from Lord Melbourne himself. Caroline's correspondence with him at this time shows painfully how the man who had been her lodestar was transformed into yet another source of suffering.

One particularly upsetting letter refers to the occasion when Caroline went in person to 10 Downing Street to break the news of Norton's action to Melbourne. 'I will not deny that among all the bitterness of this hour, what sinks me *most* is the thought of *you* – of the expression in your eye the day I told it to you . . . The *shrinking* from me and my burdensome distress.' This was, after all, the man who wrote of himself: 'You describe me very truly when you say that I am always more annoyed that there is a row than sorry for the persons engaged in it.'[10]

Caroline continued to write to Melbourne, keeping him posted with all the convolutions by which well-meaning outsiders, like the Revd Barlow and Colonel Leicester Stanhope, attempted to reconcile the Nortons. All Caroline asked for at one moment was a year's trial in Norton's company and that of her children. 'An eternal separation from them will kill me.' But Norton was beginning to talk of divorce, of which the Crim. Con. action would be the first step (although, as has been noted, not always a successful one).

There was one ominous sentence in Caroline's correspondence with Melbourne: 'N is unwilling, *most* unwilling *himself* to bring you forward. Grantley and perhaps other Tories have urged him to do it.' She ended: 'God bless you. Take care of yourself, & remember me *kindly*, are my two prayers.' She signed it with one of her pet names, Car.[11] (Caroline had several intimate signatures as well as Car, including Cary, Carey, Carly and Carry.)

The possible political conspiracy which lay behind the case was certainly the talk of the town. On 14 May, for example, Caroline's friend Edward Trelawny thought there was undoubtedly a political motivation: 'So eager are the Tories for power that they were reduced to the mean shift of getting up a private intrigue to create a public discord.' Norton himself was dismissed as a fool, in the words of Shakespeare, 'as gross as ignorance made drunk'. This foolish Norton had been persuaded to spread abroad reports 'criminating' (*sic*) Melbourne and his wife. Even if, in Trelawny's opinion, in the end it was all 'more bark than bite'.[12]

Whether it was the intention of Norton personally or not, Melbourne's position as Prime Minister was temporarily embarrassed by the action for Crim. Con. in May 1836, just as ardent Tories, such as Lords Grantley and Wynford, hoped. Melbourne himself talked of offering his resignation to King William IV – who refused to consider it.

Melbourne's role as a conservative Whig Prime Minister since the previous April (when he took on his second administration) involved endless attempts to keep together those politicians, both Whigs and Tories, who potentially agreed with each other. This attitude corresponded roughly with the wishes of the King, so his reluctance to lose Melbourne was understandable; besides, the case was yet to be heard.

Certainly, the political situation in the summer of 1836 was hardly enough to comfort Melbourne for this embarrassing development in his private life. The Whig government, trying to put through a Bill reforming Irish municipal corporations (English ones had been reformed the previous year), was defeated in the House of Lords. The radicals in Parliament were furious: the possibility of the creation of peers to alter the voting in the House of Lords was once again raised, as it had been at the time of the Reform Bill seven years earlier. Melbourne resisted it.

In private, Melbourne's main reaction seems to have been irritation – and a wish to be involved as little as possible. To Lord Holland, he made a somewhat ungallant complaint: 'The fact is He is a stupid Brute and She had not temper nor dissimulation enough to manage him.' Melbourne became ill, perhaps psychosomatically, Melbourne's body, like Melbourne's mind, being determined to spare him the ordeal of the law. He suffered from various sicknesses including 'a feeling of strangulation' so that even claret – horrors! – tasted 'quite nauseous' to him.[13]

By the last week in April, Caroline was staying at her brother Brinsley's townhouse in Grosvenor Square; her entire possessions including her clothes were left behind in her old house. All the while these tortuous negotiations, concerning the children, finances and the rest of the details of this miserable marriage, went on. Later, she moved briefly to a hotel in Spring Gardens. The tone of her letters to Melbourne becomes sombre. One ended: 'I am to be a childless mother & a disgraced wife for my *supposed power to charm* strangers, and yet the man whom I have been "charming" ever since I was two-and-twenty [the age at which she met Melbourne]—'. Then she breaks off. 'Well! I beg pardon. I dont want to torment you – all I say is, *worse* women have been better *stood by*.'[14]

The next letter, answering his note, was even more distraught: 'You need not fear my writing to you if you think it *commits you* . . .' She adds: 'God forgive you, for I do believe no one,

young or old, ever loved another better than I have loved you.'
That might seem to be conclusive about her relationship with the
Prime Minister; it still leaves unclear whether romantic passion
was ever physically consummated, and if so, to what degree. Caroline writes: 'I trust to your power & *facts* to carry you thro.'[15]
This is an important assertion – made privately to him, evidently
without fear of contradiction, that he of all people must know
the *facts* do not support Norton's accusation. It can be placed
alongside Melbourne's equally private letter to her of 23 April:
'You know that whatever is alleged (if it be alleged) is utterly
false.'[16]

Were they in fact innocent? The question can never be
answered with absolute certainty. Lord Holland succinctly represented the worldly point of view, quoting from Ariosto's *Orlando
furioso*: 'Forse era ver, ma non però credibile' (it may be true, but
it is surely not believable). Did an attractive, rakish, middle-aged
man without a wife really call regularly on a beautiful, unhappily
married young woman at her house to do nothing but discuss
Whig politics? For the cynical, Lord Holland will always have
the last word.[17]

On the other hand, there are the facts about their personal
correspondence written for each other's eyes only. First of all,
neither Caroline nor Melbourne ever admitted to having had the
affair of which they were accused – either in public declarations
or in private. This public denial, established early and maintained
by Melbourne until his death, was only to be expected. The private denial is obviously more important as evidence, although
it still could have been the result of a mutual caution, verbally
agreed. Thus, in theory, it still would be possible that they had
had a raging affair and simply lied about it in the interests of
self-preservation, as people have been known to do throughout
history. But there are various indications, trivial in themselves but
cumulative, which point in a different direction.

Caroline's teasing letter, while pregnant, twitting Melbourne on
the prospect of marrying her future daughter, has already been
mentioned. It is surely impossible for her to have written such
a light letter if both parties knew that Melbourne might have

been the father of the baby in question. Altogether, Caroline's numerous pregnancies, while not ruling out sex altogether, have to be borne in mind in view of her suggested role as a mistress. She was pregnant when she first petitioned Melbourne on behalf of her husband, bearing three children during the next five years.

This was proof of continuing conjugal relations with George Norton, who never questioned their paternity at the time. He would hardly have suggested William as the name of his third son if he suspected William, Lord Melbourne, as the father; such slurs came later. Caroline took the line that Norton himself believed her innocent, which made his action, for the sake of financial gain on the one hand and political advantage on the other, all the more reprehensible.

There was another factor which, once again, does not constitute proof but points away from full consummation. Melbourne had an acknowledged taste for flagellation in the course of consensual sex. There is no suggestion that he ever indulged in this taste with Caroline Norton – who as the indignant wife of an abusive husband was unlikely to have welcomed it. On the question of beating, she had certainly been an indignant child; on one occasion when they discussed the merits or otherwise of whipping children, Caroline pointed out that, when beaten, she had bitten the hand of the beater and rushed off to commit the crime again. 'I can recollect no single instance in which I was subdued by harshness.'[18]

Melbourne made no secret of his views. A few years later, Queen Victoria recorded his exclamation on the subject when they were discussing a French woman who deserved pity because her husband had beaten her: 'Why it is almost worthwhile for a woman to be beat, considering the exceeding pity she excites.'[19] And there was general laughter. He was evidently sufficiently open about his tastes with Caroline for her to write him a jocular letter from Rome on the subject, with details of a picture that he might enjoy. 'I saw in a shop of curiosities . . . a small black cabinet inlaid with ivory etchings . . . in the centre (to my astonishment) your favourite subject of a woman whipping a child, (or a nymph whipping Bacchus, or some such thing) . . . I had half a mind to buy it for you.'[20] This jokey epistle is not the letter a nymph would have written to her own Bacchus.

In an age without dependable birth control, dalliance of a lighter sort was of necessity popular.[21]* It seems most likely that Melbourne and Caroline indulged in caresses, of a fairly intimate sort, but stopping short of the ultimate act. As a result, she at least was convinced that she had not committed adultery.

One significant letter to Melbourne later refers to the stress that Caroline – and women in general – put on their 'actual innocence'. Melbourne rebuked her for it; the inverted commas being his.[22] Adorable flirt as she was, at least in her own estimation and the estimation of her admirers, if not that of the satirists and her own husband, she could still pride herself on her 'actual innocence'. She was a married woman beyond reproach – or anyway, beyond the ultimate reproach of adultery.

Even as Caroline's situation deteriorated, Melbourne tried hard to absolve himself from adding to her anguish. He responded to her taunts on the subject in a letter: 'I daresay you think me unfeeling but I declare that since I first heard I was proceeded against I have suffered more intensely than I ever did in my life.' He attributed his recent illness to the strain, before emphasizing: 'Now what is this uneasiness for? Not for my own character, because as you rightly say, the imputation upon me is as nothing. It is not for the political consequence to myself, although I deeply feel the consequences my indiscretion may bring upon those who are attached to me or my fortunes. The real and principal object of my anxiety and solicitude is you.'[23]

In particular, Caroline's situation regarding her children, which mattered to her more than money, more than possessions, more than reputation, was no better. From Miss Vaughan's house they were removed to the house of her agent, Mr Knapp. Having

---

* Owing to the eternal human wish to make love without physical consequences, methods of contraception, ranging from herbal preventives via primitive sheaths to coitus interruptus or withdrawal, had been known since ancient times.

discovered their whereabouts, Caroline lurked about, managing to receive a crumpled little note from Brin. Now they had been transferred, all three, to Wonersh Park, home of her hostile brother-in-law Grantley.

At one point, Caroline took a courageous decision, understandable in the circumstances but potentially disastrous. She went down personally to Wonersh Park. She was actually admitted by a footman – here was the sister-in-law of his employer, after all – and even managed to grab hold of her middle son, Brin. Then George Norton was tipped off about what was happening and had the boy wrenched away. The result therefore of her courage – or rashness – was more maternal anguish and a certain public humiliation in front of the Wonersh servants.

As Caroline herself put it in a letter to Mary Shelley: 'I failed. I saw them all; carried Brin to the gate, could not open it, and was afraid they would tear him to pieces, they caught him so fiercely. And the elder one [Fletcher] was so frightened he did not follow.' Even so, despite their 'dogged brutality', she was confident that 'If a strong arm had been with me, I should have done it.'[24]

The lawyers began to be briefed for the oncoming trial. Both counsels – for the eager plaintiff, Norton and the unwilling defendant, Melbourne – were Members of Parliament as well as barristers. It was symbolic of this case, in which political differences played a strong, if undefined, part, that the two men were respectively a Tory and a Whig.

Sir William Webb Follett, for Norton, was the Tory MP for Exeter. Clearly, he was an excellent choice since, at the age of forty, he already had a distinguished legal career: he had been knighted after acting as Solicitor General for Sir Robert Peel in his short-lived ministry which ended in April 1835. One of the ten children of a West Country timber merchant who had started life as a soldier, he had proceeded from Exeter Grammar School to Cambridge; on an Exeter plaque erected after his death, he would be hailed as 'the greatest advocate of the century'.

Sir John Campbell, who would act for the Prime Minister, was in his mid-fifties and had also had a long career; he was currently the Whig MP for Edinburgh, and had been appointed Attorney

General in both Melbourne's first administration and his current one. As a Whig he had played an active part in the proceedings leading up to the Great Reform Bill of 1832. But this was no frivolous Whig of the social Holland House variety; in fact, he rejected Lady Holland's offers of hospitality, saying he was not 'a tuft-hunter'.[25]

The first case he took on as Attorney General concerned the prosecution of a bookseller on the charge of blasphemous libel, in the course of which he spoke up strongly for divine revelation as a source of public morality. If the Ten Commandments were rejected, 'men would think they were at liberty to steal, and women should think themselves absolved from the restraints of chastity'. With such firm moral views, Campbell was clearly an excellent choice to argue that Melbourne – and by inference, Caroline Norton – had not broken the Commandment, 'Thou shalt not commit adultery.' Additional lawyers on both sides were John Bayley, an experienced older lawyer, and Richard Crowder, to assist Follett for the prosecution.

Serjeant Thomas Talfourd and Frederic Thesiger KC, both formidable men, acted as assistant counsels for the defence.

Naturally, the whole of London society buzzed with excitement, predictions, lamentations, exultations or some combination of all these emotions. The press was quick to enjoy the situation. 'Reputation is a jewel of surprising scarcity,' observed Melbourne to Mrs Norton – at least according to *The Satirist*. To which 'the Hon. Lady' was said to have replied: 'I can well imagine that by my not possessing a specimen.'[26] One of Caroline's admirers, a frequenter of her salon, was Benjamin Robert Haydon, whose diaries show a mixture of self-congratulation and self-castigation where the beautiful Mrs Norton was concerned. 'Oh you handsome, abominable hussy,' he wrote when she proved erratic in attendance as a sitter for his recreation of Cassandra.

Now, on the eve of the trial, Haydon was sure she was guilty: 'She appears to have been all I have suspected her from the first since the moment I saw her, and yet with my eyes open I sank into a species of infatuation.' And Haydon even thought

– wrongly – that his own wife might have been responsible for the case, as revenge for his infatuation. The rumour which had reached him that George Norton would produce evidence from the servants would turn out to have more substance.[27]

Charles Greville in his Diary was altogether cooler: he merely predicted that since 'John Bull fancies himself vastly moral and the Court is mighty prudish', between them 'our offhand Premier will find himself in a ticklish position.' All of this, in short, was 'inconvenient', although Lord Melbourne's friends were said to be certain of his acquittal. ('Nous verrons' was Haydon's rection to that.) It took the magnificent Duke of Wellington, whose own private life was colourful, to dismiss the whole thing. Would Melbourne resign? 'Oh Lord no! Resign? Not a bit of it. I tell you all these things are a nine days wonder . . . it will blow over and it wont signify a straw.'[28] And Wellington maintained this lofty position while some of his fellow Tories exulted at the opportunities for party-political gratification in the trial: Wellington was above such 'miserable feelings of party spite'.

There was a poignant letter from Caroline to Melbourne before the case began, dated 20 June, while she was still at Spring Gardens: 'In a couple of days, all cause for complaint, insult or reproach will be at an end . . . *If all the world advised me not, & every friend I have, knelt to me to persuade me to a different line, I would do whatever you asked – or bid me do.*' The emphasis ceased. 'I merely repeat my strong impression that you have ceased to feel the affection for me which you did.' Worse was to come: 'It is the vanity of women that always leads them to think their own an *individual & peculiar case* . . . which has misled me into a painful struggle of hope & fear, instead of quietly taking my place in *the past.*'[29] Then she named his wife – and Lady Branden, the wife in the previous case against Melbourne.

Throughout the trial, which was heard in June 1836, the care of Caroline's three sons, all under the age of seven, remained with their father, who would eventually send them far away to his sister Lady Menzies, who had detested Caroline from the start, in Scotland. The 'helpless wretch' Caroline took refuge in her mother's widow's apartment at Hampton Court Palace where she had lived as a child. News would take approximately two hours to reach her via messenger from the Law Courts.

It was the height of the English summer, and Hampton Court Palace was magically surrounded by golden fields and dark woods. Under normal circumstances, there could be no better place for tranquil retreat from a threatening world. But for Caroline personally, the prophetic lines of her poem 'Summer's Gone', printed in *The Coquette* the year before, seemed more appropriate:[30]

> Hour after hour I wander,
> By men unseen –
> And sadly my wrung thoughts ponder
> On what *hath* been.
> Summer's Gone!

LEFT: The Sheridan sisters, sometimes known as the Three Graces: Helen (b. 1807), Caroline (b. 1808) and Georgiana (b. 1809).

RIGHT: Tom Sheridan, son of the playwright Richard Brinsley Sheridan and father of Caroline. He died in South Africa when she was a child.

BELOW: Hampton Court Palace, where Caroline lived when young with her widowed mother and to which she returned for refuge.

ABOVE: Caroline by William Etty, 1839

Caroline Norton by
Daniel Maclise from a
lithograph published by
James Fraser, 1831

Caroline Norton.

THE AUTHOR OF "THE UNDYING ONE".

Published by James Fraser, 215, Regent Street London.

Engelmann, Graf & Coindet Lith.rs to his Majesty 1a. Newman St.

RIGHT: Caroline,
sketched by John Hayter.

BELOW: Caroline,
engraving by J.H. Robinson
after a portrait by
Thomas Carrick

THE CHILDREN OF CAROLINE AND GEORGE NORTON:

RIGHT:
Fletcher (b. 1829)

BELOW:
Brinsley (b. 1831)

OPPOSITE:
Willie (b. 1833)

Extraordinary Trial!

NORTON v. VISCOUNT MELBOURNE,

FOR

CRIM. CON.

Damages laid at

£10,000 !!!

A full and accurate report of this remarkable Trial taken in short
hand by an eminent Reporter expressly for this edition.

Embellished with a

PORTRAIT AND MEMOIR

OF

The Hon. Mrs. Norton,

&c. &c.

LONDON:

WILLIAM MARSHALL, 1, HOLBORN BARS.

LEFT: The proceedings of the Trial of Lord Melbourne for 'Criminal Conversation' (adultery) with Caroline Norton, 1836, published as a pamphlet

BELOW: No. 3 Chesterfield Street, Mayfair, to which Caroline moved in 1845. Her brother Brinsley had to act as assurer of the lease, since as a woman she was not legally allowed to do so, despite providing the money.

CHAPTER SIX

Extraordinary Trial

'Extraordinary Trial! Price Sixpence. Norton v. Viscount
Melbourne. Embellished with a Portrait and Memoir of The
Hon. Mrs. Norton, etc. etc.'

London; W. Marshall, 1 Holborn Bars

FROM THE VERY FIRST MOMENT the doors of the Court of
Common Pleas opened on Wednesday, 22 June 1836, the trial of
the Prime Minister provided a sensational spectacle. Long before
the time appointed for the opening of the court to the public
the galleries were crowded, it being generally understood that
as much as five guineas* had been given for seats.[1] When the
doors opened there was a tremendous rush from the hall and
every corner of the court was instantly crammed. In the midst of
the scramble, gowned and wigged barristers were prominent, but
their attempts to seek priority with cries of 'Make way for the
gentlemen of the Bar' were unavailing, and treated with laughter.

The Chief Justice of the Court of Common Pleas, who was
now to preside over this 'Extraordinary Trial' (as it was termed
in the press), was Sir Nicholas Conyngham Tindal. He arrived
in court punctually at half past nine. Tindal, who was sixty, had

---

* Nearly £500 today.

occupied the position since November 1834. A man of great learning and a distinguished lawyer (he had successfully defended Queen Caroline in her trial), he had previously been a Tory MP and Solicitor General for three years. The jury of twelve men was then called.* Of the twelve listed names, every single one, including Robert Stafford, subsequently chosen as foreman, was described as 'merchant'. Sir Robert Peel had been named among the jurors but was not called.

Still the uproar in court continued. When Mr Bayley tried to open the proceedings, no one could hear a word he said. Sir John Campbell, for Melbourne, announced that unless order was produced, it would be impossible for the trial to proceed. One of the officials pointed out that several of the witnesses in the case were among those struggling to get into the court. The Chief Justice then ordered them to stop struggling and leave the court until it was their turn to give testimony. He added that, as the court was now full, the doors should be closed and no one else admitted except witnesses. Still there was trouble. Sir John Campbell protested that *all* the witnesses ought to leave the court, otherwise they would not be heard. The Chief Justice agreed; the witnesses were duly removed to await their turn outside.

Finally, Sir William Follett, counsel for George Norton, addressed the court. He referred immediately to the responsibility of his task, in view of the 'high rank of one of the parties – from the position which he occupies in this country and the Councils of his Sovereign' and 'the well-known beauty and talent of the unfortunate lady'. As a result, the subject had become one of 'public and painful notoriety'. He urged the jury to dismiss all 'idle rumours' from their minds and approach the subject as they would any other trial.

Having said that, Follett immediately asked them to consider whether the defendant – Melbourne – had not taken advantage of his high position to lull suspicions that might otherwise have awakened, and introduced himself into the Norton family as 'benefactor, a patron and a friend'. Whereupon Melbourne

* Women were not allowed to serve on a jury until 1920.

had inflicted upon Norton 'the deepest injury' which one man could inflict upon another, in the shape of 'illicit intercourse' long continued, during which, Follett was careful to note, 'children have been born'. The jury might therefore find that Melbourne had 'poisoned that source which is the purest of all feelings – the affection of a father for his dear and lovely children'.

Follett then proceeded to summarize the facts of the married history of George and Caroline Norton, before concentrating on the subject of Storey's Gate, described as a small house looking onto Birdcage Walk, whose position is 'rather important as you will see when I come to speak of the evidence'. He related how Melbourne entered the life of the Nortons – Caroline's letter to help her husband – without mentioning the fact that she had actually written at the instigation of Norton himself. The Prime Minister now became 'a constant visitor to Mr Norton's house in Storey Street' although Norton himself, hard at work, was gener- ally absent all day, and often for dinner as well. At which point Follett stepped briefly backwards – Norton had, of course, also been there on occasion and in fact he felt 'nothing but friendship' for Melbourne – before moving in for the kill. Melbourne had been in the habit of arriving after duties at the Home Office (when he had been Home Secretary) were discharged, at about three o'clock, and leaving before Norton returned.

Follett declared with a flourish: 'I think that any gentleman, on looking at the evidence I am going to state, must be satisfied that very shortly after their first interview a criminal intercourse com- menced, and continued between the defendant and Mrs Norton.'

A great deal of detail followed, including Melbourne's use of the back entrance. How no one was admitted during his presence, the blinds looking onto the park were drawn, the servants were directed not to come in unless Caroline rang for them. Follett then proceeded to paint a vivid picture of Caroline herself: 'She goes to her room; prepares herself to receive Lord Melbourne, dresses, arranges her hair, and gets the room ready before he comes. While he was in the house she frequently goes into her bedroom. Her hair is disordered, her dress is disordered, she goes again to her bedroom to set it to rights. Having arranged her hair she comes down again to Lord Melbourne.' So much for Storey's Gate. Now for Lord Melbourne's own house, to which Caroline was frequently conveyed by a friend's carriage, which then drove round the park until it came back to fetch her again.

'Where had she been during that time? Or in what room?' enquired Sir William with a knowing flourish. It was true that he could not call Lord Melbourne's servants, but maybe the Prime Minister would do so.

All this was petty domestic detail compared with what was to follow. Most of the above was explicable and human – the rearrangement of the hair, the visits to her bedroom (never forgetting the two full-term pregnancies which she experienced during the period in question). Now Follett revealed that when Mrs Norton was ill – the nature of her illness was not mentioned and could of course have been connected to pregnancy or miscarriage – Melbourne had visited her for an hour or two in her bedroom. 'This must seem very extraordinary,' he said, according to the manners of the present day; but the case did not rest here. 'Servants who barged in, found the doors bolted and saw kisses being exchanged.' Then there was Mrs Norton 'in a kneeling posture' with her hand on Melbourne's knee. 'In that room Mrs Norton has been seen lying on the floor, her clothes in a position to expose her person.' At this point there was, understandably, a 'Great sensation' in court.

All of these allegations would have to be supported by witnesses. In the meantime, Follett moved smoothly to patriarchal rhetoric as he addressed the jurors: 'I ask you as men of the world, with a knowledge of the feelings of your brother men, I ask you what must be the meaning of the visits of Lord Melbourne to this young and beautiful woman?' And he expatiated again on all the detail before turning to an altogether trickier subject: the notes of Lord Melbourne to Mrs Norton. Here Follett showed his mettle by arguing that the undeniably brief, flat notes were, in fact, a proof of the greatest possible intimacy.

The first note simply read: 'I will call about half past four . . . Yours.' It had no commencement, unlike most letters from gentlemen to ladies: surely this was not the note of a mere acquaintance. The next letter was even more lethally intimate to Follett's way of thinking. 'How are you?' it began. (At which point there was laughter in court.) 'There is no house [of Parliament] today. I will call . . . about half past four, or, if you wish it, later.' There was more laughter.

In court at this time was Charles Dickens, who was covering the case as a reporter for the *Morning Chronicle*.[2] His new work, *The Pickwick Papers*, was currently being serialized in twenty instalments, for publication as a book at the end of November. It now included the fictional case of *Bardell v. Pickwick*, in which Pickwick's erstwhile landlady Mrs Martha Bardell sued him for breach of promise and £1,500 damages; Dickens had good fun with these allegedly passionate letters, which seemed to 'import much more than mere words convey'. (It is said that Serjeant Talfourd, a friend of his, actually checked the detail.)[3]

In *The Pickwick Papers*, the counsel for Mrs Bardell, Serjeant Buzfuz, reads aloud the following note: 'Dear Mrs. B. – Chops and Tomata sauce. Yours, PICKWICK.' It was clearly some kind of code: Buzfuz lets loose his horror at the idea of such a wicked subterfuge on the jury: 'Gentlemen, what does this mean?' He goes on: 'Chops! Gracious heavens! And Tomata sauce! Is the happiness of a sensitive and confiding female to be trifled away by such shallow artifices as these?'

Even worse was the next one: 'Dear Mrs. B., I shall not be at home till tomorrow. Slow coach.' And then followed what Buzfuz called a very remarkable expression: 'Don't trouble yourself about the warming-pan!' Buzfuz waxed eloquent on the subject of the sheer harmlessness of warming-pans before suggesting that the phrase was 'a mere cover for hidden fire'.

Dickens's genial parody, only a little exaggerated, was more amusing than Follett's indignation in court only because there was nothing at stake. Where Follett's peroration was concerned, it remained to be seen whether the gentlemen of the jury would be convinced of the secret depths of these banal communications.

Follett then moved on to Norton himself, carefully acquitting him in advance of any kind of collusion – a vital legal point

– and insisting on citing Caroline's own letters to her husband as examples of her desire to deceive him despite Sir John Campbell's attempt to rule them out. One letter produced, once again, laughter in court, this time described as 'Great Laughter'. This was Caroline describing to Norton a book of Dr Lardner's letters lent to her by Melbourne in which he proved that Mary Magdalene was the most virtuous of her sex. She had not yet read the book, Caroline wrote, and was impatient to see how Lardner proved it.

Follett concluded on the crucial, if ugly, subject of damages. Once more Melbourne's lofty status was stressed: 'his rank is an aggravation – his age is an aggravation – and the hollow pretence of his being a friend of the plaintiff is a still greater aggravation.' Once more, Follett appealed to the jury, not so much on behalf of Norton but 'as husbands – I ask you as fathers – and I ask you as men'. Then the Learned Counsel sat down.

The next act in the drama consisted of the examination of various witnesses by Sir John Campbell. These were Norton's friends, visitors to the house who testified to the conventional nature of life at Storey's Gate, including the common use of the Birdcage Walk entrance for carriages, the frequent presence of Caroline's sisters and brothers-in-law, Caroline's affectionate relationship with her husband, and lastly that 'Mrs Norton was exceedingly fond of her children.' (The centrality, in her life, of Caroline's role as a mother was something which was never contradicted.) The witness in question, George Derby, a neighbour in George Street, Westminster, stressed the point again: 'she was remarkably fond of her children – my children used to go to them. Mrs Norton appeared devoted to her children, and was an excellent mother in every way.'

Now the parade of domestics as witnesses began; reminding one with their salacious mixture of observation and conjecture that Fanny Godwin advised Mary Shelley always to keep French servants because English servants loved to gossip.[4] They began with Miss Augusta Norton's lady's maid, Georgiana Veitch, who spoke of Lord Melbourne's repeated visits, sometimes for as long as three hours. Under cross-examination from Sir John Campbell, she admitted that Miss Norton herself had always been present in the house; furthermore, visits to Mrs Norton's bedroom occurred because 'she was a great invalid at the time'. (The dates the lady's maid gave would fit with Caroline's second pregnancy.)

Ninnette Elliot, Caroline's own housemaid, who became her lady's maid, also gave evidence of Melbourne's visits, but with detail such as Mrs Norton's tendency to *rouge* when he came. When he left, 'I used to see her on these occasions wash her hands and smooth her hair again.' She also called for a clean pocket handkerchief. 'I observed a great loss of pocket hand-kerchiefs.' Possibly in reaction to the sheer banality of such statements, laughter in the court became more frequent. At least Ninnette Elliott referred to kisses which she had seen bestowed by Melbourne; then there was Caroline sitting on a sofa hand in hand with Melbourne; but since on each of these occasions she had witnessed the supposedly guilty couple because she had actually been summoned to their presence, it was difficult to envisage anything very torrid.

As for George Norton, Melbourne was 'very often gone just before Mr Norton came'. (Loud laughter.) If he arrived home and heard that Melbourne was there, 'Mr Norton was always angry.' (Much laughter.) But Ninnette also confirmed: 'Mrs Norton was very fond of her children, and seemed to be an attentive mother.' A member of the jury cross-examined the former maid, now a married woman, who denied that she had been discharged – she had left because 'she was in the family way', which Mrs Norton had accepted so long as she could do the work. The kiss? Was it on the cheek or the hand? The cheek. She saw Melbourne's face close to Mrs Norton's and heard the kiss as she was shutting the door.

Two further Norton maids were examined, the second talking of tumbled hair and a collar and hair which needed to be put to rights after Lord Melbourne's visit, along with the administration of fresh *rouge* . . . More disquieting, along with the tumbled hair – no laughs in court this time – was the mention of 'marks' on the linen of Mrs Norton, the 'consequence of intercourse'. One thing on which there was general agreement was that 'Mrs

Norton was never At Home when Lord Melbourne was at home.'
(Laughter.)

Then came Thomas Bullemen, who had been a footman with
the Nortons for a short while, but was employed at length by
a Colonel Armstrong, whose daughter was a good friend of
Caroline. A long, rambling cross-examination ensued about
comings and goings to Storey's Gate, with occasional glimpses of
intimacy when the footman had to take a note up to the drawing
room. On one such occasion he saw Lord Melbourne on the
sofa, with his hand on Mrs Norton's shoulder, and it seemed
they had been sitting close. 'He gently removed his hand, but
did not seem at all taken by surprise.' William Lawley, Colonel
Armstrong's coachman, had performed tasks such as driving
Mrs Norton to the Duke of Devonshire's, and dropping Colonel
Armstrong at White's Club; 'I don't think there was any mystery about that.' (A laugh.) He could not remember how Mrs
Norton was dressed when she went to the Duke of Devonshire's,
except that she had a white veil over her bonnet: 'I believe she
was dressed as ladies generally are when they pay morning
visits.'

After these fairly commonplace testimonies, the pace quick-
ened with the arrival of John Fluke, coachman to Mr Norton
for four years. For Fluke, returning to Storey's Gate with tickets
for a play, knocked twice on the drawing-room door without
success and, thinking the room was empty, entered. There was
Melbourne standing by the fireplace with Caroline lying on the
hearth rug on her right side, her clothes disordered and her left
leg uncovered. 'The witness saw as far up as the thick part of the
thigh.' Fluke immediately backed out and went home, mentioning
the incident to his wife and others.

The cross-examination of Fluke was, in its own way, equally
dramatic, except that it was also hilarious. He was asked why he
had left Mr Norton's service. The answer: 'Why if the truth must
be told, Sir, I got a little drop too much.' (Great laughter.) On the
day he was dismissed, the Nortons quarrelled in the carriage and
he supposed Mrs Norton was determined 'to spit her spite at me'.
(Great laughter.) 'Had you taken anything that day?' 'Yes, I had a

drop too much, and Mrs Norton was cross that evening, because the black horse happened to gallop.' (Much laughter.) 'I could not keep him in a trot.' (Renewed laughter.)

Asked about his drinking habits, Fluke readily admitted that he did sometimes drink too much. 'I don't know who don't. The best of us take it, masters and servants.' (Much laughter.) How often did he take a drop too much? 'What, Sir, in four years?' (Roars of laughter.) Pressed on the subject – 'to the best of your recollection' – and asked if he was drunk every afternoon, he denied it indignantly. 'What, then?' 'Why, I should say middling, as we are all, more or less.' (Shouts of laughter.) On the particular occasion of the black horse galloping, however, on the way to the Marquess of Lansdowne's ball, he admitted that he had certainly had a drop too much; hence his dismissal.

Fluke was also extremely shifty on the subject of his financial arrangements, his general lack of funds, and whether or not Norton had paid him for his testimony. The phrase 'moonlit flitting' was used. Emphasis was placed on his current residence, with his wife and family at Lord Grantley's place at Wonersh Park.

The next witness, Martha Morris, attested to Caroline Norton's handwriting from her years in service to her. Four letters, covering roughly four years, were then read out, all from Caroline to George Norton. They were intimate letters, as befitted the correspondence of a wife with her husband, in which if anything Caroline showed herself the more affectionate of the two.

Sir John Campbell now rose to address the jury on behalf of Lord Melbourne. He began by assuring them that he rejoiced 'unfeignedly' in the news that they wished the trial to end that evening. 'They would have the satisfaction when they laid their heads upon their pillows, to reflect that, having heard all the evidence . . . they would come to the calm and clear conclusion that it was wholly insufficient to support the accusation.' He continued in the same lofty vein. He would bring no further witnesses which might have justified a delay. But he would state that all the material facts were false.

As to criminal prosecution, that was how Sir William Follett had rightly termed the proceedings. But since the violation of the marriage vow was one of the greatest crimes, in proportion to such a deep and grievous accusation, 'the proof must be clear and convincing'. Yet here was a crime allegedly committed by two parties and neither could be called, Lord Melbourne because he was the defendant, and Mrs Norton because she was the wife of the plaintiff. In the present case, they must believe that 'the adulterous act was really committed and complete, for nothing short of it would entitle the plaintiff to a verdict'. As an authority quoted by Follett had said, it must be shown that Mrs Norton had surrendered 'not only her mind but her person'. Sir John would be able to show them that there was nothing but 'an intimacy of friendship and innocence' between the two.

Sir John went on to pronounce that, invariably in his experience of adulterers, 'a woman who forgot the duties of a wife, forgot those of a mother.' Mrs Norton, on the contrary, 'when she found she was almost deprived of her children, she was deprived of her reason, and in a state bordering on distraction.' He would make the same point about Mrs Norton's letters: Sir John had a distinct idea of what the letters of an adulteress were like, similar to an adulteress's inadequate performance of her maternal duties. Thus, Mrs Norton's tender, playful letters 'could not have been written by an adulteress'. Campbell proceeded to emphasize Mr Norton's previous friendly attitude to Lord Melbourne, which meant that now he was under some delusion: 'he had been made the tool of others, he would not say from personal but from political matters.'

Then he pitched into the witnesses and their inadequacy. Who were they? 'Discarded servants – a race, the most dangerous in all cases, but particularly in cases of this sort, wholly unworthy of belief.' He pointed out that they had generally remained in the family some time without apparently suspecting anything 'improper'. He asked of one maid: 'In the name of God, who made her suspect anything? Who put harm into her head?' Sir John quoted a law book: 'In a discovery made by a servant, it was important to shew that it was promptly communicated to the party injured,' with the crucial addition: 'If it was not made till after a quarrel, or dismissal from the service, or after a long interval, the evidence labours under great suspicion.' He pointed out that in this case the supposed discovery was made 'after a dismissal, after a quarrel and after a long interval'. All three were combined in one testimony – that of John Fluke, who had been dismissed from the service of Mrs Norton two years earlier after a quarrel which he himself had 'so graphically' described.

Sir John then proceeded to quote Edmund Burke – 'one of the greatest writers, statesmen and philosophers that had ever adorned a country' – at length on the subject of domestic servants; how they 'surrounded the bed and table with snares', and were in general nothing but instruments of terror and alarm. It was their ability in particular to come forward after many years, especially if there was hope of reward. From here, the Attorney General swooped on the fact that these ex-servants had been taken to the Grantley home of Wonersh Park and housed. Here they had been offered large sums of money if their evidence proved successful. Furthermore, the servants produced had been highly selective, and he went into details of those who might have been summoned but were not.

All of this was a prelude to Sir John Campbell's final surge, which concentrated on Norton and his family, in particular his brother Lord Grantley. Miss Augusta Norton, who had lived for some years in the house, was said to be abroad but Grantley was actually present in court – and yet he had not been called. Later he questioned why Caroline's sisters had not been called and her aunt, Lady Graham, to testify to her chastity and purity – in proof of which they had never disassociated themselves from her company.

Once again there was much detailed recounting of the comings and goings at Storey's Gate, proving that Melbourne's habitual choice of entry was perfectly reasonable under the circumstances. The letters which had been produced in court were examined and found to prove nothing except an affectionate marriage between George and Caroline Norton. Sir John then strongly rebutted the notion that Melbourne had anything to do with the break-up. So why was his name introduced? It was not spontaneous suspicion in Norton's mind, he had been 'played upon'. Thus, it was clear that Norton had been the victim of some 'insinuating rogue that devised the slander'. The separation had been brought about by a quarrel respecting the visit to Frampton, at which point Mrs Norton had left the house in search of her two children, 'in a state of horrid distraction'. Then someone must have got hold of Norton and, for indirect purposes, induced him to bring forward the accusation.

Sir John Campbell discussed the Norton marriage in some detail. A member of the jury asked: 'Did they sleep together?' The answer was that they did, cohabiting as husband and wife. He became eloquent on the subject: he argued that it was impossible that 'adulterous intercourse' had existed at the same time as this evidently happy union, starting in 1831 (the year Caroline petitioned Melbourne for Norton).

In this connection he ridiculed the concentration of the prosecution on petty domestic detail: was the fact that Mrs Norton went upstairs to wash her hands a proof of adultery? And was it not strange that every time 'something was about to happen' – the implication was, of an adulterous nature – a bell was rung for a servant who then happened to witness it? He was discreetly sympathetic on the subject of the notorious 'marks', which were perhaps of a 'feminine' nature, but he chose to conclude on the lethal question of Norton's motivation. 'Mr Norton is a tool – an instrument of shame – he had been persuaded to allow his name to be used and used, merely for party and political purposes.' Campbell denigrated the prosecution witnesses briefly again, concentrating on Fluke, who had been shown to be a 'a drunkard and a swindler'. He trusted willingly and unhesitatingly to the 'discrimination, the justice, and the impartiality of an English jury'. The Attorney General sat down.

The Chief Justice now summed up for the jury, beginning with the key legal point. Great 'familiarity' between the defendant and the plaintiff's wife had been shown, rather than adultery: the action was not brought for 'familiarity' but for adultery, and unless adultery was proved, they must find for the defendant.

He then turned to John Fluke, whose jovial evidence on his own drinking habits had so delighted the spectators. Here the jury must consider whether Fluke had shown himself by his own testimony 'a moral and honest man', and Tindal recalled it in further (unsatisfactory) detail. He considered other domestics' witness statements. But the main tenor of his summing-up was the need to prove adultery, and otherwise find for the defendant. They must not rely on facts of 'an ambiguous nature'. This was surely an important phrase to the jurors who had listened to so many colourful, diverting – but essentially ambiguous – anecdotes about the defendant and the plaintiff's wife.

The jury only conferred 'for a few seconds' without moving from the courtroom. Then the foreman said: 'My lord, we are agreed, it is our duty to say that we have agreed in a verdict that is for the Defendant.'

Someone at the back of the court cried out 'Bravo'. This was the key for loud bursts of applause and shouts of 'Good old Melbourne'. Once again it was promptly repressed while the Chief Justice expressed his surprise that a verdict could be received in a court of law 'in so disgraceful a manner'. But it was too late to quell the mob outside the court. There were shouts of victory.

Whether the mob was celebrating the defeat of what would later be called the Establishment, or was genuinely on the side of the Prime Minister and the Hon. Mrs Norton, made no difference. Either way, Melbourne and his alleged paramour Caroline had been found innocent. Innocent, that is, in a court of law.

It was twenty minutes before midnight when the court closed.

CHAPTER SEVEN

Given against Whom?

'It's given against him! Against Norton! And my children
cant grow up believing in their mother's shame.'

Caroline Norton to Brinsley Sheridan, 22 June 1836

AT HAMPTON COURT, CAROLINE NORTON began a letter
to her brother Brinsley while she was still in a state of agonizing
suspense. 'Before I close this,' she wrote, 'I will find the result of
the proceedings.'[1]

The early tone of the letter is bitter, although driving half the
day in Richmond Park with Mrs Sheridan (to pass the time)
she had tried hard to seem in good spirits for the sake of her
'poor worn Mother'. She confessed to her deep resentment,
but it was surely only human – in man's nature – to resent
being 'in this sort of scrape'. Her sister Georgia and aunt Lady
Graham were commended for their 'utmost kindness' in sitting
with her, before she raged against the coarseness of the details
provided by the witnesses, 'which drives me quite wild'. Perhaps Brinsley's young wife Marcia should not read them: 'the
result is all that signifies to those that love me, and the details
to those that hate me.' As for Norton, the 'filthiness' of the
evidence he sanctioned disgusted her, particularly since she had
performed all the duties of maidservants and manservants for

him herself – such as emptying his slop – 'rather than torture him with shame'.

Then her handwriting changes completely as she continues ecstatically: '*It's given against him! Against Norton! And my children cant* [underlined twice] *grow up believing in their mother's shame* – Oh I have spent such a long long day – truly a night – waiting – but it is over.'

Caroline went on to ask her darling brother to kiss Marcia, his wife, on her behalf and thank her for her 'little innocent welcome', when Caroline came to her house '*under a cloud*'. As a young mother with young children, she was now hoping to make this fearful disgrace fly away: 'it is all *so* false, *so* false!' She ended: 'God bless you dear.'

This was Caroline Norton's moment of pure joy. In that instant of relief, she must have unconsciously expected her life to revert to normal – whatever that was. But she knew what it was: the children once more in their mother's care, home life of sorts, anyway a home, possessions, the life she wanted, not the one devised by George Norton. After all, the verdict had been given against him. Had it not? Time would show whether the verdict of society might be somewhat different.

In Parliament, the reaction was similarly enthusiastic in its own rather different style. When Sir John Campbell (after twelve hours in court) arrived back in the House of Commons, news of the victory had preceded him. The Whigs roared their approval and waved their order papers wildly. Sober Tories in the Lords were busy disassociating themselves from the alleged plotting of Lords Grantley and Wynford. Greville summed up that point of view: 'old Wynford [was] at the bottom of it and persuaded Lord Grantley to urge it on for political purposes.' In this cynical world, however, it was generally felt that Lord Malmesbury had the last word when he quoted 'an old Tory' as saying that he couldn't see why Lord Melbourne was so triumphant at the verdict, given that it had been proved: 'Never had a man had so many opportunities and missed them all.'[2]

The Times in its issue the following day, 23 June, was already advertising '*Norton v. Melbourne – A full and accurate report of this extraordinary trial, specially taken in shorthand by an expert author'* – for sixpence. But on 24 June, the newspaper felt it necessary to make a solemn declaration: Lord Melbourne had been acquitted of a crime 'against the laws of God and man', the imputation of which must have caused him and the lady concerned enormous embarrassment and distress. But he did *The Times* a great injustice, if he thought that the newspaper 'felt any other sentiment than sincere concern' at the proceedings.[3]

Furthermore, *The Times* added piously, 'we defy the grossest slanderer of the press or party to say that we have ever exhibited the slightest wish to encourage' the case concerned. Similarly, the newspaper denounced the 'stubborn malice' with which a strong Conservative – it referred to Lord Wynford – had been accused of pushing it forward for political motives.

All the same, *The Times* managed to print a highly critical report from the hostile *Standard* because it was so 'well expressed'. There would be many members of society, including friends of both Melbourne and the Nortons, for whom this was the true verdict on the recent trial. While 'cheerfully admitting' that the Prime Minister was innocent (which meant 'the unhappy lady' was also innocent), the *Standard* piece went on to denounce 'Lord Melbourne's waste of the time so amply paid for by the public – his indulgence in trifling amusements unbecoming his age, his station and his office', which communicated some of its shame to the lady herself.

Mrs Norton was characterized as young, lively and maybe vain: her conduct had been imprudent, indiscreet and undignified, 'the very last that we would hold out to an English wife'. There was, however, a final reservation of some importance for the future: 'it does not appear that the authority most bound in conscience and in interest to interrupt it ever interposed.' That so-called authority was of course Caroline Norton's husband.

There was a certain irony in the fact that alongside this report lay an advertisement for Richard Brinsley Sheridan's most famous play, with its all too appropriate title. That evening, at the Theatre Royal, Haymarket, *The School for Scandal* would be performed. Ellen Tree would play Lady Teazle. Beset by what

Caroline Norton would call 'the demon of gossip', this beautiful, vivacious heroine has trouble caught between her husband Sir Peter and her admirer Joseph Surface; it was a splendid part for an actress that Sheridan's granddaughter was now far less happily enacting.

The reaction of King William IV was altogether more gracious than that of *The Times* or the *Standard*. In Greville's words, the monarch behaved 'very handsomely' about the whole affair. He now expressed his satisfaction at the result in terms 'sufficiently flattering' to his Prime Minister.[4] Naturally, Mrs Norton's welfare did not feature in this Royal judgement.

At this point the world, not only the wider world but also the intimate world of her adored sisters, would have liked Caroline to fall silent. The fate of Maria Bertram, the beautiful, flirtatious cousin of modest Fanny Price in *Mansfield Park*,* provides a perfect example.[5] After Maria's adulterous affair, ending in an elopement with Henry Crawford, she is divorced by her husband and endures public calumny. Crawford not only abandons her, but soon finds another girl to marry. Maria, on the other hand, in Jane Austen's words, 'must withdraw . . . to a retirement and reproach which could offer no second spring of hope or character'. The retirement in question consists of living in another part of the country with an elderly aunt.

Where Caroline was concerned, a grave, suffering, silent woman of great beauty and great sadness would have suited society, both close and distant, perfectly. Caroline Norton did not fall silent.

It is true that her first published work after the trial, a poem, concerned sufferings which were not her own. Although, since it directly concerned the sufferings of children, it could be argued that there was, in fact, an emotional connection. But Caroline felt the need to return to her normal life – which had been the life of a writer, as well as the life of a mother. For one thing, there was a need to earn money, even if legally such money accrued to her husband.

* Jane Austen's third novel, first published in 1814.

Caroline duly wrote to the celebrated publisher John Murray what she hoped was a beguiling letter, confessing that she had always wanted to be published by him – 'it is a vanity of mine.'[6] She also admitted that he might be affected by the recent scandal and hoped that his name on the book, together with that of Lord Ashley (Shaftesbury), to whom the poem was dedicated, might give a different impression. Murray's idea of publishing the book with the author described as anonymous was one she instantly accepted: 'my name has been (God knows!) before the public, enough to make me hate the letters which compose the word.'

After this piece of self-abnegation, Caroline, throughout the preamble to the publication of the long poem, reverted to the more characteristic behaviour of an author. She had been disappointed by the low financial offer Murray made. Proofs went to the wrong address, the book was not yet out despite there only being two days left until November, the Irish woman in charge of the house had not realized the importance of the papers, would Murray send out copies in his name, it would come better from him . . .[7]

A Voice from the Factories was dedicated to Lord Ashley because it was related to his Bill to protect young children working.[8] A particular amendment of 15 March 1836 may have provided the impetus. This was designed to exempt older children of eleven and twelve from the new Factory Act passed in 1833, which (compassionately for the times) set children's working hours per day at a maximum of eight.

The fate of children in factories was not a new passion. Caroline wrote a subsequent letter to a correspondent, who has been identified as Lord John Russell, on the subject of her involvement in social issues.[9] Russell had expressed astonishment 'at our female eyes perusing the parliamentary reports, on the subject of the Factory Question'. Caroline, while denying that she was 'a political lady', pointed out that, with her sister Georgia, she had read the reports on the Factory Question, and the reports on the Poor Laws 'as they came out, just as you, oh! elevated MP, might have done'. Then she pleaded motherhood: quite apart from the interests of the people concerned, the fact that they had *sons* (her emphasis) made them want to see 'how the wheel goes round', how their security of position and property might be affected by what 'their Papas and Uncles are doing'.

After this modest preface, she changed her tune. 'As I am in the humour for boasting,' she points out that, just after the death of William Huskisson in a rail accident in September 1830, she missed the mail because she had wanted to test for herself what nerve it took to stand still by the railroad while one of those 'machinnes infernales' [*sic*] went by. With the rest of the day to fill in, she was taken by her husband to see two factories. 'I believe this was long before any reports were thought of, or at least *I* had never thought of the subject before.' Significantly, she added: 'but even *then* I meant to have written on it.' Norton, on the other hand, 'laughed at the notion – you know he professes the greatest contempt for female intellect.'

Caroline, however, declares herself glad that she waited: at that earlier date she would have written with 'infinitely more confidence and proportionately worse'. Her aim is merely to show what an impression the sight made on her at the time: 'I never forgot it or missed an opportunity of hearing or reading what I could on the subject since.' So Caroline admonishes Russell: 'Dont give your votes carelessly under the impression that the fair sex are indifferent to politics.' Then she added a postscript which was to be strictly confidential: 'It may be that I may canvass your vote this session on a question . . .'.

The tone of the dedication to Lord Ashley was reverential. Caroline began by describing the reason for her anonymity: the author has no right to expect that their personal opinion (there is no clue to the author's sex in the dedication) would carry any more weight than anyone else's. But two great reformers are cited: John Howard, 'immortally connected with the removal of the abuses which for centuries disgraced our prison discipline', and William Wilberforce, whose perseverance created 'the long-delayed emancipation of the negroes'. So the author hopes to see Ashley's name 'enrolled . . . as the Liberator and Defender of those helpless beings', the factory children, 'on whom are inflicted

many of the evils both of slavery and imprisonment, without the
odium of either."*

The poem begins by describing 'CHILDHOOD, the weary life's
long happy holyday', contrasting it with the 'vexatious sympathy'
which we feel at the sight of 'infant skill'. In general, 'ever a
toiling child doth make us sad'; as adults feel 'when we hear the
shrill faint cries / Which mark the wanderings of the little sweep'.
In this particular case, a child trapeze artist who is preparing to
play his part 'glances below for friend or father's face', then lifts
his small, round arms and feeble hands:

> With the taught movements of an artist's grace . . .
> And with a stare of numbed and childish fear
> Looks sadly towards the audience come to gaze
> On the unwonted skill which costs so dear

Then Caroline moves to the 'Poor little FACTORY SLAVES' for
whom the poem is written; for them, the 'low whirring of the
incessant wheel' and the summer curse of 'stifling withering heat'
instead of the simple joys of childhood:

> His fellow-labourers (playmates hath he none)
> Walk by, as sad as he, nor hail the morning sun.

There are further glimpses of the pathetic lives of these little
slaves even at night: in broken sleep the victim mutters: 'Mother!
Oh Mother! Is it yet THE TIME?'

Caroline appeals to Parliament and its Members to do something:

> Oh, Men! blaspheme not Freedom! . . .
> Forbid it, Spirit of the glorious Past
> Which gained our Isle the surname of 'The Free'

---

* Caroline's wish came true: the revolutionary Factory Act of 1833 protecting children is forever associated with Ashley, although under the name of
Lord Shaftesbury, the new title which he inherited from his father in 1851.

After all, if the weight and unfairness of the social order gets too heavy, 'the dog that watched and fawned prepares to bite'. In sum, Mercy should sit beside the Ruler's throne: 'Lest due authority be overthrown.' From this vague political message, Caroline moves finally to the New Testament: 'Suffer that little children come to me.'

By the time *A Voice from the Factories* was published in late November, Caroline had left Hampton Court and was installed at 16 Green Street, Mayfair, at the house of her uncle Charles Sheridan. She was also, as before, welcomed by Brinsley and Marcia Sheridan at Frampton. Charles was twelve years older than Caroline, an unmarried diplomat described by one of his nephews as 'perhaps the handsomest of all the Sheridan men, and an enchanting companion' (his weakness was the proverbial Sheridan tendency to consumption).[10] From Green Street in the late summer, Caroline wrote to Melbourne a letter which began well; she had been following the parliamentary debate: 'it is the first thing for *three weeks* that has made me forget my own affairs for a while.' Then she worries: 'Let me know that you were not the worse for the fatigue & late hour of breaking up.' This is the familiar, tender 'Car', as she signs herself.[11]

After that, it gets worse, much worse. Norton has ordered that Willie's name should be changed to Charles (his middle name), the implication being that Melbourne's name was William: 'the affectation and insincerity of the whole thing makes my heart *burn*.' A lot of painful domestic detail derived from maids follows: '*petty* things' that Norton has done to spite her such as taking Fletcher to the dentist to perform a procedure which Caroline had forbidden. In Norton's own words: 'I can do what I please *now*, my boy.'

Then Norton has cross-questioned the servants as to whether they had not remarked on 'my poor Brin's' likeness to Melbourne. The answer was yes: he was handsome and more cheerful than the other children, and he seemed especially 'like' a few days after the Prime Minister had visited. Caroline went on: 'Now mark the answer of a *servant* to a man who is called a *gentleman*'. When Norton asked: 'Didnt you think all along that he was *his* child?', the answer came: 'No Sir, we none of us thought it, because *the Mother would never have let a joke be made about the likeness,* if there had been a *reason for it.*'

'If I had had to defend myself,' wrote Caroline, 'I know no better answer!' And one might add that the whole tone of her letter was utterly implausible if Melbourne had actually been the father of either child.

The rest of the letter gave further upsetting details concerning the children. Fletcher, aged seven, had been taken to the lawyers in Lincoln's Inn; that was the day before Norton had desired Brin, not yet five, to tell him the truth about his mother, otherwise he would lock him up in a dark room for a week. Poor Brin looked round the room fearfully, reddened and said: 'Mamma wont *let you* lock little Briny up.' Caroline went on: 'Ive told them [the servants] to tell me nothing more than I maynt go frantic before it is settled – and yet I cant help asking questions every five minutes.'

The conclusion of the letter demonstrated another kind of pain. 'And all this time you wont see me,' wrote Caroline to Melbourne. 'And God knows, with your ways of thinking when I shall see you again.' At the finish, she wrote simply: 'Send me a line. Car.'

The position with the boys, and indeed the whole Norton marriage, had fluctuated since the verdict of innocence on 22 June; but it never wavered in Caroline's favour. How could it? Innocent or not, the law was entirely on the side of the husband, not the wife. The fact was that Caroline's children might not grow up believing in their mother's shame, but they might grow up without actually seeing her . . . It remained to be seen whether a change in the law would provide a more effective weapon than the personal efforts of a desperate woman. Caroline now attempted to combine both.

Negotiations for some regularization of the position between herself and George Norton continued. It has to be borne in mind that, legally, all this time Caroline Norton had no money of her own. In the autumn of 1836, she refused an offer of £35 quarterly until she could see her sons. Even an event which might have brought some kind of bizarre comfort – the death of the dreaded Miss Vaughan on 22 November – failed to do so. Caroline felt nothing but hatred for her, based on her behaviour towards the boys, hitherto 'so gently and tenderly treated', which included the use of flogging as a method of correction.[12]

Already in the late autumn of 1836, Caroline was planning the pamphlet which would eventually emerge as *Observations on the Natural Claim of the Mother to the Custody of her Infant Children as affected by the Common Law Right of the Father.*[13] Whatever her own sufferings, which she never wished to underplay, Caroline Norton the campaigner was well aware that she was not the only mother who suffered from the cruelty of the law in this respect. For example, she sent the pamphlet to her friend Mary Shelley. She had in mind Mary Shelley's own troubles when Sir Timothy Shelley threatened to separate Mary from her son, also named Percy, after the death of the poet. In Mary Shelley's own words: 'There seems to be something incomprehensible in a state of society that should admit of the propriety, or rather, enforce the necessity of a boy of nine being separated from all maternal care.'[14]

She contacted Charlotte, Countess of Orkney, her contemporary, for details concerning her mother-in-law, the Viscountess of Kirkwall, who had lost access to her children in 1809 and then divorced her husband. Caroline also consulted another very different friend, the writer and lawyer Abraham Hayward, and on his advice omitted what had evidently been a 'personal attack' on Lord Wynford for his Tory plotting. Although Caroline believed such an attack was justified (evidently convinced of the political pressure put on George Norton to prosecute): 'however I have enemies enough already so it is as well.'[15]

There was one important person in Caroline's life at this time who was horrified at the idea of such a publication. Her mother, Mrs Sheridan, thought that pamphleteering was an 'indelicate' activity for a lady.[16] She was not alone. Unfortunately, her disapproval stood for the conventional disapproval of society where Caroline was concerned – despite being found innocent. In the same way, Mrs Sheridan was actually sure that Caroline had been

Melbourne's mistress, and would probably have agreed with the cynical Lord Malmesbury that if she wasn't, Melbourne had missed an awful lot of good opportunities.

Caroline Norton's social life did not surge forth in a way that it might have been supposed to do, given the now perpetual absence of George Norton and her own popularity before the case. On the contrary, she began to hear unpleasant stories about her besmirched reputation. On 19 October the old family friend Douglas Kinnaird, an associate of Byron and a man of both the theatrical and literary worlds (who had given the fatherless Caroline away at her wedding), jokingly reported: 'I caught *cold* last night where I dined . . . and I also caught a dislike of *you* there was so much abuse and fault-finding.'[17] It was the beginning of a trend which would affect the once high-spirited Caroline for the rest of her life.

It has been seen that there was already felt to be something racy about the Sheridan girls, a reaction which came mainly from the envious. Most, if not all, of this was concentrated on Caroline. Emily Eden was Lord Auckland's intelligent novelist daughter, sometimes mentioned as Melbourne's ideal second wife; she had described Caroline in 1834, with a shade of jealousy, as being 'beautiful as I think it possible to be . . . but tiresome society . . . affecting to be so much more wicked than there is the slightest call for'.[18] Now, unfortunately, there was no need for affectation: there really was something opprobrious about Caroline's reputation.

Ten years later, it would lead someone like the Revd William Brookfield, a witty Anglican preacher who numbered many writers among his friends and was subsequently honorary chaplain to the Queen, to dismiss her to his mother in a vivid turn of phrase. Although he personally believed Mrs Norton to be as free of impropriety as three women he named as 'the most spotless virgins the chaste moon ever sees putting on their nightcaps', he still wouldn't approve of her as an intimate friend.[19]

And as we shall see, the uneasy feeling about Mrs Norton among women in particular – who, unlike men, might be put off by her glamour – would come to have an effect during the early stirrings of feminism. Paradoxically, as Caroline herself developed into a campaigner for particular women's rights, she declined in the estimation of women themselves.

Caroline's nervous feelings of social exclusion, spotting slights in tiny social incidents, which were to become an important part of her emotional make-up, date from this period. Humanly, she could not help being aware that Melbourne, on the other hand, was enjoying his own social round as keenly as ever – or as keenly as he wished.

Observations was offered to John Murray, publisher of *A Voice from the Factories*, with the proviso that if he would not publish it, she intended to print it privately at her own expense. In the event, Murray printed 500 copies in the summer of 1837, but for private circulation only. The main message of the pamphlet was that all children below the age of seven should be in the care of their mothers. The fate of the older children should be decided not by the father, but by the Court of Chancery. Ironically, Caroline used her husband's law books to study the subject.

To Lord John Russell at the end of her letter about factories, Caroline confided that she had written 'a longish pamphlet'.[20] She summed it up as 'the claims of the Mother of legitimate children to be allowed the same privilege as the Mothers of illegitimate, and to keep their infants under seven years of age'. This description, which stresses the contrast between the apparently moral and apparently immoral – to the latter's advantage – seethes with Caroline's resentment. It was, after all, her Christian marriage which had resulted in the legal deprivation of her children, whereas a (presumably sinful) unmarried mother would have retained full rights. Altogether Caroline would write three pamphlets on the subject about which she felt most strongly in her whole life, access to her children, compared to which retaining married women's property (her royalties from her books) came a poor second.

The first case of a contest between husband and wife over the custody of infants had occurred in 1804.[21] In a shocking incident by any standards, Leonard De Manneville had grabbed his tiny daughter from his wife, who was actually breast-feeding her at the time; she then applied to the Court of the King's Bench for a writ of habeas corpus for the return of the baby – without success. The rights of the father over a daughter until the age of twelve and a son until fourteen were held to be paramount.

Mrs De Manneville then turned to the Court of Chancery seeking custody, or at any rate to stop her husband fleeing with the baby to his native France. Here she encountered more sympathy from Lord Eldon – 'I am much struck with the case' – but he still maintained the power of the father's rights, given that the couple were not legally separated: 'This is an application by a married woman, living in a state of actual unauthorised separation, to continue . . . that separation, which I must say is not permitted by law.' Lord Eldon did at least agree that the child should not be taken abroad, but his whole attitude to a married woman – Mrs De Manneville, or as it were Caroline Norton – was that she was subject to 'couverture' by the act of marriage and could not sue her husband. The court could, in fact, grant a mother custody, but a mother could not legally ask for it.

There had been twelve other cases since 1804 seeking parental rights: seven were brought by mothers, six of whom lost, the rest by third parties. The exception was an unopposed mother, Mrs Bailey, where the father of the child was in prison, having been 'late convicted of felony, and was now in custody at the hulks, under sentence of transportation'.

The case of Emily Westmeath in 1818, on the other hand, was an outstanding illustration of the weakness of the married woman at law; once again, the fact of 'couverture', lack of legal separation of the couple, meant that she was deprived of her children, one of whom died after being taken away to Ireland. As a recent authority has written: 'We see in these cases the creation of two separate custody standards . . . fathers received custody of their children so long as they had not forfeited their paternal rights through endangerment of life and limb.'[22] In general, the courts applied quite a different, 'much less stringent' moral standard to the father than to the mother.

On 25 April 1837, Serjeant Thomas Talfourd, one of Melbourne's defence lawyers, introduced the Infant Custody Bill into the House of Commons. It was described later as the first feminist legislation ever to be brought before Parliament.[23]* Talfourd, the son of a wealthy Reading brewer, was now in his early forties and had combined a successful career at the Bar with a literary life: as has been noted, he was a friend of Dickens, and would ultimately edit Charles Lamb's letters. He had written poetry, had plays performed, and contributed, for example, to the *Edinburgh Review* and *Quarterly Review*. Talfourd also wrote well-regarded articles on legal subjects. This combination would lead him to publish an important article on the law of copyright 'of the Highest Importance to Authors', which, if it did not yet succeed in awarding authors their due, was at least much respected.

As a practising barrister, Talfourd had personal experience of cases when – even if he had been acting for the father – the sufferings of the mother concerned had been all too evident. It seems likely that he was already contemplating some kind of action on the subject when Caroline Norton contacted him through her friend Abraham Hayward. It was a natural match of campaigners: one an eloquent, compassionate, knowledgeable man, the other an intelligent, if much less educated, woman spurred into action by her own tribulations.

In the present instance, Talfourd's language was restrained but evidently heartfelt. He asked for leave to bring in a Bill to empower the Lord Chancellor and the judges to make the orders relating to the custody of infant children in cases where the parents were living apart, on the application of either such parents, or on the order of a writ of habeas corpus issued by the father.

* In 1913, in the full throes of suffragette activity, as he saw it, the Earl of Lytton in a life of his grandfather Bulwer Lytton wrote that the debate on the Infant Custody Bill was the first occasion on which the agitation 'with which we are so familiar' found expression.[24]

Talfourd allowed himself to comment briefly that 'by this Bill he sought to empower the judges to do that which he had often heard them deplore their inability to do'. He then reserved any observations on the subject he had to make until the second reading. To this, the Attorney General, who did not rise or initiate any discussion at this point, simply remarked that the subject was 'one of such extreme delicacy and difficulty' that he wondered whether the law could be improved even by the Bill of his Honourable and Learned Friend. But he was glad the first step had been taken. There were, in fact, two readings of the Bill but, as yet, no prolonged debate on the subject.

Caroline herself withdrew her active support for the Bill when the children were said to be arriving from Scotland, and Talfourd, it seems, respected the delicacy of that situation.[25]

At this point, Great Britain was about to undergo a seismic change. The life of King William IV, in his early seventies, was visibly moving towards its close. A bad attack of his chronic asthma in April was succeeded by a collapse at Windsor Castle; there were fainting scenes at lunch and dinner; he did manage to attend a final Council meeting on 27 May, but in a wheelchair. He never left Windsor again. There was, however, one huge consolation in having lived to pass the date of 24 May, in whatever condition. William IV had no legitimate children (although plenty born out of wedlock). May 24 was the date on which Victoria, the young daughter of his late brother the Duke of Kent, was able to write in her Journal: 'Today is my eighteenth birthday! How old!' She added: 'and yet how far from being what I should be'.[26] But from the point of view of William IV, it was her age not her character that was crucial. At eighteen, Victoria had officially passed outside the control of her mother, the Duchess of Kent, whose dominance (together with that of her chamberlain, Sir John Conroy) had been dreaded.

The immediate consequence of the succession of a new monarch in June, whatever age, was the suspension of Parliament. According to tradition, there would need to be a General Election. Under the circumstances, Serjeant Talfourd could not proceed with his Infant Custody Bill, which had not yet been debated.

The last female Sovereign, Queen Anne, daughter of James II, had died over a hundred years ago in 1714, way outside living memory. Perhaps there would prove to be something appropriate about the whole discussion of Infant Custody during the reign of a female Sovereign, since it was the rights of females – females who were mothers – which were at issue.

CHAPTER EIGHT

Hungry for the Children

'I am hungry for the children'

Caroline Norton, 3 June 1837

At the beginning of June 1837, Caroline Norton wrote a long letter to her husband in the midst of the endless, anguishing negotiations concerning their – theoretically – shared family. 'God knows nothing was further from *my* wish than to exist fourteen long months without ever seeing or hearing directly from my children.' She concluded: 'I am hungry for the children.'[1]

Then, at long last, she met the boys with the agreement of their sole legal guardian, their father. At this point, Fletcher was just eight and Brin was five and a half. Willie, who would be four in August, was still at that early period of his life which both God and nature designate as only fit for female care, as Caroline would describe it in pamphlets later. There were to be daily visits, with nights spent at Norton's house in Wilton Place.

She described their appearance in a letter to Melbourne.[2] The boys were looking tolerably well, with the exception of Brin. 'A perfect skeleton', he seemed to Caroline to be growing 'crooked' and she was allowed to show him to Sir Benjamin Brodie, surgeon to royalty, the next day. All the same, Brin was 'very merry'. As for Willie, 'the little one is the sharpest fellow you ever saw, & speaks as fluently as I do.' But even as she rejoiced, Caroline managed a swipe at her husband: Fletcher and Willie both boasted of their purses full of sixpences, but she had not yet heard from Brin: 'I am in great hopes I have one son who does not resemble his Father, thinking money *the* object of life.'

The situation was improved for the time being, but there was one touching sentence about the boys' reaction to it all: 'They were very happy at returning but cannot understand going away in the evening.' And Caroline allowed herself to say at the end of the letter: 'I have no more to say except that I feel very sad, and still miss *a child*, for this sharp talkative little being does not seem to me to be my fat fair baby.' This halcyon period – for such it was for the long-deprived mother, despite the unhappy ending to each day – was not to last. A day came when Caroline was once again refused admittance to the house and, after a painful scene, the children were sent back to Scotland.[3]

Meanwhile, the negotiations as to the children's future, and that of their parents' union, went on. There was even a meeting between them proposed by George at the house of the late Miss Vaughan, which Caroline ducked in favour of Norton's own house, where the servants would serve as witnesses. By Caroline's own account, it was long and very distressing. Norton proposed that she return '*and forget the past*'. A very strange correspondence followed about the terms of her return, which involved practical if unromantic matters like her contribution of furniture. It was at this point that Caroline unwisely but characteristically – the Sheridan in her which made her blood 'dance' – allowed herself to make a joking reference to a recent sensational murder case.[4]

A certain Greenacre had murdered his fiancée, Hannah Brown, having lured her to the house to discuss the distribution of their property before their marriage, which was planned for Christmas Day. Caroline asked whether George intended to do a Greenacre, as it were. George Norton seized the opportunity to have a bit of fun himself, asking her to come round; 'bring all you have got and we'll be married on Christmas Day.' He signed it Greenacre.

A series of letters signed Greenacre followed, involving other jokes relevant to the criminal case (which had ended in Greenacre's conviction and execution), leaving Caroline to suspect her husband was now half mad as well as physically violent given the opportunity.[5] At the same time, the bizarre correspondence, in which the warring couple freely took part, does throw some light on another aspect of their marriage. It was, after all, Caroline who first introduced the name of the murdered Hannah Brown: their relationship did include that light-heartedness, frivolity even, which was never totally eliminated from Caroline's nature. This was the lady, after all, who had horrified observers by kicking Melbourne's hat.

A serious effort at reconciliation between the warring parents was made by Sir John Bayley, George Norton's lawyer in the recent case, the barrister son of a judge, who was not disposed to encourage Norton in his wilder threats of permanent deprivation on the simple basis of a father's overruling rights, since the question of the mother's immorality had been excluded.

To Bayley's surprise Caroline Norton agreed that he should act for them both; but it was, in fact, an extremely sensible decision if any practical settlement was to be brought about. Given the two characters involved, however, what followed was not so surprising: Bayley came to sympathize with Caroline and later had to defend himself against the charge of acting unfairly towards his original client, Norton. His self-defence was honest enough. He had discovered all Caroline's anxieties to be centred on the children. Towards money she displayed 'perfect indifference'. George Norton, on the other hand, displayed himself as only anxious about money, 'so obviously making the love of the mother for her offspring a means of barter or bargain'.[6] The result was that Bayley declared himself unable to be part of anything that denied Caroline 'fair and honourable access' to the children.

We must remember, perhaps, as did sly contemporaries, that Bayley, despite his experience of the law and his legal background, was here dealing with one of the most famously charming women of her time. But the truth was that the facts of Caroline's case themselves spoke clearly enough to convince an honest lawyer. This was particularly relevant when details of Norton's physical abuse of his wife began to emerge. Bayley found confessions in Norton's own hand '*of the grossest personal violence*' (his italics), in spite of which he found Caroline both 'reasonable' and 'tractable'. George Norton, on the other hand, blamed the trial on his advisers, and Caroline's own declaration that she would never return.

With Bayley's help, a letter was written and posted, sending once more for the Norton children from Scotland. Then George Norton changed his mind. At this point Bayley ceased his efforts at mediation, which ended one possibility of a harmonious agreement between the warring couple. Correspondence continued throughout November 1837 and into the next year, before efforts to agree were abandoned.

Some indication of Caroline's frame of mind can be got from her letters to Mary Shelley. 'Dear Mrs. Shelley,' she wrote on one occasion: 'I have been and *am* as ill and worn-out as I can possibly be . . . I have been ever since I saw you "arranging" with Mr. N. and we are just where we were, except that I *hate* him more than I ever thought I could hate so weak a nature.'[7]

All this left the financial situation of the couple wide open and unresolved. George Norton might be the legal owner of his wife's literary earnings since she was non-existent under the law, but, by the same principle, he was legally liable for her debts. The only measure that would protect a husband from his wife's debts was a legal separation. And the Nortons were not legally separated. No arrangements had been made about Caroline's finances. George Norton, therefore, had found it necessary to place a series of three advertisements, declaring himself without responsibility for his wife's debts; this, however, had no validity in law, in keeping with the whole anomalous position of a married woman herself.

A prominent advertisement in *The Times* on 5 September 1837 (four times the length of all the adjacent advertisements), which was given wide publicity, ensured that anyone who had temporarily forgotten about the Norton case would remember it again.[8]

Beginning 'Whereas on the 30th March 1836, CAROLINE ELIZABETH SARAH, my WIFE, left me, her family, and home,' it continued by declaring that G. C. NORTON had given his said wife a 'liberal and ample' annual allowance in accordance with the advice of his legal advisers. Elaborate details followed of proposed methods of payment and rejections. The advertisement then proceeded to cite 'articles of luxury', altogether unnecessary for her, and inconsistent with his means, for which actions for recovery of debt had recently been threatened. As a result: 'I hereby give notice of my said offer of such provision for my said wife and that I will not be answerable for any debts she may have contracted since the 30th of March 1836, or may contract hereafter.'

Such a public – and humiliating – declaration demanded some kind of public retraction. A letter to *The Times* from Jennings and Bolton, lawyers to Caroline's brother, followed on 12 September. 'With reference to the public advertisement which appeared in your paper on the 5th inst . . . we are directed by Mr. Brinsley Sheridan to state that the whole of it is false.'[9]

In contrast to these squalid and unhappy discussions involving the once peerless Caroline Norton was the new life of her former admirer, Lord Melbourne. Caroline had signed off her letter to him regarding her children, written five days before the death of William IV, on a dolorous note.[10] This indicated how things were already proceeding between Melbourne and herself – or rather, not proceeding. 'I hear nothing of you, as I used to do,' she wrote, 'and feel much the same dreariness of heart that one does when watching by a sick bed: – everything very cold, very dim, & very silent, & the clock ticking very loud.' But Melbourne as Prime Minister was doing the very opposite of sitting by a sickbed as he began to develop a relationship with his new Sovereign.

The eighteen-year-old Queen, who greeted her Prime Minister at nine o'clock in the morning on the day of her accession, was already prejudiced in his favour. Her uncle and mentor, King Leopold of the Belgians, had given her instructions as William IV moved inexorably towards death. 'You will entrust Lord

Melbourne with the office of retaining the present Administration as your Ministers.'[11]

The young Queen saw a man no longer young – Melbourne was by now over sixty – but still in his own Whiggish way handsome, still carrying with him that air of aristocratic indolence which was at such variance with his known career: by this time it included not only two cases for Crim. Con., but the experience of a wife both mad and unfaithful, and the tragedy of an only child, Augustus, who was seriously handicapped ('the poor sickly lad' died in 1836 in his late twenties).

Melbourne, for his part, saw a little rosebud of a woman, her tiny figure – she was four feet eleven inches – adding to the childish impression, whereas Caroline was already a flourishing rose (Caroline was eleven years older than Victoria). Above all, the young Queen Victoria was in clear need of Melbourne's paternal guidance. As a father figure, he would fulfil the role that she had never known in real life since her own father died when she was eight months old; Caroline, who had last seen her father when she was five, had at least some childhood memories of him.

John Hobhouse, an acute observer of the political scene, was quick to make the comparison: 'Victoria's demeanour with him was that of a child to a parent. He was easy but respectful.'[12] When the young Queen read her Declaration on her accession, 'everyone appeared touched with her manner', particularly those two distinguished veterans, the Duke of Wellington and Lord Melbourne: 'I saw some tears in the eyes of the latter.' Very soon it became the custom for Melbourne to sit next to the Queen at dinner, where 'he kept up a conversation which seemed to amuse her for she often laughed.' There were further paternal scenes when Melbourne tried to teach the young Queen how to play chess, before handing over to Hobhouse, in a situation in which there was considerable confusion, as he put it, with two Queens on the board, and a third one just sitting there.

As events moved towards the coronation of the new monarch – which would take place on 28 June 1838 – there was an increasing concentration on the new Court and its courtiers. Presentation to the young Queen, the right to curtsey respectfully before her, was the kind of access to which the socially insecure naturally aspired. As with all such public ritual events, as Caroline put it herself, it was not so much presence at the Court and the Court balls which were desired – they were 'nothing in themselves' – as exclusion from them, 'the badge of shame', which was feared. Some six weeks into the new reign, Caroline wrote Melbourne a bitter letter, focusing on her possible rejection, and, even more humiliatingly, Melbourne's unwillingness to help her.[13]

She began ominously: 'I congratulate you on your influence at the palace,' before complaining about the presence of the notorious Lady Stanhope, who had already dined there for the second time, despite being 'your brother's mistress (if she hasn't also been yours)'. After denouncing Lady Stanhope at some length, she moved to her real complaint. 'You have treated me with the most selfish ingratitude . . . We will see whether under the mask of justice, I shall be told by the Queen that I am not fit to associate with the ladies of her court, while she makes a companion of one whom your "guardianship of royalty" does not consider an unfit associate.'

This complaint about the privileged acceptance of certain grand ladies, whose social status rendered them apparently immune from disapproval, despite their egregious moral failings, remained a preoccupation of Caroline Norton. Why should others be granted an indulgence which was not allowed to her, an infinitely lesser sinner – if sinner at all? A few years later, she was wailing in a long letter to William Cowper-Temple (Melbourne's nephew) that it was 'in vain to place opinions in the score of *virtue* which are in truth the results of *worldliness*'. Not until these grand ladies were being 'cut' like her, that is ostracized, would she believe that her lack of social support was not because 'they consider me a person unnecessary to support – but a person unfit to be supported.'

Particular examples were Emily, Duchess of Beaufort, and Lady Holland. The Duchess had caused a scandal by marrying her erstwhile brother-in-law, the 7th Duke, in 1822, a year after her sister's death, in theory outraging convention. Lady Holland, the celebrated Whig hostess, had undergone a divorce. 'Shew me the Duchess of Beaufort sitting alone among her deserted card tables,' wrote Caroline bitterly, 'and Lady Holland vainly expecting company to dinner.'[14]

Melbourne's idea that Caroline would have to wait for Presentation until the Queen was married was especially enraging. Greville, in his Memoirs, described the new Court as 'a stainless Camelot' (how unlike the home life of the Queen's uncles George IV and William IV!). Caroline now found not only that she was excluded from Camelot for being, as it were, stained, but that her Sir Lancelot in the shape of Lord Melbourne was an integral part of it. 'If he thinks I can be brought to bear tamely what the Royal Girl considers a fit punishment for me in being her predecessor,' fumed Caroline, 'I can't help it.'[15]

In contrast to this neurotic, if sympathetic, preoccupation with her social status, the return of Talfourd's Bill, as the Infant Custody Bill was known, to the political arena raised a very different issue for Caroline's concern. She continued to circulate her views in another privately printed pamphlet, following *Observations* the previous year. This was entitled *The Separation of Mother and Child by the Law of 'Custody of Infants', Considered*, and targeted at her influential political friends when she could reach them – this, despite her family's despairing disapproval expressed among themselves.[16]

On 21 December, Talfourd moved the Bill in the House of Commons for its second reading. In the debates which followed, the most tenacious opponent proved to be Sir Edward Sugden, currently Tory MP for Ripon, formerly Solicitor General and Lord Chancellor of Ireland.[17]

Sugden was a prominent lawyer, an expert on the laws of property, the subject of many of his publications. His brilliant career had been meteoric in its rise: Sugden actually began life as the son of a wig-maker and hairdresser in Westminster; in consequence his opponents were wont to challenge him at election time for being the mere 'son of a barber'. From this humble background had emerged not, as might be supposed, a radical but an energetic opponent of reforms of many different sorts. He had opposed not only the Great Reform Bill of 1832 but also

Jewish Emancipation on the grounds that the Jews 'had possessed nothing; they held nothing'.

Now Sugden pitched into Talfourd's suggested measures (extremely modest by later standards). Talfourd's original Bill had centred on the particular relationship of a mother and a child – one can here discern the influence of Caroline Norton's well-publicized situation – and did not attempt to limit the existing rights of a father over his legal offspring. Sugden, however, led the opponents to the Bill by attacking the whole principle of 'this absolute right' of a mother to have access to her own children.

The kernel of his argument was summed up by a hostile pamphlet published in Fleet Street in which the Bill was described as 'directly immoral, antichristian'.[18] While Sugden 'readily admitted' that there was 'no more painful source of regret' to a mother than to be debarred from access to her own children, he used precisely the point as an argument for denying this access to her in the event of separation. He dreaded the effects of this 'unchristian' new Bill concerning custody, which would actively encourage women to feel the freedom to separate. After all, 'the great tie which prevents the separation of married persons is their common children,' and if the Bill was passed, this tie would no longer bind them. Crudely put: 'you opened a door to divorces and to every species of immorality.' Sugden even suggested at one point that women might actually be glad to have this emotional excuse to submit to their capricious husband's will. 'It was some satisfaction for an angry woman to say "I would leave him immediately but for my children."' (This was certainly an optimistic forecast where Caroline Norton was concerned.)

Sugden waxed eloquent in a series of comparisons by which an established marriage, among other things, was compared to a vine stiffened into hardness by the warm embraces of the sun, which could thus endure the storms of the north. And he quoted a fable in which an acrimonious married couple had been confined to one room, given one chair to sit on, one table at which to eat and one place in which to repose. The result was reconciliation. While the idea of a couple like the Nortons in such confinement might cause a realistic person to shudder, Sugden accepted that togetherness was the best way to reconcile differences.

Throughout the debate the evil social consequences of allowing women this maternal right continued to be stressed, with further suggestions that the Bill would positively encourage adultery; although at all points it was the adultery of women which was contemplated with eloquent horror, the mood of the times drawing a sharp practical (rather than moral) distinction between the adultery of the mother, which might result in foisting another man's child on her husband, and the adultery of the father.

In a later debate, a supporter of the Bill, the Tory MP William Tyringham Praed, once again stressed this distinction between the sexes.[19] But he then pointed out, accurately, that unlimited access for mothers was not actually being offered. On the contrary, it was being suggested that with a separated couple, an impartial person should have the power to take the circumstances into consideration before granting limited access to the mother. This meant evaluating the mother's personal conduct: 'Nothing was so likely to keep her conduct correct as to give her licensed interviews with her children.' (There was no mention of any evaluation of the father's conduct.)

Praed then outlined a counterfactual situation in which a law was proposed 'to declare, even if the husband should have been guilty of the grossest debauchery, and had by his brutality driven his wife from his roof, yet that the husband should have the custody of the children, and that his virtuous and injured wife should not have even a limited access to them'. This time, he was sure that no one in the House would be found to second it.

Serjeant Talfourd, summing up in reply, pounced on his opponent's argument and turned it round. 'What was more deplorable than that this depth of [maternal] feeling should be the last link to prevent a virtuous woman from separating from her husband who ill uses her': 'This iron bond' of a mother's love, as he called it, was supposed to induce women to remain under their husband's roof, regardless of whatever cruelties he chose to use towards them.

Serjeant Talfourd and his allies convinced the House of Commons; it voted in favour of the Bill, 91 Ayes to 18 Noes.[20] The Ayes included the young Benjamin Disraeli and the Earl of Surrey MP, heir to the premier peer the Catholic Duke of Norfolk, who nine years earlier had been the first Catholic MP elected under the new rules of Catholic Emancipation.

Before the Infant Custody Bill could become law, it had to run the gauntlet of the House of Lords. The debate on the second reading took place on 30 July 1838.[21] Lord Lyndhurst led the debate: a leading lawyer, he had already been Lord Chancellor twice, most recently in Sir Robert Peel's ministry ending in 1835, and had generally shown himself opposed to liberal measures such as Catholic Emancipation.

In terms of background and private life, however, Lyndhurst was not a conventional Tory. Born in America, he was the son of a painter, John Copley. Then there was the question of his wife: Dolly, Lady Lyndhurst was an extremely handsome woman, so dark, according to one diarist, that she was 'very nearly a woman of colour'.[22] Others thought she resembled a painting by Leonardo da Vinci. Her reputation, including rumoured links to the Royal Duke of Cumberland and Lord Dudley, was scandalous. If Caroline Norton was described in discreet terms as 'not quite nice', the same female misogyny found Lady Lyndhurst quite openly described as 'an underbred creature'.

Whatever the influence of his colourful private life, Lyndhurst made a long speech, dwelling on various cases of obvious unfairness towards a virtuous mother. In one horrific case, as he related it, the mother was of 'irreproachable character' and had separated from her husband due to his 'barbarous usage'. Her husband was now openly living in adultery with a woman named Delaval, his six-year-old daughter having been properly left with her mother. The husband then exercised his rights to custody of the child – despite by this time being himself confined in prison, which meant that the little girl had to be carried to him 'day by day', cared for in the intervals by her father's mistress: in short, the mother was allowed no access at all. Lord Lyndhurst left it to the House to conceive what must have been this virtuous woman's sufferings.

In another case where a child taken from her mother had begun to suffer from 'a scrofulous complaint', the mother in question begged to be able to care for her. In spite of the fact that the judge specially referred to 'the devotional watchfulness and care of a mother', which by implication a father could not match, by law he could still not restore the child to her mother. In another case, that of a Mrs Greenhill and her three daughters, taken from her, the court similarly expressed regret that it had no power to act.

Lyndhurst ended by appealing: 'let it be remembered to what tyranny and oppression on the part of the husband the existing law led.' He had merely suggested the mildest of remedies. All he was asking was for some impartial judge to decide 'to what extent a virtuous mother might have access to her children when separated from her husband'.

The next speaker, who opposed the Bill, was in fact the liberal Whig Lord Brougham, a former Lord Chancellor, who had strongly supported the Great Reform Bill of 1832 as well as the abolition of slavery and was famous for defending Queen Caroline, wife of George IV. Despite his support for reforming causes, currently that of public education, Brougham made a long speech of opposition. Its tenor was later summed up in a letter from the sympathetic Whig Lord Holland to Caroline Norton, who criticized it for both 'logic and feeling': 'Nothing could be worse than Brougham's speech on the Bill. His message was that, several legal hardships being of necessity inflicted on women, *therefore* we should not relieve them from those which are not necessary, although repugnant to the feelings of our nature, and indeed to nature itself.' Lord Holland declared that he personally would always vote for the Bill.[23]

In view of Brougham's uncharacteristically illiberal stance (scarcely masked by his tortuous legal arguments), it seems more than possible that some personal grudge against Caroline Norton was involved here: there were rumours that Brougham blamed Caroline's influence with the Prime Minister for his exclusion from Melbourne's 1835 ministry. Apart from his detailed criticisms of the Bill, his speech also dwelt on what appeared to many to be the crucial question, that of the wife's possible adultery: 'What could be a more powerful tendency to make a wife faithful than the knowledge that infidelity on her part would sever her connexion with her offspring?' The Bill, as a whole, would be a channel 'through which the floods of immorality would be sure to overthrow the character of the institution of marriage'.

The final intervention of the Tory Lord Wynford, the man believed to have spurred on George Norton to sue Melbourne, stressed once again the incentive the present law gave to women to remain chaste in the shape of access to her offspring. Basically, he spoke up for the George Nortons of society: 'There were cases in which the greatest injustice would be done to husbands by the Bill.' He recalled, for example, the Hampshire case, which their Lordships would probably also remember, of a husband who actually found his wife in the arms of a *servant*! 'Yet this chaste and virtuous lady', as Wynford sarcastically termed her, would be entitled to apply for access to her own children if the Bill became law.

This combination of the entrenched patriarchal arguments of Wynford and the tortuous legal arguments of Brougham convinced the Lords. The Bill was rejected by a majority of two: nine votes content, eleven not content.[24] An exceptionally small House of Lords thus demolished the hopes of women throughout the country who were, in the words of Caroline Norton, 'hungry for the children'.

Serjeant Talfourd and Caroline nursed their disappointment, Caroline with a bitterness she did not hesitate to express subsequently: 'You cannot get peers to sit up till three in the morning listening to the wrongs of separated mothers,' she wrote.[25] While the fashionable world rejoiced in the coronation of the young Queen, Caroline had to endure the advertisements of George Norton denying responsibility for his wife's debts.

No agreement had been reached yet about her financial situation, which depended on the nature of the separation, legal or simply practical, between the married couple. All her personal property, including her dead father's pension and her earnings, continued to belong to her husband. It was symbolic of such omnivorous possession that among her personal property, Norton even retained relics of Caroline's grandfather Richard Brinsley Sheridan.[26] The latter had proposed an allowance of £300 a year after the failure of the Melbourne case. George Norton was, in fact, now being sued for £142, the cost of a small phaeton which Caroline had used the year before to enable her to visit her children. There were other costs Norton had refused to pay, such as jewellery Caroline had undoubtedly bought. On the other hand, this jewellery was, like her other so-called possessions, actually possessed by George Norton.

This lawsuit had a very different atmosphere from the House of Lords, with its lofty oratory on the subject of infant custody, that novel issue of principle. The 'non-existence' of a married woman in the financial sense was age-old; as a result of her lack of legal rights, any husband could be sued for his wife's debts at any time. In the course of it, there were attempts to bring in the private affairs of the Nortons, including their correspondence. Caroline eagerly cooperated, feeling that the justice of her case (in a different context) could only be reinforced. The case came before Lord Abinger, with Caroline (once again, in something which directly concerned her) forming no part of it. The letters between husband and wife were not admitted. George Norton's rebuttal of his wife's debts in advertisements now proved similarly useless from the legal point of view. He was simply told to pay up.[27]

Whereupon Caroline determined, in a modern phrase, to go public with the whole affair. This was entirely in keeping with her new life as a campaigner. Her family was horrified. Her mother had called campaigning indelicate; it was not, however, her mother or sisters but Lord Melbourne who actually held her back. For the Prime Minister, struggling with attempts to repeal the Corn Laws, to name only one of the political issues of the day, a return to the hideous personal publicity of the 1836 case, thanks to tempestuous action on the part of his erstwhile lady friend, was the last thing he needed. As usual, Caroline heeded him. This was, after all, the man she had regarded as her protector, who she passionately wanted to believe had her best interests at heart. As she summed it up: 'I listened [to him] then as at other times.'[28] More public spats between the Nortons would be 'beyond measure vexatious and embarrassing to him'. She could 'rest assured' that no patience shown would be forgotten. At Melbourne's request, 'I gave up what I prepared.'

March 22, 1838 had marked Caroline Norton's thirtieth birthday, verging on middle age according to the average female life expectancy of the time.

There were beginning to be references to her health in her letters to her family, increasing as time went on. The mention of spitting blood 'two or three days at a time' was particularly troubling to one of Sheridan descent, given the sad family tendency in that respect.[29] She also suffered from what she described as rheumatism, 'which pains my head and blinds my eyes', so that she could not work by candlelight. These headaches became an unpleasant feature of her existence, sometimes confining her to the house for several days when the doctors forbade her to go walking.*

She was separated from her children, but, equally unfortunately, not separated officially from her husband. And there was little to comfort her in public life. The recent Bill for Infant Custody, more accurately termed maternal access, had failed. She was no longer welcome at Court, nor indeed in several sections of society. Her notorious beauty, the languorous dark eyes under the heavy eyebrows, which inspired artists, was in itself a fertile source of gossip: any man connected to her was liable to be accused of either seducing her or being seduced; this included Serjeant Talfourd, her friend and collaborator on the Bill. It was becoming the fashion to look for scandal in any situation in which she was involved.

---

* They might now be described as migraines.

With a courage and determination which were far from Burke's chivalrous notion of feminine delicacy, Caroline Norton picked up her pen and wrote again on behalf of the cause in which she believed.

CHAPTER NINE

Woman's Tears
and the Law

*'The question of the propriety and necessity of the
ALTERATION OF THE LAW is the question the House has
to consider, and not the paltry and ridiculous doubt whether
Mrs. Norton used her woman's tears and her woman's
arguments.'*

A Plain Letter to the Lord Chancellor on the Infant Custody
Bill, 15 December 1838

THE ATTACKS ON CAROLINE NORTON and her feminine
wiles continued. For those opposed to the whole idea of separated mothers' access to children, Caroline's notoriety since the
1836 case provided a convenient scapegoat. Surely it was her
wicked capacity for enchantment which had brought about
the whole immoral campaign? As ever in such attacks, the
fact that there was some truth in the charges, if not the whole
truth, helped them to gain currency. That is to say, Caroline
had indeed used her political friendships to bring attention to
the unfair suffering of mothers; while her own manifest woes
gave reality to the picture. None of this meant the law did not
need changing.

Another charge against her was similarly untrue. This came from exactly the other point of view, that of early feminists such as Harriet Martineau.[1] It was suggested that the Bill had been held up by her selfish preoccupation with her own needs – in this case, the delicate situation regarding access to her own children. In fact, it was the ongoing need to improve the Bill after its original rejection which had held it up, not Caroline's fear of compromising her negotiations with Norton. But the timing made the accusation possible. Besides, there was always a body of opinion determined to assert that all Caroline's campaigning – and quite possibly all female campaigning – was totally selfish, based entirely on self-interest, not the interests of the female sex as a whole.

The British and Foreign Review, for example, launched a huge spray of acid upon her reputation.[2] This was the work of John Mitchell Kemble, brother of the actress Fanny Kemble: a painful connection for Caroline, who rated Fanny as her friend. The malevolent John Kemble, roughly Caroline's contemporary, was a brilliant if erratic man; ironically, his own marriage would break up a few years later, although in this case it was his wife's adultery and his drinking which were to blame. Now he mounted numerous accusations, of which the most perverse was the suggestion that Caroline had married George out of 'lust' rather than love. The most damaging was that scandalous linkage between Serjeant Talfourd and Caroline Norton.

MPs were accused of intending to destroy 'the very principle of the marriage law altogether', and to set up in its stead the principle of the separate existence of the wife as if she were a 'feme sole', the legal term for a single woman. There was a sanctimonious reference to the *Review*'s reluctance to cite the subject. 'It is not we but Mrs. Norton who has forced her case upon the public. She has courted publicity.' And throughout, the *Review* stressed the shocking nature of Talfourd's contention: 'all women, even convicted adulteresses' had a prima facie right to demand access to what the *Review* described as 'their husbands' children'.

The British and Foreign Review even invoked the purity of the new monarch. 'God and the people of England defend, that, in the second year of the reign of our gracious and noble sovereign lady, our virgin Queen,' such a Bill should be sent up to her, considering its 'abominable immorality'. This was another cruel reference from Caroline's point of view: she continued to remonstrate embarrassingly with Melbourne by letter about his preference for the 'Royal Girl' over herself while watching his movements avidly via the newspapers. In a typical letter written at the beginning of 1839, she began by worrying about his health: 'Have you had a cold? I thought all my cold journey down, whether you had taken cold or not, & then when I saw you dined at the Palace, I felt the usual mixture of irritation and satisfaction – satisfaction that at last you were *well* and out.'[3] The cause of the irritation was obvious.

Caroline was appalled by Kemble's attack. When there was a question of him succeeding his father as Examiner of Plays (an early censor's role), she remonstrated with Lord Conyngham, the Lord Chamberlain, who had the power of the appointment.[4] Caroline found such an appointment 'monstrous and incredible', given that Kemble had actually called her a 'she-devil' and a 'she-beast', so that even his friends felt the need to apologize for him. Now it was suggested he should monitor the language of other people. Thanks to such abuse, 'I have for three years *walked on hot ploughshares*,' she wrote. She ended by positively raging against 'that perfidious aristocracy' who had been ever ready to avail themselves of her talents; let them beware: 'I may be a worm – and they may cut me to pieces – but they shall find, *like* the worm, that every atom has life in it still.'

The self-styled worm, Caroline Norton once more used her pen to defend herself, in her own words, 'as the soldier relies on his sword to cut his way through'. But her next campaigning pamphlet, published after the failure of the original Infant Custody Bill, was put out under the pseudonym of 'Pearce Stevenson Esq.'. It was entitled *A Plain Letter to the Lord Chancellor on the Infant Custody Bill* and dated 15 December 1838.[5] Caroline took the opportunity to hit back at the *Review*, which had wrongly ascribed to her an anonymous article, 'An Outline of the Wrongs of Women', and then proceeded to treat the said article with 'abhorrence and indignation'. The imaginary Pearce Stevenson proceeded to give a solemn avowal, quoting Messrs Saunders and Otley, that Mrs Norton was 'NOT the author of the article' and the accusation was consequently 'WHOLLY DESTITUTE OF FOUNDATION'.

One of the main features of *A Plain Letter to the Lord Chancellor* was its dismissal of any connection between the proposed Bill and feminine weakness: 'The question of the propriety and necessity of the ALTERATION OF THE LAW is the question the House [of Commons] has to consider, and not the paltry and ridiculous doubt whether Mrs. Norton used her woman's tears and her woman's arguments.' It went on to stress that any attempt to link the maternal sufferings of Mrs Norton with the parliamentary efforts of Serjeant Talfourd was full of 'false and malignant representations'.

There was a full narration of the various stages of the breakdown of the Nortons' marriage, including Norton's physical assaults on his wife, and Mrs Norton's efforts to see her children. Care was taken to point out that all this occurred before Mrs Norton got to know Serjeant Talfourd: 'it was after this unsuccessful struggle [for access to the children] that Mrs. Norton was introduced to Serjeant Talfourd (with whom she had no previous acquaintance).' She contacted him, in fact, because of his previous work with the Greenhill case. The pamphlet then related a number of painful stories of mothers denied access, as speakers had done in both Houses of Parliament, before denouncing Lords Brougham and Wynford in particular.

She pointedly contrasted their liberal efforts in other directions with their attitude to women's legal rights. Brougham had exercised his 'skilful and laborious pleading' in defence of the liberties and social rights of the black population in his anti-slavery work. Wynford had waxed indignant against the presumed defects of the new Poor Law. Now, 'we hear with surprise the one advocating the oppression of bad men over their unoffending wives, and the other upholding as a fit legislative enactment the parting of a guiltless mother from her helpless child.'

Caroline Norton saw to it that the pamphlet was disseminated as widely as possible to people of influence and authority. In England in 1839, there was no one who fitted that description better than the seventy-year-old Duke of Wellington, veteran soldier and veteran politician. Caroline duly asked her sister Georgia to tackle him the day before the Bill would be in the Commons, when she feared 'they mean to try to pull it to pieces'. 'I *beseech you* to send to the D. of Wellington the pamphlet and a note from yourself. – He reads everything sent him and answers the meanest petition *himself* – so I am assured . . . I really am in a fever – write also to Palmerston.' After all, in the words of Caroline to her sister, when she was in anguish over the result of the vote, 'it is but *one* night out of any body's life to do a kind thing to many a poor brute of a woman & many an innocent child.'[6]

Serjeant Talfourd returned to the House of Commons with his third attempt at an Infant Custody Bill. The first reading of the new Bill took place on 25 April 1839.[7] He took the trouble to refer glancingly to the unpleasant aspersions which had been cast on his relationship with Mrs Norton. 'He had been subject, as everyone who embarked on such a cause must be, to scandal and to slander; for this he cared not.' He would, on the contrary, proceed so long as he was supported by such a respectable majority of MPs.

Talfourd mentioned the amendments he had made to his previous Bill, while making the point that it had been defeated in the Lords by only two votes. He was now, for example, asking for a mother to have actual custody of her child up to the age of seven, not mere access, pointing out that this would simply give virtuous women the same rights as the mothers of illegitimate children. In short, he was attempting to mitigate the lot of innocent and injured mothers and give them 'something more than empty rights'.

Of course, the stigma of female adultery remained: that enduring belief in the double standard. It was specifically stated: 'Provided always, and be it enacted, That no Order shall be made by virtue of this Act, whereby any Mother against whom Adultery shall be established by Judgment in an Action for Criminal Conversation at the Suit of her Husband [for example, Caroline Norton, if her husband's case had been successful] or by the Sentence of an Ecclesiastical Court, shall have the Custody of any Infant or access to any Infant.'

This time the Bill moved forward quickly, and after a successful second reading moved to the Lords.[8] Once again, Lord Lyndhurst made a powerful speech in which he related some hard cases where children had been separated from their mothers, including that of the baby still at its mother's breast when its father got hold of it 'by a stratagem' and put it in the care of a stranger.

Once more also Lord Wynford attacked the Bill, but the atmosphere had changed. This time it was allowed to proceed. Finally, on 17 August 1839, the young Queen Victoria gave Royal Assent to the Infant Custody Bill. Given that she was not yet married herself, it was appropriate that 17 August was the birthday of her own mother, the Duchess of Kent. Victoria's Journal for the day dwelt in detail on the many presents her mother was given. Otherwise, it was a long record of her concerns for Lord Melbourne, who was present at Windsor Castle, much resembling Caroline's own frequently expressed care. For example, was he having enough to eat? (The answer to the latter question was surely yes, since Melbourne revealed to the agitated young Queen that he had begun his day with a cold grouse before proceeding to three mutton chops at twelve noon.)[9]

Victoria made no record of the fact that she, the virgin Queen, had signed a momentous Bill which has been described as 'a landmark in the history of English law', even if to some it remained unchristian and immoral.[10] Thus, for the first time in English history, a mother had some legal rights over her own children – those 'who had lain beneath her heart and drunk of her life', as the writer and feminist Elizabeth Lynn Linton would put it later.[11]

A mother was now able to petition the court for custody of her own children up to the age of seven – those of tender years, as it came to be known – and for access to other, older children. The

Court of Chancery could transfer legal custody to the mother, if she was judged to be best suited to the care of the child. In short, up to the age of seven a father's rights were no longer absolute. One reservation, however, remained: that of the 'double standard': the proven adultery of the mother (not of the father) still ruled her out.[12]*

What then of Caroline Norton, whose unhappy story had served to focus public attention on the true implications of the existing legal situation? Unfortunately, she now got to experience the peril of the Scottish connection: the new law for England, Ireland and Wales did not apply in Scotland. So, despite her efforts, both by the pen and by persuasion, she was still for the time being immersed in those negotiations to see the boys which left her so distraught.

Through all this hideous time, Caroline's family, principally her sisters Helen and Georgia, sustained her, even when expressing private disapproval to each other.[13] The exquisite Lady Seymour and the graceful Lady Dufferin (Helen's husband Price Blackwood succeeded to the title in November 1839) loyally continued to entertain their 'scandalous' sister. While Caroline continued to be based in Bolton Street, at the house of her uncle Charles Sheridan, there were trips abroad in their company.

These were evidently merry occasions. Caroline described to Helen their future sleeping arrangements, quoting Ariel in *The Tempest*: 'Dear Nell, "Come unto those [sic] yellow sands" for Wednesday being our quarter day, we shall depart *after* as soon as possible, packing up our sheets and towels, and altogether dismantling our habitation. You can enjoy a dressing room and bedroom, & bed in dressing rooms. Pricey shall have an extra shaving glass for his whiskers.'[14] In October 1840, Caroline went to France and Italy with the Dufferins. The visit, above all the stay in Rome, restored her equilibrium and some of that jauntiness which originally captivated Melbourne returned to her

---

* By an Act of 1873, the mother was able to get custody up to the age of sixteen. It was not until the Guardianship of Infants Act 1925 that the law made men and women formally equal.

letters to him. It was from Rome, for example, that she wrote that wicked letter describing to him a cabinet inlaid with ivory etchings, including one of 'his favourite subject', which was whipping, and declared that she had half a mind to buy it for him.[15]

The difference in Caroline and Georgia's relative positions in society was, however, vividly expressed ten days after the passing of the Infant Custody Bill. At the end of August 1839, Georgia, Lady Seymour, eighteen months younger than Caroline, was hailed as the Queen of Beauty at the extraordinary Eglinton Tournament.*

Georgia was generally felt to be worthy of the august title even by a rival Queen; for the young Victoria expressed her contentment with the choice to Lord Melbourne. She had previously approved Georgia's sweetness and gentleness in her Journal at the time of her accession, two qualities incidentally she did not find either in Mrs Norton or the then Mrs Blackwood.'[16] Georgia's nephew, in a memoir about his mother and her sisters, wrote of Georgia that she had 'large deep blue or violet eyes, black eyebrows and eyelashes, and a complexion of lilies and roses – a kind of colouring seldom seen out of Ireland'. If Benjamin Robert Haydon (who was tormentedly in love with Caroline) complained on the other hand that there was no music in Georgia's soul, he admitted that she was 'a love, a Venus in figure', which was probably more appropriate for a Queen of Beauty than that dangerous music which presumably possessed Caroline.[17]

Now Georgia provided the central feature of this prodigious fake historical tournament, organized by the Earl of Eglinton in Ayrshire and said to cost £40,000 (three and a half million pounds today). A very British festival, it was marked by prodigious rainstorms; but wild weather could not affect the title which Georgia so publicly enjoyed. Crowned with pearls and ornamented with diamonds, she reigned in splendour even if, due

---

* Her husband was styled Lord Seymour at the time of their marriage until 1855, when he succeeded to the Dukedom of Somerset and Georgia became a Duchess.

to rain, she had to be conveyed in a closed carriage, instead of leading a brilliant procession mounted on 'a palfrey'.[18]

While Georgia reigned, Caroline was allowed at last a somewhat lesser recognition: that reception at Court which she craved. The tacit ban on her Presentation, based on a diktat of William IV – something Caroline furiously resented, given the previous King's own record of mistresses – was lifted. She was presented at a Drawing Room at Court in May 1840. There was some Royal sympathy for her situation at this point. King Leopold of the Belgians, a supporter of Caroline, who was present, told his niece Victoria that it was 'a very generous feeling' which had prompted her to receive Mrs Norton. He commented further that Norton was certainly an extremely unpleasant husband. The Belgian King also understood why Caroline had appeared nervous: 'I can well believe that she was much frightened having so many eyes on her, some of which, perhaps, not with the most aimable [sic] expression.'[19]

Caroline, according to the Court Journal, wore lace over white satin, and a train of pale Irish lilac poplin. Her headdress was made of lilac flowers which, with her black hair, clearly created a strong impression. Ostrich feathers and pearls further adorned the outfit. As a result, Lady Holland found Mrs Norton 'in greater beauty if possible than ever'.[20]

Afterwards, however, Caroline did not find all arms and doors open to her as she had expected. Nevertheless, it is clear that something fundamental in her nature – her personal sense of social justice – was at last satisfied by this development. It had never seemed fair to her that Melbourne, her co-defendant in the case in truth if not in law, had emerged smoothly from the process, the favourite of the Queen, while she suffered ignominy. She made that point quite frequently to Melbourne himself. Now that wrong was righted.

On 10 June 1840, Queen Victoria and her new husband, her cousin Albert of Saxe-Coburg, were involved in the most alarming incident. Their wedding had taken place earlier in the year: Hobhouse, who was at the ceremony, found it affecting that when she turned round from the altar, Victoria 'smiled playfully'

at Melbourne, who was standing behind her holding the Sword
of State. It was perhaps a kind of farewell. Now Victoria was a
few months pregnant.

The Royal pair were leaving Buckingham Palace in an
open carriage for Constitution Hill when the Queen heard an
explosion; immediately Albert flung his arms round her and
shouted: 'My God! Don't be alarmed.' Two shots were fired
by an eighteen-year-old youth named Edward Oxford, later
found guilty but insane. The brave young couple actually proceeded on their way to Hyde Park in order, in Albert's words,
to show the people that they had not lost confidence in them.
It was a courageous gesture which duly made a great public
impression.[21]

Caroline, newly acceptable since her Presentation, seized the
opportunity to send her own form of sympathy to the Queen:
what Victoria called with approval in her Journal 'a very pretty
little manuscript poem', but Caroline herself described as a
'Song'.[22] This was a very different Caroline from Melbourne's
jealous correspondent who had derided the Royal Girl. Her
'Song' had, on the contrary, a positively feminist slant. The
three handwritten pages entitled 'Lines on a late occasion' were
'Humbly dedicated to her Majesty'. The poem itself was inspired
by the remark attributed to 'the Traitor Oxford that "A Woman
should not rule this Realm"'.

Caroline Norton went on to give a history lesson in verse
lauding the Elizabethan era: 'To stamp that term of *Woman's*
rule / As Britain's 'Golden Age'. Then Richard Coeur de Lion
was invoked. Although the days of 'brute strength, and mail-clad
forces' were past,

> But not from England's crown is lost
> What never can depart, –
> The courage of her Royal blood, –
> Though shrined in woman's heart . . .
> . . . a lion-heart still holds
> The sceptre and the Crown.

The courage of Victoria in continuing on her way smiling, tranquil and serene immediately after the 'bolt of death' had flown past, was saluted, before the conclusion:

> And Heaven shall bless the brave young Queen
> Who feared no traitor's might
> And guard our Coeur de Lion still
> In all her sacred right!

Caroline Norton sent Victoria this loyal handwritten tribute bound in with her latest publication: *The Dream, and Other Poems*. It included 'The Creole Girl', to which allusion has already been made as an example of the aching sympathy for children, including those of mixed race, which had possessed Caroline since her troubles with her own family began. Throughout *The Dream* a mother's love was celebrated: a widowed mother contemplates her innocent sixteen-year-old daughter as she sleeps, a girl who is, in fact, on the brink of marriage:

> Sweet is the image of the brooding dove!
> Holy as Heaven a mother's tender love . . .
> The *only* Love which on this teeming earth
> Asks no return from Passion's wayward birth

It ends with the daughter resolving to go forward courageously into marriage, as her mother did, despite suffering: 'And from her mother's fond protecting side / She went into the world, a youthful bride.'

The unfortunate (other than deprived mothers), as in Caroline's previous works, were also not forgotten:

> The poor – the labouring poor! whose weary lives
> Through many a freezing night and hungry day,
> Are a reproach to him who only strives
> In luxury to waste his hours away.

And of course, the workhouse orphan, both poor *and* a child 'left without a friend', was mentioned. A comparison was drawn by one critic between the work of Caroline Norton and that of Elizabeth Barrett Browning. Mrs Norton was obsessed by the struggle of a woman towards happiness, whereas Miss Barrett wrote of the struggle of a soul towards heaven: 'the one is all womanhood: the other all wrongs.' The womanly Queen duly found *The Dream* 'very beautiful', just as she had approved the 'Lines on a late occasion'. This was not surprising, because among the poems was an ecstatic one entitled 'The Chapel Royal, St. James. On the 10th February 1840' – the place and date on which Victoria had got married:[23]

> All-hallowe'd be thy love;
> And still with proud content the day allied,
> When Princely Albert claim'd his Royal Bride!

Caroline had produced the book in part to provide money, of which she was in continual need, while the unsatisfactory negotiations continued. It produced one classic comment from Hartley Coleridge in September 1840 in the *Quarterly Review*: Caroline Norton was 'the Byron of Poetesses', a huge compliment but one in which it is also possible to discern a reflection on her private life. Coleridge believed the poem was 'deeper, plainer, truer' for the dark hours Caroline had endured over the loss of her own children, 'when loss brought her to the verge of unreason'.[24]

Choosing to assign flowers to each of the poetesses he saluted as the nine Muses (putting Caroline ahead of Elizabeth Barrett Browning), he chose for Caroline 'the Rose, or, if she likes it, *Love-lies-a-bleeding*'. *The Dream*, which appeared with a portrait of Caroline by Landseer as a frontispiece, was immensely popular and soon went into a second edition. There was also a question of it being pirated in North America, where the British laws of copyright did not obtain: a compliment, if a dubious one.

In the meantime, the negotiations between the Nortons continued along the distressing lines of one step forward, and almost immediately another step back. A seemingly endless

correspondence ensued in which Caroline made elaborate commitments such as this: 'I am perfectly ready to give my most
solemn promise (and whatever feasible security you may point
out) that I will not any time attempt, by my own or other
people's means, to remove the children, wherever they may be;
or interfere in any way with their health, dress, or education:
they are no longer infants, and what I felt while they were so,
and in the rashness of my first sorrow, would not influence me
now.' Under the circumstances, the next promise was particularly
significant: 'I will also solemnly swear never to attempt, or suffer
any person to attempt, to weaken their respect and affection for
their father or their father's family.'[25]

George Norton persistently used his trump card – access to
the boys – to impose his own terms. He was also thoroughly
wayward in promising the boys' arrival and then changing his
mind. On one occasion, Caroline actually waited for them in a
house on the Isle of Wight – in vain. Understandably, she became
extraordinarily suspicious of George and as a result she wrongly
suspected an unpleasant stranger, who, in modern parlance,
stalked her, as being somehow connected to George or what she
held to be his odious family.[26]

Throughout this period, Norton had still not returned his
wife's possessions to her – those possessions, including clothes
and jewels, which she had abandoned when she left the house in
1836. There was another case for debt, respecting carpets ordered
for Caroline at the Bolton Street house in which she now lived.
The other side to the harsh marital laws of the time was the
husband's liability for his wife's debts. In this instance, the judge
proved sympathetic to Caroline, who had after all been excluded
from her original house, which explained the need for carpets
elsewhere. It was the jury who took the side of George Norton,
as a result of which the carpet-supplier went unpaid and Norton
got away free.

The financial terms Norton proposed were never generous,
despite the fact that some of the money he promised was at least
morally Caroline's because it came from her marriage settlement.
But as the boys grew older, and the question of an English school

to prepare them for Eton College arose, reality meant that she could no longer be left completely out of the picture.

Although the situation might not be totally satisfactory from Caroline's point of view, it was better than it ever could have been, thanks to the existence of Serjeant Talfourd's Bill.[27] That is to say, George Norton did not send the children to live with Caroline, as she had expected, but would extend no further opposition to her seeing them as they progressed from preparatory school to Eton. It seemed that there could be, at last, some kind of stability, if not perfection, in her maternal arrangements.

Eighteen months later, when all the boys were in Yorkshire at Kettlethorpe Hall, George Norton's family estate, tragedy struck. Willie Norton celebrated his ninth birthday on 26 August 1842. The youngest of the three, this was the unfortunate child whose name had been ostentatiously changed by his father from William (Melbourne's Christian name) to Charles (his middle name), a gesture described by his mother at the time as full of 'affectation and insincerity'.[28] In any case, the order seems to have been generally ignored. Willie he remained, and it was as Willie, on the afternoon of 12 September 1842, that, riding out all alone, he fell off his pony.

Such accidents were hardly unusual. What was unusual was that there was no care for him, either to keep him safe on his pony, or to cope with his injury after the accident; there was only an old woman, the gamekeeper's wife, who was at the gate to deal with admittance and departure. The boys had 'no attendance', as Caroline told her mother later.[29] Willie's arm was injured and bleeding from the fall, and, in the absence of his father, he went to nearby Chapel Thorpe Hall. This owner was also away but his servants tried in vain to tend him. The little boy got blood-poisoning.

His condition worsened. His mother was, at last, sent a message, which had to be forwarded to Tunbridge Wells, where she was taking the waters. Caroline set out for Yorkshire, but it was too late.

When she arrived at the railway station, a Lady Kelly, another guest at Kettlethorpe Hall whom she had never met before, greeted her. 'I said: "I am here. Is my boy better?" "No", she said, "he is not better. He is dead."'[30]

Willie died, having prayed, asked his father to pray, and, as he was dying, twice asked in vain for his mother. It was clear that the accident itself would never have happened if there had been proper care of him. As Caroline described it: 'My poor little spirited creature was too young to rough it alone as he was left to do.' She had a further bitter comment: half of what was spent on decorating his little coffin at his funeral could have been spent on 'some manservant' to look after the boys at play.

Caroline admitted in a letter to Samuel Rogers the next day: 'It may be sinful to think bitterly at such a time.' She had at least not expressed these thoughts to Norton himself, 'to spare pain to one who never spared it to me. But it is not in the strength of human nature not to think: "This might not have happened had I watched over them!"' To her sister Georgia, at least, Caroline managed to be more philosophical: 'He died without fear, so young as he was, I can feel he is in Heaven – I saw little enough of him in this life – God grant that I may meet him in another.'[31]

The image of the little coffin lying alone in the Kettlethorpe dining room where Willie used to play haunted her for the rest of her life. As did the horror of her 'vain journey' north when Willie was already in his coffin: other deaths within the family would always bring back the tragic memory. Thirty years later Caroline would commend an epitaph from a child's grave to Lady Anna Stirling-Maxwell which ended with these words: In the last day when Earth and Heaven meet, we shall find our child again.[32]

It was true that the law had been changed. But a terrible cost had been paid by Caroline Norton in the form of a woman's tears for her lost boy, lost forever in the absence of his mother's care.

PART THREE

HALF IN SHADE, HALF IN SUN

As half in shade, and half in sun,
This world along its course advances,
May that side the Sun's upon
Be all that shall ever meet thy glances!

Tom Moore's epigraph to *The Child of the Islands*,
Caroline Norton, 1845

CHAPTER TEN

Heavenly Norton

'That he may not have the Heavenly Norton on one side of him and the Blessed Seymour on t'other (for this is too much to bear) is my prayer'

Daniel Maclise to Charles Dickens, 1840

CHRISTMAS 1842 WAS SPENT BY Caroline Norton with her surviving sons, Fletcher and Brin, aged thirteen and eleven respectively. They went to Frampton Court, in Dorset, home of her brother Brinsley and his wife Marcia, to whom Caroline was close, having been appointed godmother to their latest child. In January 1843 she was able to take her boys to one of Charles Dickens's famed Twelfth Night parties: magical tricks were performed by a conjuror, such as the ingredients of a plum pudding being tossed into a gentleman's hat and reappearing in perfectly cooked form.

It was the first Christmas Caroline had spent with her children for seven years: in 1839, for example, she had spent the day alone reading a pamphlet. This was some small consolation in her grief: that tragedy which, as she told Charles Mulloy Westmacott, editor of *The Age* and her supporter, in a letter written on black-bordered paper, had made 'all indifferent to her on this side of the grave'.[1]

The unexpected and horrifying death of Willie Norton, to which lack of care undoubtedly contributed, had accelerated the process by which George Norton gradually and grudgingly relinquished his sons' upbringing to their mother. At some point, some kind of unofficial deal was done with Chancery, as recent research has uncovered, although no publicity was given to it.[2] The Nortons were not legally separated, but Caroline was able to ease their path from Laleham Preparatory School in Surrey to Eton College. Fletcher went to Eton in the autumn of 1843 and Brin a year later. The obstacles Norton had previously placed in Caroline's path with regard to involvement were abandoned.

Given what the two boys had lived through – most recently the death of their little brother, but in the past incidents such as being physically wrested out of their mother's grasp – it was scarcely surprising that from time to time they had nervous problems. And then there were health issues, which seemed to be endemic in the Sheridan family.

Caroline herself continued to be plagued with troubles like coughing blood and debilitating headaches, while her correspondence becomes increasingly laden with references to doctors, advice to stay in bed, and unhappy health experiences. At one point she suggested whimsically to her brother Brinsley, 'if the days of witchcraft were not past, I should think someone had made a wax figure of me, to roast before the fire.'[3] (But she did not go further and suggest that the maker of the wax figure might have been George Norton.)

As to the boys, Fletcher in particular was a delicate child with periods of 'weary illness', although that merely brought him closer to his mother – now that she was able to care for him again. Once Fletcher and Brin were safely established at Eton, very much within reach of Caroline, it was hoped that a new period of calm would follow. While Fletcher's health continued to cause problems, the younger boy proved to be gratifyingly clever: Caroline happily boasted to her brother about the brilliance of 'my little, or rather my *stumpy* Brin'.

She made every effort to promote her boys: clearly the pent-up energy of a mother over the years was now at work. On 10

April 1845, for example, she wrote to Sir Augustus Clifford, Gentleman Usher of the Black Rod and former MP: 'I *entreat* you to put me and my second boy Brinsley, into some rat-hole or creak in the wall in the House of Commons tomorrow to hear the debate on Maynooth & I will ever feel obliged to you for the opportunity of making my shaggy little Lion of a boy "taste blood". He exactly resembles a *caricature cupid* from *old Mr. Sheridan's pictures* and is very intelligent and eager.' On the same occasion, Caroline told Disraeli's wife Mary Anne, whom he had married in 1839, that her elder boy, 'whom you patronise', was feeling better and her younger boy was 'wild to hear a debate' on the last day of his holidays, this being his first attempt at taking an interest in 'politics'.[4]

Caroline Norton was now able to enjoy again not only the periodic company of her beloved children, but also the distinctly unmotherly activities of her previous London life. There were, however, changes in the political scene, equivalent to the changes in her personal horizon. In September 1841, Lord Melbourne was succeeded as Prime Minister by the Tory Sir Robert Peel – to the considerable regret of Queen Victoria, who continued to consult her mentor Melbourne in a way that caused understandable annoyance to her new administration. But the days of the convenient stroll from 10 Downing Street to Storey's Gate were long gone in more than one sense. For in July 1845 Caroline moved into her own house for the first time in her life. And the area she chose was no longer close to Parliament but tucked away in the heart of Mayfair.

No. 3 Chesterfield Street was an elegant townhouse in a side street not far from Berkeley Square, overlooking the garden of Lord Wharncliffe, Lord President of the Council in Peel's government; Caroline found it agreeably tranquil compared to previous lodgings, where 'the rolling over the stones of the carriages' and 'the raps at the door' had been so disturbing. The house next door had once been frequented by the future George IV, who visited Beau Brummel there; recently various politicians and diplomats had found Chesterfield Street convenient. No. 3 had, in fact, been rebuilt only fourteen years before following a fire and was, as a result, 'all very new and sound'. In a letter to Disraeli's wife Mary Anne, Caroline referred to it as 'my future Palace'.* As she told Brinsley, it was the perfect residence for a lady able to support herself by her own activities.[5]

But there was a complication. By the laws of the time, such a lady was not, in fact, able to sign the lease. Caroline had to ask Brinsley to act as assurer. As she wrote with indignation to her brother: 'I can sign *nothing*: no one will admit me as a responsible party.' And she contrasted her legal position angrily with her actual working life: 'It is a bad thing to feel *legally* so helpless and dependent, while *in fact* I am as able to support myself as an intelligent man working in a moderate profession.' Fortunately, Brinsley agreed to help, buoyed up no doubt by the thought that John Murray had agreed to pay £500 for his sister's latest publication. There might be a delay in the deal 'but the lease is a present and pressing necessity', wrote Caroline. If Brinsley helped her now, she promised to repay him in two or future years, if she earned enough money by writing.[6]

It is notable that even during this discussion about sponsorship and the lease, there were unhappy murmurs from Caroline on the subject of her reputation: some people might not want to associate their name with hers.[7] There were also superstitious references to her own health (Caroline was in her late thirties) and what Brinsley should do '*in case* I get worse – knowing that you think my expectation of being worse foolish'.

Caroline Norton's London circle, quite apart from writers such as Dickens and Samuel Rogers and Thackeray (whom she helped to meet Lord Melbourne), included several artists: her appearance coupled with her equally colourful character clearly had a mesmerizing effect upon them. One gets the impression that this aspect of her public life – as it became – was a positive pleasure not only for the gratification of vanity, as anyone would feel, but for another reason peculiar to Caroline. It acted as a

---

* Still to be seen today, between Curzon Street and Charles Street, Mayfair. In 2021 English Heritage put up a Blue Plaque to Caroline Norton unveiled by the author.

contradiction of those charges of mannishness and of conversation 'often coarser than even a man should use', which her increasingly outspoken comments attracted.[8] The Caroline that the painters portrayed was unquestionably beautiful and she often depicted a strong female character from history or legend; but there was nothing masculine about her.

Lady Blessington included a character in one of her novels which she made easy to identify as Caroline by using the name of the family title, slightly misspelt: 'the celebrated Mrs. Grantly'. Exclaiming over Mrs Grantly's beauty – 'her deep lustrous eyes beat in languor, as if she thought not how many were seeking to catch their recognition' – Lady Blessington asked the rhetorical question: 'Does she not look the very personification of a Muse?'[9]

Benjamin Robert Haydon for one would certainly have agreed. So would Sir Edwin Landseer (who provided the frontispiece of Caroline, meditative but voluptuous, for *The Dream*), along with Daniel Maclise, John Hayter and his brother George, and many others. John Hayter, in fact, was responsible for the earliest portrait of Caroline, a charcoal drawing which became the frontispiece for her collection *The Undying One*.

In the spring of 1833, Haydon had been hard at work on a vast depiction of the Guildhall Banquet marking the Great Reform Bill. At this point, Mrs Norton called on him with the daughter-in-law of Lord Brougham (who featured at the banquet) and cheerfully suggested: 'You should paint *us*, Mr. Haydon.' 'Sweet creature,' commented Haydon in his Diary, 'I should be delighted to do so.'[10] This was a welcome compliment from 'so handsome a darling'; surely other women must have been irritated by Mrs Norton's good looks, which made everybody else look ugly beside her.

Haydon proceeded to call on Caroline in return and was soon dining with her. His Diary continued to rave on the subject of her beauty, with frequent mentions of her as a Sybil, interlaced with references to her amusing conversation. At a bazaar, for example, the famously overweight Lord Andover was being plagued to buy from the stalls; grumpily he referred to himself as being like the

Prodigal Son, persecuted by ladies. 'No,' said Caroline, more like *the fatted calf!*'[11]

News of the riposte spread: as a result, numerous fat lords – at least according to Caroline – called on her and begged her to explain 'it was not *them!*' All this was interlarded by Haydon with references to her 'fine black eyes', 'her Egyptian mouth' (corrected to 'a Greek mouth cut by an Egyptian sculptor') and 'her sublime head'.

These were the happy days before the case – and by the time the scandal broke in 1836, Haydon was sufficiently enmeshed and in love to convince himself (quite wrongly) that his wife Mary had played some part in the revelations because she felt her own domestic happiness was threatened by Caroline. He also persuaded himself that Caroline was guilty – this was the siren who had enchanted him – but then contradicted himself by saying that Caroline was innocent when his wife (like much of the rest of the world) declared her to be guilty.

As it was, Haydon's torments enabled him to envisage Caroline Norton all too vividly as the Cassandra in his own life presaging doom. He decided to paint her as the tragic prophetess of Greek mythology, destined to foresee the future with hideous accuracy and equally destined not to be believed. *Cassandra Predicting the Murder of Hector* was exhibited at the Royal Society of British Artists and sold to the Duke of Sutherland for £420 (about £35,000 in modern values). Caroline continued to flirt atrociously with Haydon, if his own Diary is to be believed, to the extent that Lady Blessington (evidently unaware of the existence of his wife) believed that he would marry her directly were George Norton to die.

When Parliament burnt down in 1834, Haydon was horrified by the scene: 'Good God, and are that throne and tapestry gone with all their associations!'[12] However, the celebrated historical artist immediately saw the possibilities and visited the then Prime Minister, Lord Melbourne, to convince him of the need for historical pictures in Parliament's recreation. In fact, the exhibition of 1843 at Westminster Hall of art for possible use in the rebuilding included two pictures by him, one being a study of

Edward, the Black Prince. But Haydon's brilliant, if tumultuous, life was already degenerating thanks to his recurring financial difficulties: he committed suicide in 1846. It was Daniel Maclise, twenty years younger than Haydon, who was destined to give Caroline Norton's figure permanent fame, so long as the British Houses of Parliament were to survive in their nineteenth-century form.

Maclise was among the many artists who had experienced with wary delight the glamour of Caroline Norton as a person. In May 1840, for example, he heard that Charles Dickens was going to a dinner party given by Samuel Rogers. Maclise hoped that Dickens would not have to sit between the sisters, 'the Heavenly Norton . . . and the [Blessed Seymour]' – 'for this is too much to bear'.[13] Here was the enchanting woman Edwin Landseer had admired, a friendship which evidently had its ups and downs. 'If you don't bring to cheer me the great Artists you promised, you shall be devoured by my new dog who is a Skye Terrier and a most ludicrous and friendly beast,' wrote Caroline at one point.[14]

Maclise was an Irishman, born in Cork, the son of a shoemaker who had previously been a Highland soldier. His breakthrough came when he made a secret sketch of Sir Walter Scott, whom he spotted while touring Ireland, and then widely disseminated it as a lithograph. In 1827, Maclise came to London, had the same success with a lithograph of Charles Kean the actor, and exhibited at the Royal Academy for the first time in 1829, becoming an RA in 1840. His speciality became historical subjects, apart from his portraits, which were mainly literary, including Dickens, for whom he illustrated Christmas books. Now that the Houses of Parliament were being rebuilt by Charles Barry, Maclise was an obvious choice to contribute, since the Parliamentary Committee concerned made a recommendation that fresco painting should be given official patronage. A further Select Committee, which included Sir Robert Peel, and a new Commission set up in 1841 with Prince Albert as President, both favoured it.

So there were to be six arched compartments for frescoes in the space above the chamber of the House of Lords: the subjects chosen should illustrate the function of the House and its relationship to the Sovereign. The decision was made in favour of three allegories: Religion, the Spirit of Justice and the Spirit of Chivalry, with three historical scenes opposite. The subject of Justice was duly assigned to Daniel Maclise.

Who best to symbolize Justice? The answer was the Hon. Mrs Norton, especially since one of the Commissioners had requested that 'female beauty was intermingled without which pictures, at least a series of them, will be generally unattractive'.[15] The result was a magnificent full-length picture approximately eight feet high and five feet wide.

Caroline Norton has one arm raised holding the scales of justice; her huge, baleful eyes are cast upwards, while all around her are numerous figures, each in its different way emblematic of the search for justice. There is, for example, the powerful presence of the emancipated slave at the bottom of the picture, his discarded chains nearby, and the grieving widow opposite, accompanied by her pleading child. Justice is situated between a dulcet female figure of Mercy and Retribution, represented by an angel with a sword. To admirers of Caroline, her appearance as the Spirit of Justice had then, and always will have, a double meaning: she both administers it to the unfortunate and demands it for herself.*

Caroline Norton continued to combine her passive life as a Muse with her true vocation as a writer. Whether out of pride or desperation or a mixture of the two, she was not backward in promoting her own worth. On 21 March 1843, the Poet Laureate, Robert Southey, died. Four days later, Caroline wrote to the Prime Minister, Sir Robert Peel, a letter which began: 'Sir, I trust you will not deem my writing to you impertinent,' and went on to suggest that 'though you may consider my request ridiculous', he should submit her name as Poet Laureate, following the death of Mr Southey. It is noticeable that Caroline deliberately alluded to a female Sovereign: 'I do not know if there is any precedent for

---

* Maclise's fresco *The Spirit of Justice*, featuring Caroline Norton, can still be seen in the House of Lords today high up in an arched compartment to the left of the throne, facing the entrance from the House of Commons.

appointing a female Poet Laureate, even in a Queen's reign.'[16] The inference is clear: if a woman can rule, why not other possible promotions?

The letter which follows is highly personal and, seven years after the case, does not try to evade her possibly scandalous story: 'The Queen is well aware of all the circumstances connected with my misfortunes, and I have been assured is kindly disposed towards me.' She mentions how she suffered 'without a shadow of justice' and might have given up 'but for my boy's sake' (presumably she referred to the dead Willie Norton). Caroline then relates how she worked hard at home, and 'so far as my literary abilities enabled me' supported herself and her sons without costing Mr Norton a farthing. There is a note of pride: 'I made more in a month [by writing] than he did in a year [as a barrister].' Finally, she pleads in the name of these sons: 'not to appear disgraced at least in *their* eyes would make any mark of notice such as this appointment more welcome than court vanities generally are.'

Sir Robert Peel did not respond to this naked appeal. William Wordsworth was appointed as Poet Laureate to replace Robert Southey on 6 April. It would be over one hundred and fifty years before the step of appointing the first female Poet Laureate was taken, although that too was during the reign of a female Sovereign.*

Caroline Norton's next published work, in 1845, *The Child of the Islands*, was in fact, regardless of the Laureate disappointment, a long poem.[17] It took as its epigraph some lines by the great Irish poet Tom Moore. In 1831, he himself had dedicated a poem to Caroline with 'every feeling of admiration and regard': 'The Summer Fete' commemorated an occasion 'of which she was one of the most distinguished ornaments', and was inscribed 'with every feeling of admiration and regard' by her father's 'warmly attached friend'.[18] Moore's lines now could indeed serve for the hopes of her well-wishers for her future:

* Carol Ann Duffy, the first female Poet Laureate, was appointed in May 2009.

As half in shade, and half in sun
This world along its course advances
May that side the Sun's upon
Be all that ever meets thy glances.

The innocent child concerned, it was made clear in the Preface, was Albert Edward, Prince of Wales, born on 9 November 1841, that is, the infant heir of the British Islands destined for a magic childhood:*

Thou shalt enjoy the kitten's frolic mood
Pursue in vain gay painted butterflies
Watch the sleek puppy lap its milky food
And fright the hen with all her clucking brood

Caroline also mentioned that she had intended to publish earlier, but 'domestic conflict' stopped the work.

Her declared aim was the inculcation of 'Kindliness' between the higher and the lower classes, just as in the new reign of Victoria, 'The Feeble are calling (not Vainly) on the Strong.' Her Preface suggested that the arrival of the Prince marked a return to innocence and goodwill in all spheres of public life. Affection for the Royal child would inspire a feeling of gentle concord throughout the land, leading to the end of discrimination and deprivation. As the poem had it, the arrival of a new baby was the universal experience: 'Of all the joys that brighten suffering Earth / What joy is welcomed like a new-born child?'

She proceeded to cite a whole range of parents. There is the squire happily saluting his heir, and the couple where the father of the wife had objected to the match now feeling 'the Angel Hope' as they gaze at the baby. Each parent sees what they want: 'The Soldier, laurels on the field of blood – / The Merchant, venturous skill and trading fair'. Even 'she that is a mother, but

* It is to be hoped that the future Edward VII enjoyed at least some of these pleasures in his boyhood before he discovered very different ones.

no bride' will start out of her 'lethargy of woe' and plan with renewed courage for the future and the best protection of her child. There is only one 'dread exception': when the child is left to die by the unmarried mother who chooses to end 'the life her sin had made'.

In general, Caroline continues to show that compassion for the weak – including the disabled – which she had shown for the character of Catherine Dalrymple, 'born crooked', in her novel *The Wife and Woman's Reward*, ten years earlier. Caroline's motto for the Royal child was to stand 'Above, but not Aloof', still near enough to stretch out a friendly hand: 'And let thy Smile be like the Summer Sun / Not to one Class alone – but all Humanity!' The final message of the poem is that the rich, too, suffer personal tragedies (Princess Charlotte, daughter of George IV, died in childbirth), but at least they can help the poor economically. Throughout the self-indulgence of the rich is stressed, and the suffering of the poor, as for example the woman who has to pawn her silk dress, and the woman who buys it: 'Careless of all conditions but her own / She sweeps the stuff along, to curtsey to the throne.' Or there is the woman who impulsively sends for a dozen servants resting on the Sabbath because she wants to 'whirl . . . to Hyde Park' in order to take the air.

The poem went well, and there was a second edition the following year. Among approving correspondents, it must have been especially gratifying to Caroline to receive a letter from her sons' Headmaster at Eton, Dr Edward Craven Hawtrey. But the material success of the book was obviously vital to her. In the copy sent to her friend Sidney Herbert, Caroline marked two particular passages: the death of a gypsy girl in prison and a description of a ballet class, before adding: 'Don't lend it to anybody because I depend on it for some bread and butter.'[19]*

One letter of about this time from Caroline to her sister Georgia gives a glimpse of the many-faceted literary world in which she moved. Caroline refers casually to a visit from 'the gallant

* A sentiment with which any author in search of sales – and in the opinion of Dr Johnson at least, which author is not? – will sympathize.

old creature', the writer Samuel Rogers, who came to see her despite being all swathed and splinted up from two broken ribs; under his auspices Caroline had met the 'youngish' poet Alfred Tennyson – he was actually thirty-four and would be appointed Poet Laureate five years later. 'And I like him.' She proceeded to describe him: extreme short-sightedness gave a peculiar expression of deadness to his eyes, which were black; this was 'a dark, untidy man – gruff and blunt in manner but with a fine profile'. Somehow Tennyson reminded her of the hero of one of her own novels, 'so extremely sensible of his own value – and yet, he is not conceited'.[20]

Rogers also promised to bring round Alexander Kinglake, the young barrister who had recently written *Eöthen*, a highly popular account of his travels in Syria, Palestine and Egypt; Caroline rated *Eöthen* all the more highly because it was the first book she had enjoyed since her recent illness: 'there are offences against taste in it – but oh! how clever and entertaining and what a vivid picture of Eastern travels!' These offences against taste, it should be noted, did not prevent Caroline Norton from subsequently entertaining Kinglake at her Chesterfield Street salon. She was welcomed in turn at his Greenwich house, where a clergyman found her – in unconscious reprisal for her judgement on Kinglake – 'a bit free and easy', before relenting: 'it seems only the overflowing of an open disposition.'[21]

There were, of course, inevitable consequences to this free association with writers: just as Caroline Norton mesmerized and inspired artists with her 'biblical' – a word sometimes used – beauty, so the equally colourful, if less biblical, life story of 'the Heavenly Norton' inspired writers, not only Lady Blessington with her 'Mrs. Grantly'. Anthony Trollope's mother Fanny Trollope had worked for Caroline when she was editor of *The Court Journal*; there are traces of her character in Lady Laura Kennedy in Anthony Trollope's *Phineas Finn*, an unhappily married woman with political connections. Disraeli's Lady Berengaria Montfort, the Whig hostess in *Endymion* who admires Lord Roehampton (Melbourne), is another fictional reference. These were all, as it were, in retrospect, Trollope publishing in 1869 towards the end of Caroline's life and Disraeli in 1880 after her death.

Anne Brontë was the exception in that she did not belong to these literary circles and had never met Caroline, although Caroline was on record as admiring her sister's *Jane Eyre* when there was some question about the true identity of Currer Bell: 'it is a very remarkable book whoever wrote it,' she told Lady Dacre in 1848.[22] In the same year, in *The Tenant of Wildfell Hall*, Anne Brontë featured a heroine, Helen Graham, 'a tall, ladylike figure' whose characteristics are those always attributed to Caroline by observers: the raven-black hair, clear and pale complexion, above all the apparently submissive eyes with their 'drooping' lids and long black lashes beneath 'expressive and well-defined brows'.[23] Helen Graham turns out to be a scandalous figure in public terms because she has fled her abusive husband with her child for the anonymous security of her maiden name and the tenantry of Wildfell Hall (Caroline contemplated flight, even if she did not succeed in achieving it). Helen, as the wife of Arthur Huntingdon, also tries to make a living from her own artistic endeavours, in her case as a painter. As her child, little Arthur, observes: 'Mamma sends all her pictures to London . . . and someone sells them for her there, and sends us the money.'

There was one notorious recreation of Caroline Norton which was dated shortly after her death, yet soon enough to affect her reputation in subsequent years, as though it were an actual historical record. This was *Diana of the Crossways* by George Meredith, published in 1885. It featured a scandal – a new scandal, not one associated with the case. But, like the case, it concerned a developing male relationship in Caroline's life. It was one which waxed in importance as the connection to Lord Melbourne waned; and Melbourne himself, in his sixties, after a life lived to full, began to fail.

CHAPTER ELEVEN

Lost Companions

*'That I grieve, and shall grieve, many and many a day, for my
lost companion, may be true – is true'*

Caroline Norton, 1846

THE POLITICAL SCENE IN THE mid-1840s was dominated
by the decision of the Tory Prime Minister Sir Robert Peel to
repeal the Corn Laws. This was against the wishes of most of
his own party. These laws, passed in 1815 and imposing a tariff
on imported grain and other foodstuffs, had protected home
producers including the Tory landowners and farmers.

In the past, Peel himself had voted constantly for their preser-
vation. Now, as with Catholic Emancipation in 1829, he changed
his mind, and the 'free trade' doctrines of Richard Cobden
prevailed. He had become, once again, 'Sir Robert REPEAL', as
he had been scornfully designated in 1829. The beginnings of
the appalling Irish Famine in 1845 and the need for food – any
food – in a country which was starving to death were among
the factors which played their part. This change of policy by the
government would, according to custom, have to be announced
by the Prime Minister in the House of Commons. Obviously,
regardless of rumours, no one could be quite sure of the outcome
until the announcement actually happened.

The London world was therefore agog when, in suitably por-
tentous fashion, *The Times* made the following announcement of
its own on the subject on 4 December 1845:[1]

> The decision of the Cabinet is no longer a secret. Parliament,
> it is confidently reported, is to be summoned for the first
> week in January; and the Royal Speech will, it is added,
> recommend an immediate consideration of the Corn Laws,
> preparatory to their total recall. Sir Robert Peel in one house
> [of Commons] and the Duke of Wellington in the other [of
> Lords] will, we are told, be prepared to give immediate
> effect to the recommendation thus conveyed.

In fact, Peel resigned on 6 December, only to return on 20
December when Lord John Russell and the Whigs failed to
form a government. Thus, he duly made his speech announcing
repeal in late January. The question remained: since someone
was responsible for the leakage? – who was it? The name of
the leaker became the subject of gossipy conjecture, both furious
and prurient. Then the delicious answer came which pleased
both parties: it was the scandalous Caroline Norton, once again
demonstrating the evil influence of a beautiful woman in politics;
she had learnt the news from Sidney Herbert, who was a member
of Peel's Cabinet. And proceeded to sell it – according to one
story – to the editor for £1,300.[2] She was, after all, acquainted
with the young editor John Thadeus Delane, as well as being
Herbert's friend, and well known to write letters to *The Times*.
Was any more proof needed? Who needed the truth where 'a fiery
scandal' – Meredith's subsequent phrase – was concerned?

George Meredith, whose *Diana of the Crossways* featured
the Cabinet leak to the press, would have been eighteen at
the time of the so-called scandal. His Diaries of the time are
full of references to a lady then becoming famous for beauty
and wit, including reflections which Caroline Norton certainly
would not have regarded as insults, such as: 'a witty woman is
a treasure, a witty Beauty is a power.'[3] The novel, in all its main
aspects, so clearly draws on Caroline that it is easy to see why,

published after her death, it came to be regarded as historical record rather than essentially fiction. The unhappy marriage of the Nortons, their age difference, the Irish connection, the fact that the English husband felt himself 'but a diminished man' by his wayward wife's behaviour and the famous appearance – dark, large eyes, the heavy brows, the proud line of a straight nose, and the 'reposeful red lips' with 'their curve of slumbersmile at the corners': the recognizable elements are all here.

Caroline–Diana's famous wit is summed up in a scene at a cricket match at which Diana lightly mourns woman's lack of opportunity. Diana: 'I think the chief advantage men have over us is their amusement . . . I wish I could bat half as well.' The answer comes: 'Your batting is with the tongue.'[4] What is totally missing from *Diana of the Crossways* is the fundamental tragedy of the Norton story, that is, the disputed position of the children. The actual course of this fiery scandal was, in fact, quite different to Meredith's colourful version; although it did result in grief of a very different sort, in the severing of Caroline's intimate connection to Herbert.

To begin with, Caroline Norton's friendship with Sidney Herbert owed a lot to her silvery tongue on the one hand and his marvellous good looks on the other, coupled with his intelligence and ambitious liberal ideas. It is thought by Herbert's most recent biographer to have begun with an introduction by their mutual friend Lord Lincoln.[5] The second son of the Earl of Pembroke and a Russian Countess, born in 1810 and thus two years younger than Caroline, Herbert was described as 'beautiful as an angel'. If his image by the fashionable portrait painter Sir Francis Grant does not exactly confirm his divine status, it does show an extremely handsome human being. Herbert was first elected as Tory MP for Wiltshire South in 1832, appointed a junior minister in 1834 and by 1845 had risen to be Secretary State for War in Peel's Cabinet.

Clearly, in many ways Sidney Herbert represented to Caroline exactly the kind of ideal man that George Norton was not and never had been, even before his abusive tendencies became apparent; someone she could admire and who would admire her in his turn. He helped her, for example, over the Chesterfield Street lease. It was significant that towards the end of her life she would compare Herbert with Ralph Leveson Smith, her lost love. Herbert also had something of that 'aristocratic listlessness', masking 'plenty of courage and not a little force', which had marked Melbourne. Caroline's teasing references to Herbert as 'My Secretary' are reminiscent of the banter of the early Melbourne years.

At the same time, Sidney Herbert had a genuine interest in the plight of the less fortunate of society. These were the ideas which had influenced Caroline in writing *The Child of the Islands*. Looking ahead, Sidney Herbert's scheme for female emigration, the Female Emigration Fund, which helped unemployed young women workers find a proper future in another country, was exactly the kind of cause which suited Caroline's philanthropic nature, with its strong sense of justice, predisposed towards her own sex.[6] Looking still further, Sidney Herbert's relationship with Florence Nightingale when he was minister in charge at the time of the Crimean War would prove to be another example of his ability to relate to an interesting and complex woman.

There seems every likelihood that Caroline Norton and Sidney Herbert were lovers before the Corn Law scandal cast a shadow over their relationship. One sighting of the pair on holiday on the Isle of Wight, first on a beach and later on a yacht on the Solent, does not seem to make much sense otherwise.[7] Caroline, at this point, had nothing to lose. Whatever the legalities of the situation, she had long regarded her marriage as over. It is true that she was known to bewail her scandalous reputation, which led to some unfortunate assumptions. As she confided to her friend Richard Monckton Milnes: 'The saddest moment for me, is when a man seems uneasy at being left alone with me, when his voice lowers and he draws his chair nearer – I know I am about to lose a friend I love, to get a lover I do not want.' On another occasion, Caroline told Charles Mulloy Westmacott that if she was helped by any gentleman, the world will say 'he is my *lover*.'[8]

The truth about the Corn Law scandal did not actually involve Caroline and Sidney Herbert: it is plausibly thought that it was actually Peel's Foreign Secretary Lord Aberdeen who murmured in the ear of the editor of *The Times*, John Delane.[9] But the whole incident serves as an indication that the scandalous *timbre* with which the Melbourne case had smeared Caroline's reputation was likely to be permanent. In short, Caroline presented too easy a target: she lived to discover that striking looks and a silver tongue could be a curse as well as a blessing.

Sidney Herbert's reaction was quite simply to get married himself. It had always been on the cards, as Caroline had been aware, even if she may have allowed herself romantic dreams of a very different solution, supposing her marriage to George Norton ever magically evaporated. Sidney Herbert was in his mid-thirties. Although a younger son, his brother the Earl of Pembroke was childless and there was a possibility of succession to the family title (as with George Norton), so that it could be argued that it was time for marriage. In August 1846 he duly wed Elizabeth Ashe à Court-Repington, an intelligent woman in her early twenties, with whom Caroline now proceeded to establish polite relations.

Herbert's marriage was nevertheless a palpable blow to her, given her own vulnerable situation, both legally and emotionally; furthermore, it was a public blow. In July, three weeks before the actual event, she revealed her hurt and anger to her friend Lady Duff Gordon, as she deplored 'the coarseness of representing me as the forsaken and lamenting *mistress* of a man whose marriage I could not prevent'.[10] Then she gave her own version: 'That I was weak, nervous, shaken, by many worries, & a sore heart struggle that I grieve, and *shall* grieve, many & many a day, for my lost companion, may be true – *is* true.' But she had left town in express expectation of this event. In short, 'I did my best, without reference to myself, for Sidney Herbert's happier destiny.' So that it was a little hard that she should be represented as 'a *sacrifice*' when she was actually more of 'a *priest*' offering up her own vague but impossible dreams, to bring down 'the blessing of real happiness on his path'. She ended by pointing out that Lord Pembroke's 'heirless marriage' had long made Sidney Herbert's own marriage, for the sake of an heir, 'necessary and unavoidable'. She did not need to add that she herself was ineligible for this role: not only was she legally married but she was approaching forty, definitely not the conventional young childbearing bride.

To Samuel Rogers, Caroline was even more outspoken on the subject of the marriage: 'it was a struggle in the doing, it was not a sorrow, *done.*' After all, the tricky circumstances surrounding her friendship with Sidney Herbert had been such recently that 'the rose has been almost shut out by the thorny briars.'[11] Caroline concluded with a bitter reference to the Crim. Con. case: 'Do not think of me as *grieved*, dear Mr. Rogers: my griefs and my beliefs were of *the year 1836* when I thought (in my youthful credulity!) there was justice in "the world", and eternity in impossible friendships.'

When George Herbert, the desired male heir and future Earl of Pembroke, was born in July 1850, Caroline wrote a warm letter of congratulation to Sidney Herbert, on 'the greatest and happiest event of your life – the birth of your boy – that link between you and the generations to come . . . I hope the little new soul will be as like you as possible.' She was then frank enough to continue: 'I envy your wife, what I have envied other women, the thorough respect for the father of her children which must make the wish that they should resemble him the best and most earnest hope she can form for the future.' Only too clearly, this was not a respect that Caroline herself had ever harboured for George Norton.

It was hardly helpful that the relationship with Lord Melbourne – given that it was great familiarity, not full-blown adultery, in the words of the judge's summing up in the case – had changed utterly. Her 'Dearest old Boy', as Caroline now addressed Melbourne, was visibly failing. In November 1842, just over a year after he left office as Prime Minister, Melbourne had a stroke. He was also plagued with gout. Henceforth he spent a great deal of time not only in London but at his home in Hertfordshire, Brocket Hall. Here Charles Greville found him accepting his situation philosophically with the lines from Milton's *Samson Agonistes*: 'My race of glory run, and race of shame, / And I shall shortly be with them that rest.'[12]

Melbourne and Caroline continued to correspond. Or rather Caroline continued to write letters, many of which plaintively questioned why Melbourne had not written back to her. In December 1844, for example, she wrote: 'Dearest old Boy, pray do write – I am ill in bed myself and if you don't write, I shall think you are *ill in bed too*.' Then she appealed to that fatherly, instructive side of Melbourne treasured by Queen Victoria: 'I did imagine I had coaxed you into scribbling by asking you about information for my poem [*The Child of the Islands*].' Finally, Caroline attempted that saucy tone which Melbourne had once valued so much: 'Do write . . . See now, I have written to *you*, tho' I am in bed, with leeches for my *Pillow-Fellows*. I call them *Pillow-Fellows* because *Bedfellows* take up more room.'[13]

Her playful jealousy of the other women in his life continued to operate. There was 'the virgin Eden', Emily, the clever Jane Austen-like novelist, once mentioned as a possible second wife for Melbourne after the death of Lady Caroline. It was to Emily Eden that Melbourne had once expressed contempt, significant where Caroline Norton was concerned, against people 'who complain too much'. 'Who have you got at Brocket?' Caroline went on. 'Does Emily hang her long gowns up? . . . Does Lady Holland *cut herself in four* to help and serve you? . . . or does the "Minny" who rivals our "Georgy" rouse you to any love and admiration of your own relations?'[14*]

There were also visits. At this point, Melbourne's carer, in the modern phrase, during the last three years of his life, Miss Cuyler, aroused a slightly different reaction. 'I wish her no ill. I only *shrink* from her,' wrote Caroline. The presence of Miss Cuyler signified Melbourne's mortality, the sad state of him who had once been her idol of strength and worldliness. It was evident that the spectacle of this weakness agonized Caroline. As she told Edward Ellice, in charge of his affairs, 'His death itself was scarcely so mournful and shocking to me, as the first day I saw his handsome careless head combed smooth and

* The references are to Melbourne's niece, Lady Emily Cowper, and Caroline's sister respectively.

formal by his servant's care – . . . the impatient helplessness with which he said – "I have no choice – it is such a damned helpless life."'[15]

Lord Melbourne died on 24 November 1848. Caroline described it afterwards as 'a long dim death, like a winter's sunset at sea', comparing it with the sudden death of Sir Robert Peel who fell off his horse two years later. Writing to Ellice shortly afterwards, she made a request for the return of her letters, if any were discovered. Caroline confessed that, in spite of everything, his death came as a shock to her:[16] 'Say what one will about "expected events" and looking forward to the decease of a friend under the circumstances in which for years he lingered out the close of his brilliant life – when Death comes, actually before one – it comes as a surprise – and however slowly, it *seems* to come suddenly.'

This was a reflection on the universal human experience. But there was a small, touching addition to her request for the letters. Would Ellice also give her 'those spectacles he wore' – she named an old servant who would identify them, adding: 'I gave them to him – no one will care to have them so much.'[17]

Lord Melbourne had, in fact, left a very different legacy from spectacles to his old friend. He wrote a letter to his brother, Lord Beauvale, asking him to pay Mrs Norton an annuity of £200 a year. (His generosity to old friends did not stop there: his previous *amour*, Lady Branden, was to be paid the same amount.)[18] Melbourne's instruction to his brother also contained a solemn declaration that what he had told Sir John Campbell to say on his behalf at the 1836 trial about Mrs Norton's purity was true. He felt that he owed it to her to renew this statement because of the fearful obloquy which she had suffered on his behalf.

When Caroline received news of the legacy, she did not flinch from the resurrection of memories of an unhappy time: 'I was simply glad (let those sneer at it who please) that with such a husband and such a destiny of never-ending troubles, the family of the man in whose name I suffered so much were willing to prove, not for my sake but for his, that his kindness to me outlived him.'[19] Technically, of course, this was not actually a legacy, since Caroline was not included in Melbourne's will: this was a gift at the discretion of the family.[*]

Caroline's final comment to Edward Ellice, in her long letter after Melbourne's death, summed up what was surely the truth of their relationship: 'I was *not* his mistress but I would rather have been what I was, his favourite companion, than any other man's wife or mistress.'[20]

By the time of Melbourne's death, frequent trips abroad, resulting from the varying fortunes of her sons, were beginning to reshape Caroline Norton's pattern of existence. At the same time, in London the close jesting friendships continued which, while they could not make up for the lost companions, appealed to that convivial side of Caroline which even at the direst moments she never quite lost.

Abraham Hayward, the lawyer she nicknamed 'A for Avocat' and who gave her good advice on her pamphlet *Observations on the Natural Claim of the Mother*, was one example. Caroline duly gave him a clock (known as the Horloge du Tic-Tac) for legal help in 1842. Hayward's admiring review of *The Child of the Islands* in the *Edinburgh Review* was certainly the work of a very friendly critic: 'This is poetry, true poetry, and of the sort we unfeignedly approve – the genuine product of a cultivated mind. The aim is noble, the tone elevated, the train of thought chastened though singularly fearless, the choice of images and illustrations judicious, and the language often beautiful and always clear . . .'. And so it went on.[21]

Caroline's jocular verse on her recent medical treatment with leeches, mentioned to Melbourne, which she despatched to Hayward, is in rather a different vein to this 'true poetry'. 'Dear Avocat,' she wrote in November 1846, 'I think I am better . . . this evening, for a sick poetess, I may say I feel "pretty bobbish".' 'Lines to a Leech' followed:[22]

---

[*] It also post dated her unofficial settlement with George Norton, who was later, ignoring the chronology, to reproach her for not declaring it.

Oh, thou dark Leach
If I could teach
Thee sound and speech,
I'd thee impeach
Of wish to bleach
My cheeks – and each
At once to reach,
Making maids screech!

Caroline's life as a working – that is to say, writing – mother continued to be combined with her activity as a political campaigner. Her editing of annuals, a money-spinner that she had discovered in her early twenties, belonged to the first category. In the late 1840s she edited *Fisher's Drawing-Room Scrap-book*, which, according to the publisher's wish, was now filled with her verse, along with pictures and engravings of beautiful country houses.

Very different was the pamphlet called *Letters to the Mob*, three letters originally published in sequence in the *Morning Chronicle* with the byline 'Libertas' and then put together as a pamphlet.[23] *Letters to the Mob* was written in direct response to two events which took place in 1848: the Chartist Riots in England and the February Revolution in France, by which Louis-Philippe lost the throne he had acquired in 1830. There were also folkloric memories of the 1789 Revolution, twenty years before Caroline was born. These had possessed Louis-Philippe himself, passing through the Place de la Concorde on his way to exile and realizing this was the spot where Louis XVI, Marie Antoinette and his own father, Philippe, Duc d'Orléans, had been executed: 'the frightful magic lantern' of everything the place had witnessed 'flashed through my memory'.

The demands of the Chartists in their petitions – which can be summed up as the full male suffrage not granted in the limited reform of 1832, with additional changes such as a secret ballot – do not have an extreme ring in the twenty-first century. But at the time these demands were carried out in an atmosphere of increasing ferment, including a vast meeting on Kennington Common, south of Westminster, in February 1848.

Letters to the Mob was therefore written in direct response to what Caroline Norton (and many others) saw as an attempt to rule by means of physical violence. It should be put together with her attitude to men since childhood as supposed protectors; George Norton's attacks should also not be forgotten. Certainly, her revulsion against violence as a weapon is clear throughout the *Letters*, specifically when used against women: an eternal problem of one sex in relationship to another, even if her views on the natural order have a nineteenth-century ring to modern ears.

It begins: 'I thought to head this "A Letter to the People" but you are not people. On the contrary: the true people disown the mob and look with alarm on your tumultuous gatherings.' Caroline Norton denounces, among others, the Irish rebels who have crossed the sea 'to whine and crouch, like beaten hounds', asking for help to raise the standard of rebellion at home, as well as 'the general scramble for concessions all over Europe' headed by the French.

She then moves to her main, bold principle: 'The Chartist dream of equality is the most cruel of all the temptations with which the mob-traps are baited; for it is at once the most specious and the most false. There can be no equality, any more than there can be a sea without a shore! Superiority is not a thing of man's devising, but of God's appointing.' In short, 'the mass must be governed: a change of governors is all that the most complete revolution can achieve.'

If there is one text she would recommend to the mob, this is it: '*Fear your governments less and your leaders more.*' Coriolanus, for example, was working to avenge his own wrongs, not to forward the Volscians. Gray's *Elegy Written in a Country Churchyard* made 'touching allusions' to 'village Hampdens' who protested nobly on behalf of their fellows; Caroline Norton makes the point that 'a Brummagem [Birmingham] Coriolanus' is the exact opposite, sparing his followers nothing and with no thought for their welfare, when they are sent to prison or hospital as a result of his oratory: 'rioting is the one employment for which no wages can be had.' Again: 'To revolt is to overshoot the mark of reform. I write, not to check their advance, but in dread of their failure.'

This emphasis on violence is maintained throughout, in which connection the young Sovereign and her child are evoked: 'I feel ashamed as an Englishman [*sic*] of the recollection of that paltry riot that sent pickpockets and lamp-breakers to shout at the very gates of the palace where a Queen and her new-born babe lay sleeping.'

Letter II moves to the question of the English rioters 'fraternising' (the 'cant phrase', as Caroline put it) with the new Republic in France as well as 'The United, or rather Disunited Irishmen'. The 'cold ferocity' of the original French Revolution involved the fate of another, rather different woman, when the world shuddered at such antics 'as dressing the hair on the severed head of the Princess[e] de Lamballe'.*

Further details of atrocities performed by the French mob follow, before the reflection: 'They have taught the working men to look for a sort of Utopia of labour, an imaginary system of independence of all mutual obligation between masters and men – which can never exist.' Then there is the economic reality: 'The rich man's pleasures were the poor man's earnings' (true enough, but perhaps a more satisfactory state of affairs for the luxurious rich man than the hard-working poor man).

At the end of Letter II, Caroline turns again to her own position, fully agreeing that 'there is still much to do for the people of England', while passionately disagreeing that violence is the way to achieve it. In Letter III, she comes out strongly for the upper class as leaders. 'A few certainly of our aristocracy are licentious, idle, useless – their women, insolent, overbearing, capricious. How would you yourselves like to be judged by, as a class, the bad drunken characters among you?' This is the class which was fashioned to rule and the best among them do it very well indeed.

---

* The head of the Princess was taken by the mob to a barber en route in order to show it gloatingly on a pike to the imprisoned Marie Antoinette.

Finally, Caroline Norton returns to her main message, the denunciation of revolution as such: 'Be warned: When you urge your rights, or when you would enforce them, be sure that you are bartering value for true liberty and not paying forfeit for empty rebellion.'

For all her political campaigning, the future of her surviving boys continued to constitute Caroline's most passionate cause, if a private one. Eton College had not been her choice of school for the boys: she preferred Harrow, which her celebrated grandfather Richard Brinsley Sheridan had attended. Reasonably enough – for once – George Norton insisted on the school of which he himself was an old boy. Caroline was left to console herself with 'the cheerful exercise and free air' at Eton, which improved Fletcher's health after 'the gravel yard of his private school'.[24]

The improvement did not last. Fletcher Norton left Eton in the summer of 1846 and Brin a year later. Fletcher's departure was directly inspired by Caroline's determination to defeat the dreaded consumption which dogged her family. Not only had her father died in his early forties, but two of her brothers, Frank and Charlie, had recently died before either of them reached the age of thirty.

Caroline and Fletcher got on well, not only because of his need for her care. In view of the tricky past and the scandalous picture she feared his father might have presented to him, she was touched by his attitude towards her. In the winter of 1846, she described to her mother Mrs Sheridan how nothing could be kinder, 'more tender, or more sweet-tempered than Fletcher is to me, even in little matters'.[25] Apart from being tender-hearted, Fletcher was also a reflective character. At Eton, he already had an inclination towards religion. He showed an interest in the Oxford Movement (a form of High Anglicanism close to Catholicism). The most famous member of the Oxford Movement was the future Cardinal Newman; in the course of time Fletcher, like Newman, would become a Catholic.

Caroline's idea was that a hot, dry climate would be more conducive to health than the dank atmosphere of Oxford University. In this way Fletcher duly arrived with a tutor in Lisbon

and Caroline was able, by the pulling of a few strings, to secure
a post for him at the British Legation. The next few years of
Caroline's life were spent basically caring for Fletcher. Lines from
her poem 'The Invalid's Mother, to the Sun, at Lisbon' expressed
her hopes:[26]

> I loved thee, as a careless child
>   Where English meadows spread . . .
> Now, with a still and serious hope,
>   I watch thy rays once more
> And cast life's anxious horoscope
>   Upon a foreign shore

Naturally, life on 'a foreign shore' did not exclude social acquaint-
ances as well as the performance of maternal duties. There were
other travelling friends to be encountered. In particular, there was
one young man, currently in Spain, whom Caroline hoped to see
in Portugal. This was a certain William Stirling.

Caroline had first encountered Stirling at Keir, his family estate
in Scotland. Ten years younger than Caroline – he was born
in 1818 – William Stirling was handsome as well as markedly
intelligent, with a special interest in Spanish art: his work *Annals
of the Artists of Spain* established him as an authority in the
field. It is easy to understand why Caroline took pleasure in their
friendship. They began to correspond. She urged Stirling to come
on from Spain to Portugal, although she was honest enough to
admit that she was rather dubious about the pictures he might
find there. Nevertheless, she wrote: 'I wish you would come.'[27]

William Stirling did come to Portugal. What was more, he
arrived at a critical moment in the development of poor Fletcher's
illness. Thirty years later she would remember: 'I first knew of his
goodness when my poor son [Fletcher] first spit blood, at Lisbon,
in 1848, and he helped nurse him.'[28] The likelihood must be that
they also became lovers at this early date; although as always
with Caroline – in relationships outside marriage – physical love
and friendship happily coexisted, so that one remained after the
other ceased.

In symbolic fashion, 1848 had marked the death of Melbourne; and Sidney Herbert's marriage had ended their intimacy, if not their friendship, two years earlier. Stirling was the kind of companion Caroline was searching for, to replace the companions lost to death and marriage, in spite of all the obvious disadvantages of Stirling's age and Caroline's murky marital status.

CHAPTER TWELVE

The Name of Writer

'The power of writing has always been to me a source of
intense pleasure; it has been my best solace in hours of
gloom; and the name I have earned as an author in my
native land is the only happy boast of my life.'

Caroline Norton, dedication, *Stuart of Dunleath*, 1851

WHERE CAROLINE'S MARRIAGE WAS CONCERNED, the
'arranging' with Mr Norton, as she had once called it to Mary
Shelley, showed no signs of ending.[1] During these negotiations,
which were basically for the separation of two incompatible
people, money became the main problem once the more emotional issue of the children had been, in a sense, resolved.

There were periods of respite when it seemed that accord
would be reached, as for example in 1848.[2] It was proposed
that Norton would be allowed to raise money on the trust
property settled on Caroline at her marriage, in exchange for
an annual allowance of £500; a crucial restriction was also
placed on Norton's liability for Caroline's debts. It was the
lawyer acting for Caroline who backed out on her behalf,
believing that these terms were manifestly unfair to her. Three
years later, with the death of Mrs Sheridan, the situation
changed.

Caroline Norton in fact spent much of the time before her mother's death in June 1851 nursing her, as she had spent the previous years looking after Fletcher. At the age of seventy-two Mrs Sheridan, who had been still 'handsome and sparkling' in her fifties, according to Benjamin Robert Haydon, was nearly blind. A daring elopement with Tom Sheridan had led to a quiet but creative life – she herself had written novels and poetry – as well as an early widowhood; that life was now drawing to a close. Based at 3 Chesterfield Street, Caroline constantly visited and cared for Mrs Sheridan. That left her juggling her newly demanding life as a mother with that of a daughter.

With astonishing resilience – or perhaps the natural resilience of the writer needing to earn money – Caroline Norton continued to write commercially. *Stuart of Dunleath* was published in April 1851.[3] Sending a copy to her friend Georgiana Cowper-Temple, she issued the author's plea she had once sent to Melbourne: 'Please do not *lend* it; as my publisher complains of that.'[4] The book, in three volumes, was dedicated to a new friend made while travelling abroad with Fletcher: the Queen of Holland.

Tall and stately, Queen Sophie spoke English virtually without an accent; impeccably Royal, she was the daughter of the King of Württemberg and a Russian Grand Duchess. There were two obvious unhappy parallels between the Queen and Caroline Norton. Sophie's marriage to King William III of the Netherlands was disastrous, she being famously more intelligent than her wayward husband. The second parallel was even sadder: Queen Sophie also lost a son, Prince Maurice, who died in 1850 aged seven.

Caroline Norton now addressed her, confident 'that I shall find in your Majesty, with an ardent sympathy, the most competent and indulgent of judges'. She added that owing to the Queen's command of English, 'my heart will need no translator to convey its thoughts to yours.' Caroline then made the heartfelt declaration: 'The power of writing has always been to me a source of intense pleasure; it has been my best solace in hours of gloom, and the name I have earned as an author in my native land is the only happy boast of my life.'

The final passage refers to their tragic bond: 'When last I saw your Majesty, you were mourning a child of extraordinary beauty and promise.' It might interest the Queen to know that in the course of the novel, the description of a child and 'the instance of early piety and resignation which prompted it [the child] to utter a prayer, instead of a vain call for rescue, is not an invention, but a fact taken from real life.' The allusion to the death of Willie eight years before, the tragic details related to his mother after the event, is clear.

The novel itself is a fervent, highly readable book in which romantic love, on the whole, rules over worldly values. It is also extremely sad, including the *dénouement*. The beginning, however, is engaging as the heroine, an orphan called Eleanor, has an innocent, happy relationship with her guardian, David Stuart of Dunleath, who has been left in charge of the child – and her fortune. Eleanor is 'pale, tranquil with slight limbs and bright spiritual eyes, at once wild and shy and gentle'. As Eleanor grows up, the slight limbs extending to make her an exceptionally tall young woman, her love for Stuart changes and increases. When a marriage is proposed for her, she tries in vain to convey to her guardian that the marriage is impossible because she loves another man – none other than Stuart himself. He does not comprehend.

Tragedy follows when 'Guardie', as the child Eleanor had nick-named David Stuart, is responsible, in his own despairing view, for losing her fortune. He commits suicide in the roaring local river. Then Eleanor is burdened with an unsympathetic husband in the odious Sir Stephen Penrhyn who begins badly by beating her dog and goes on, among other things, to criticize Eleanor for being too tall. Later, in a violent attack in which it is only too easy to see the shade of George Norton, Sir Stephen breaks her arm. Furthermore, Sir Stephen's sister, Lady Macfarren, is a malevolent force, furious with Eleanor's lack of fortune and determined to humiliate her where possible. Caroline herself admitted in a letter to a friend that here was another obvious parallel: in Lady Macfarren, 'I am conscious of my sister-in-law Lady Menzies.'[5]

As so often in Caroline Norton's fiction after September 1842, the topic of children is pervasive, the 'unswerving rule' of the love of a mother for her child. Both Eleanor's twins die when young, the basic sadness of her life. 'Children! They are a sacred happiness. Their place in our hearts is marked out in every page of the Holy Writ.' But there is also compassion for the poor, another constant theme. Caroline attacks the lack of education given to the lower classes and the unfair rage of the rich at the consequent lack of intelligence in the poor: 'we sow tares and we want to reap wheat.'

There is a different kind of compassion which Eleanor feels for Maya, who was once her ayah. She finds her former nurse crouching on the ground, weeping, because the special vessels that, as a 'Hindoo', she needs for cooking have been roughly taken away by her current employer, Lady Macfarren, with the words: 'Out with all those pots and pans – I never saw such heathen nonsense in all my life! If she can't eat plain wholesome food like the rest of the servants, she's welcome to starve, for me, till she's learned better.' Eleanor offers to buy Maya more pots and pans and, when Lady Macfarren sneers at her for that, continues to bend over the pathetic woman, murmuring the Indian terms of endearment she had learnt as a child.

The real trouble with Sir Stephen and Eleanor erupts when Eleanor recovers her missing fortune, left by her father. She wants to use it to buy Dunleath, once the home of beloved 'Guardie'. This brings an outburst from Sir Stephen. As usual he begins with 'a peal of blasphemous expletives'. Then he rages on: 'Everything that's yours is mine. The clothes you have on, the chain round your neck, the rings you have on, are mine. The law don't admit a married woman has a right to a farthing's worth of property.' To add to his sins, Sir Stephen's own bastard son by a beautiful village girl is gradually introduced into his household.

There is a dramatic development with the emergence into their lives of a certain Mr Lawrence of Quebec, who is in fact David Stuart of Dunleath himself. 'Mr. Stuart's no deed [dead]', as one

Scot in the know puts it, although others do not recognize him. Far from dying in the roaring river, he had been rescued; fleeing the country, he had made his life across the Atlantic. Will Eleanor find happiness at last with 'Guardie' as one can't help hoping she will?

Stuart outlines the possibility of Eleanor ridding herself of the philandering Sir Stephen under Scottish law which, unlike the English law, allows wives to sue husbands. But in the end Eleanor nobly decides to renounce Stuart, and renounce also 'the dear dream of byegone companionship'. She feels she has herself sinned in marrying in the first place when she had vowed secretly to be faithful to Stuart forever. David Stuart, for his part, tells her he will always think of her 'not as a woman – not as my ideal of love and loveliness' but as that trusting little child.

The title of the two penultimate chapters are 'Others are made happy instead of Eleanor' and 'Eleanor ceases to be unhappy'. David Stuart marries Lady Margaret, a jolly woman who has been a good friend to Eleanor, and their child, little Eleanor, will be David Stuart's favourite. Eleanor senior dies; her last thoughts are not for Stuart but for her dead children: 'I see them . . . There, there, waiting for me!'

This tale of tragedy and romance, good and evil, all set against a wild and picturesque Scottish background, was an enormous success both with reviewers and the public. The *Morning Chronicle*, for example, talked of the pathos of Dickens, the wit of Sheridan 'with a story worthy of Sir Walter Scott'. It is true that Elizabeth Barrett Browning, in a letter to her sister Arabella, was less enthusiastic, suggesting it was 'ill-written' while praising the story itself.[6] But Caroline had become satisfied with her life as a writer, if nothing else.

She certainly retained all her interest in political affairs, which had once made her the ideal lively companion for her 'Dearest Old Boy'. In January 1850, in a letter to Henry Howard, Caroline reflected with approval on Sidney Herbert's recent efforts to help unmarried jobless English women – mainly embroiderers – with emigration to Australia.[7] Whereas one census of 1841 had shown that there were 320,000 more women than men, in South Australia alone there were said to be 17,000 men to 13,000 women. *The Times* pontificated on the subject of the putative female emigrants: 'They will not be missed from Great Britain, but will be welcomed in Australia.' A more sympathetic approach was shown by the poet Arthur Hugh Clough in lines from *Dipsychus* concerning prostitutes. The Spirit tells Dipsychus not to sentimentalize about their fate:[8]

> They die, as we do, in the end . . .
> Or Sidney Herberts sometimes rise
> And send them to the colonies.

Whatever his motivation, Sidney Herbert presided over and encouraged the scheme, the Female Emigration Fund, by which the costs of emigration were paid, with enormous success.

Henry Howard, son of the Earl of Carlisle, was a young diplomat Caroline had encountered in Lisbon with Fletcher. He was currently deputizing for the Ambassador. They had made friends, this particular letter beginning with a characteristic expostulation about his laggardly correspondence: 'Oh Harry, Harry . . . you are certainly a pig!' And it ended: 'Write, Mr. Harry.'

In between, as well as relating a great deal of family gossip, Caroline reflected on the current Protectionist (anti repeal of the Corn Laws) meetings, which were very stormy, and Sidney Herbert's new campaign. 'S. Herbert has, as you will see by the paper, been busying himself about Female emigration. There is only *me* who do not feel rather jealous of his success.' She referred to the fact that others had attempted something of the sort for years, without Herbert's flair for practical philanthropy. But there had to be a joke somewhere. Caroline added: 'One amusing circumstance was Lord Verulam's saying to him that he had thought of it, long ago; but had been deterred from the fear of people saying he was getting rid of the females he had known too intimately – "God bless me, why there are *30,000 of them*!" says S.H. – and indeed it *was* too many!'

ABOVE: Lord Melbourne, Prime Minister of Great Britain, at the age of fifty-nine, two years after the case against him; by Sir George Hayter.

ADMIRERS OF CAROLINE NORTON:

RIGHT: Sir William
Stirling-Maxwell

BELOW: Sidney Herbert,
later Lord Herbert of Lea

LEFT:
Edward John Trelawny

BELOW: 'Well I shall leave the old Goat to take care of our *Poor little Lambe*': caricature of Caroline with her 'Pet' Lord Melbourne (whose family name was Lamb), and George Norton as a goat, with the horns of a cuckold.

ABOVE: Bust of Caroline by Francis John Williamson, 1873

ABOVE: Bust of Sir William Stirling-Maxwell by Francis John Williamson, 1873

ABOVE: In her own handwriting, with a characteristic little sketch at the end, Caroline's poem 'Farewell' from *The Sorrows of Rosalie: with Other Poems*. It begins:

'Farewell! in tearless agony I part

Beloved the fray can cost thee little now . . .'

RIGHT: Mariucca Federigo from Capri who married Brinsley Norton in 1854. Her peasant origins aroused unpleasant comment among the English.

RIGHT: Albumen *carte de visite* by John and Charles Watkins, 1863, when Caroline Norton was fifty-five.

BELOW: Caroline with her grandchildren, Carlotta and Richard Norton.

ABOVE: *The Spirit of Justice* by Daniel Maclise, 1847-9, commissioned for
Parliament as part of the decorations after the Great Fire of 1834. Caroline,
supported by angels, dispenses Justice to pleading figures. This fresco is still to be seen
in its archway in the Strangers Gallery high up in the House of Lords.

With friends, a loyal family in the Sheridans and a professional career as a writer, even with her children so strongly back into her life, Caroline could still never establish tranquillity as long as the situation with George Norton was unresolved. She described her feelings of gloom to her sister Georgia in the summer of 1851, although it is fair to say she began by admitting that the root of her depression could be found in 'not thinking enough of other people's destinies, and keeping too steady a view of what frets you in your own'. Caroline then turned to melancholy recollection of Ralph Leveson Smith, the fiancé she had lost so long ago: 'I begin life with the person I wish to marry – and who loved *me*.' Whatever others pretended subsequently, 'when he was dying it was only of *me* he spoke – only to *me* he sent little tokens – . . . Only *me* he pitied, for the grief he said it would be to me.'[9]

The sad tale continued: 'I marry a very bad husband – and go thro' a disgraceful trial for a friend who never was my lover. I lose the only robust child, by a very painful sudden death . . . I work all my life and very hard at literary pursuits to make out my income.' The sicknesses of her surviving sons are then related: 'neither of them very strong. Brin nervous almost to disease and stammers enough to make his profession still a matter of doubtful possibility. Fletchy is always sick . . .'. Georgia had generously rented a cottage in Hampstead's Vale of Health for her sister and her invalid son, but even that did not seem to mark an improvement.

The fact was that the brilliant Brin had brought his own problems of temperament to compound those of health of his elder brother. Apart from being clever, he had been rebellious at Eton, a course of education which had in any case not been particularly smooth, since Caroline took him out of school on occasion to go to Lisbon with her. Brin, at the instigation of his father, then went to University College, Oxford. Unfortunately, in the words of a relation, Brin was 'kindly, clever, handsome, but wild'.[10] At Oxford, his reckless extravagance and consequent debts led to his withdrawal after a year. He joined Caroline in Naples, where Fletcher's diplomatic career was progressing with a post at the British Embassy.

Through all this period, Caroline Norton worked extremely hard on her books for the sake of the income she needed to cope with her boys, George Norton persistently shifting the problem over to her. In 1853, matters came to a head in a grisly law case. There was one marked difference between this case and the previous one involving her name. This time Caroline appeared in court, although as a married woman in theory she had no individual legal existence. She was, however, accompanied by Abraham Hayward. As he explained: 'Which I did simply to prevent her going alone.' It was no good offering her advice, because she never followed it.[11]

The trouble began with the death of Mrs Sheridan: while George Norton inherited the property, which came from Caroline's father according to the law, she herself was able to receive an annual £480 (just over £40,000 in modern values). Norton promptly reduced her allowance so that she had trouble with her withdrawals from the bank. Norton was then sued by another of Caroline's creditors, who was unable to collect the debt which she owed to him. The plaintiffs were carriage-builders in Oxford Street named Thrupp and the bill was for repairs to Caroline's carriage, which she had bought herself with money from *The Dream*. Although Norton had once signed a document agreeing to pay such debts, it was argued that a man could not sign a contract with his own (still legally married) wife.[12]

The case was heard at the Westminster County Court on 18 August 1853. The Nortons were by now a middle-aged couple: Caroline was in her mid-forties to her husband's early fifties. Caroline was still a strikingly good-looking woman. Although there were occasional reports of her appearing worn and 'faded in beauty', these were generally associated with some recent crisis. People were more inclined to refer to her air of perpetual youth.[13]

The amazing dark eyes retained the power which had enchanted so many artists. Even Lady Eastlake, who was derogatory about her age – 'above forty' – commented that Mrs Norton still used her eyes 'so ably and wickedly'. According to the American historian John Lothrop Motley, who was on a visit to London, the hair remained 'raven black – violet-black without a trace of silver'.[14]*

Over half of the Nortons' twenty-six-year marriage had been spent in bitter contention. This time, Norton was himself the defendant, the role of Melbourne previously. Caroline described her feelings when she first saw her husband in court:[15] 'my courage sank; the horrible strangeness of my position oppressed me with anger and shame; my heart beat; the crowd of people swam before my eyes; the answers I had begun to make . . . choked in my throat, which felt as if it were full of dust.' Then Norton himself rose and sneered at her weakness: 'What does the witness say? Let her speak up; I cannot hear her!'

There was only a thin skirting-board between them and this proximity (which was indeed questioned by some of the lawyers present) added to her agony. 'The glare of the angry eyes' so close to her reminded her of the bygone days of her marriage when Norton had been determined 'to crush me at all hazards'. She got the impression that he saw in her 'neither a woman to be spared public insult nor a mother to be spared shameful sorrow', only 'a pecuniary encumbrance he was determined to be rid of'.

Norton's argument against paying the debt included the re-introduction of the dreaded name of Melbourne. As has been seen, Caroline had chosen not to inform him of the annuity which Melbourne had instructed his family to pay to her.

Norton now used this point against her, suggesting that Caroline had sworn in 1848 that she had received no money from Melbourne. He added an unpleasant domestic detail, the fact that she had also solemnly sworn this to their son Fletcher, whom he used as a messenger. It has been pointed out that Norton's chronology was nonsense: he had stopped her allowance before he discovered about the annuity, while the contract itself had been drawn up while Melbourne was still alive.[16]

Nevertheless, this was the opportunity for Caroline herself to state in public, for the legal record, the innocence of her

---

* Whatever art may have been employed to preserve the colour, since hair dyes were much in use in the nineteenth century.

relationship with Melbourne, something she had never been able to do before, despite being a central character in the previous case.

As to whether she would rise to the occasion, it was to be hoped that her Sheridan blood would make her welcome being the centre of attention, even in the dire circumstances of a vicious court case. The courtroom was crowded – when were the marital trials of Mrs Norton not an attraction for an audience?

Unfortunately, Norton began with allegations of the wildest, as well as the most inaccurate sort. He shrugged off the contract he had signed, saying that both of them had known it was not valid. Then he pleaded Caroline's declaration at the time that she had never received money from Melbourne as being a sign of her duplicity (and proof of her guilt in that respect, whereas he had previously accepted her innocence).

But Caroline was devastated: 'I lost all self-possession . . . I felt that I no longer stood in that court to struggle for an income, but to struggle against infamy.' She had, after all, been here before: it was seventeen years since she had waited at Hampton Court for the result of the previous case. Now the calumny was back. 'I felt giddy; the faces of the people grew indistinct; my sentences became a confused alternation of angry loudness and husky attempts to speak.' She proceeded to make a fervent denial of her adultery with Lord Melbourne: she had never been his mistress, she was young enough to be his daughter, he had never treated her otherwise than as a friend. As to the bequest, it was not in Melbourne's will, merely a recommendation to his family, which they had fulfilled 'because his memory was dear to them'.

The audience in the courtroom began to turn in her favour: 200 or 300 people applauded Caroline when she had finished. She herself felt they were manifesting a 'strong and obvious sympathy' for her. Things did not go so well for George Norton, however. The court found for the Thrupps on the grounds that the expense had been incurred before Caroline signed the famous contract.

It was at this point that Caroline Norton the campaigner spoke up. Accepting the verdict, she said: 'I do not ask for my rights.

I have no rights; I have only wrongs,' before adding: 'Now that I know that my husband can defraud me, I will not live abroad with my son.' George Norton responded with incoherent abuse and threats, at one point moving even closer and clenching his fist at her. Then the judge ordered the court to be cleared 'and so ended this disgraceful scene'.

The dispute between the Nortons, on the other hand, did not end there. Caroline had referred in her dedication of *Stuart of Dunleath* to the power of writing as being her solace in hours of gloom. Her 'power' did not only enable her to write novels and pamphlets. There was also the possibility of letters to the press: a form of conflict which, in contrast to her literary works, was distasteful to many, including members of Caroline's own family.

A bitter correspondence now took place between husband and wife in the pages of *The Times*, which may have delighted the editor but did not serve to gain that public approbation which Caroline was so keen to receive. The name of writer was something of which she had professed herself proud. She now used it in a much less sympathetic manner, so far as the world was concerned.[17]

The first letter came from Caroline pointing out the mistakes in George Norton's allegations which surely destroyed his argument. Caroline the writer could not be silent. But nor could George Norton, now her maniacal enemy. His response to *The Times* related the whole course of their marriage, from his point of view, starting with his blind love at the start, and ending with remorseless accusations about her guilt with Melbourne, the paternity of two of their children. Ironically, he also cited her lack of legal existence as a married woman and then accused her of using this against him in their financial dealings.

Various other letters then followed, including one from Norton's own lawyer, denying everything he said about the contract. The next long letter from Caroline caused further shudders in her supporters by prolonging this distasteful literary boxing match interminably in the public eye. The tone became increasingly vitriolic about George Norton. The loyal friend who had accompanied Caroline to court, Abraham Hayward, now believed rather less loyally that she ought to be forbidden the use of pen, ink and paper.

The conclusion of this letter put Caroline's own point of view. 'I will, so far as I am able, defend a name which might have been only favourably known, but which my husband has made notorious . . . Since my one gift of writing gives me friends among strangers, I appeal to the opinion of strangers as well as friends.' Not only strangers but women as a whole were in her sights: 'Let those women who have the true woman's lot of being unknown out of the circle of their homes thank God for that blessing – for it is a blessing. But for me publicity is no longer a matter of choice.' In other words, the campaign of the married woman would go on.

CHAPTER THIRTEEN

Let Him Claim
the Copyright

'I deny that this is my personal cause; it is the cause of all the
women of England . . . Meanwhile my husband has a legal
lien (as he publicly proved). . . on the copyright of my works.
Let him claim the copyright of THIS!'

Caroline Norton, *A Letter to the Queen on Lord Chancellor*
Cranworth's Marriage and Divorce Bill, 1855

F OR THE GOVERNMENT AND THE military establishment, as
well as the soldiers themselves, 1854 marked the development
of the Crimean War which had begun the previous October. The
underlying cause was the determination of Britain and France
not to allow Russia to encroach on the failing Ottoman Empire.
For other politicians and feminists, it marked the beginnings of a
serious campaign to reform the English divorce laws.

Now that the Infant Custody Act had righted at least some of
the wrongs endured by her sex, Caroline proceeded to consider
the legal fate of women in general, illustrated by a great deal of
personal detail. It worked both ways; at the same time her own
case was widely used by others to illustrate the cruelty to which
married women had been subjected by the law itself.

Yet at a moment when the question of divorce had become a major issue, it was notable that Caroline's own views on the subject were more complicated. This was in contrast to the question of child custody on which she had felt straightforwardly passionate.

The title of her next work was *English Laws for Women in the Nineteenth Century*.[1] It turned out to be more book than pamphlet, its length arousing criticism even from her supporters. Caroline Norton wrote it while staying at Clandeboye in Northern Ireland. This resulted in Helen making a gloomy prediction to their other sister, Georgia: 'I fear Caroline is at some legal devilry.'[2] *English Laws* was printed for private circulation in 1854. Caroline was now able to lobby MPs by sending them this account of her views. One of these MPs was William Gladstone, with whom she entered into correspondence.

The essence of the proposed Divorce Bill was to remove the authority of the Ecclesiastical Courts and establish a secular system. Through this, marriages could actually come to an end without invoking Parliament (an expensive process as has been noted, which was consequently only available to the rich).

Gladstone opposed the new Divorce Bill and told her so. In reply, Caroline Norton agreed that 'the ceremony of marriage' was 'utterly indissoluble'. Even if there had been a time when she wished for an end to her marriage, it would have been with 'a secret conviction' that no law could really annul it: if she had then married another man, it would have been 'with secret remorse'.[3] Her point was different: she wanted women to have full protection within the law, for themselves and their property, as they did in Catholic countries where marriage itself was similarly indissoluble. Caroline then appealed to Gladstone 'to take the lead among other men'; to admit the necessity of change, 'which meaner men either fear to admit, or sneer away with gross and stupid ridicule'. Surely this was the duty of Gladstone 'and such men as you'. After all: 'Do you think women would be less worthy – if more entirely protected by the law?'

English Laws begins with a quotation from Dickens's *Bleak House*: 'It won't do to have Truth and Justice on our side; We must have Law and Lawyers.' Caroline Norton then proceeds: 'I take these words as my text.' She goes on to relate how, for a number of years, she has been 'insulted, defrauded, and libelled' by her husband without possibility of redress under the present law. But this is not her individual cause: her aim is to prove 'not my suffering or his injustice', but that the present laws of England cannot prevent such suffering.

The question of female submission is raised from the beginning. Caroline cites the shocking (true) story of the Duc and Duchesse de Praslin. In August 1847 the Duc, a French politician, murdered his wife in the night, and when the household awoke and found the body there was bloody evidence of her desperate resistance and agonized efforts to escape. 'Do the advocates of the doctrine of non-resistance consider that her duty would have been to submit tranquilly to the fate predetermined for her?'

Caroline continues histrionically: 'If not, then waive judgment in my case; for if choice were allowed me, I would rather be murdered and remembered by friends and children with love and regret, than have the slanders believed which my husband has invented for me.' She then states firmly, as if to contradict those critics disgusted by her public stance: 'It is he [George Norton], who has made silence impossible.'

Caroline Norton's next stage was to relate the story of recent English reforms, none of which concerned women. Two examples of legislation concerned 'the great question of Roman Catholic Emancipation' and the Parliamentary Reform Bill which followed. She then moved to slavery: England had rightly offered an 'ovation' to Harriet Beecher Stowe, author of *Uncle Tom's Cabin*, so that her book became 'a household word'.

Caroline added: 'I hold her task to be a holy one, and slavery an accursed thing.' She cited horrifying details of the way slave women and children were treated, including deaths. The real-life slave-owner Arthur Hodge, said to be the original of the slave-owner in the book, took the line that as the 'negroes' were all his property, it was no worse than killing a dog.

In general, England had an honourable record of protesting about foreign wrongs. 'We have rebuked America, taunted

Naples, complained of Sweden, remonstrated with Tuscany, con-demned Portugal and positively shuddered at Austria . . .'. But when it came to her own laws: 'I will venture to say that in no country in Europe, is there *in fact*, so little protection of women as in England, England the fault-finder; England the universal lecturer.' England – where, to add to the 'absurd anomaly' of its laws so hostile to women, there is a female sovereign, unlike foreign countries where the Salic Law forbids it.*

Caroline Norton then moved to the extremely personal. Every kind of detail was supplied, making the reaction of her family at this outrage of privacy at least comprehensible. The whole story of her relationship with George Norton was recounted, begin-ning with the proposal via her mother, which took place before she was aware of speaking more than six sentences to him. She ended with Melbourne and the 1836 case: 'He was my friend, though not my lover.' Cynics might point out that Melbourne could plausibly have been *both* friend *and* lover, but this is the position from which she never deviated, including in her letters to Melbourne himself.

Caroline did not shrink from relating the details of her hus-band's violence towards her and her submission: on the floor, 'dragged down by the nape of my neck, I only moaned'. She accused him of causing a miscarriage and being indifferent to her suffering. She did not spare the reader the constant ups and downs of their relationship. 'I answered him; I pitied him; I went back to him.' A different kind of suffering was stressed over the death of Willie.

But it is in the injustice of the English law where all women's finances are concerned, beginning with her own, that Caroline the campaigner is best seen. She makes the point proudly that she has 'a position separate from my women's destiny; I am known as a writer'. This means that she has the power of benefiting herself by literary labours in which 'I do not "exist" for the claim in my

---

* The Salic Law, observed notably in France, took its name from the ancient tribe of the Salii, and had been part of the Frankish code; it forbade female succession, or succession through the female line.

own copyrights: – that is the negative and centralizing law for married women in England.'

Throughout *English Laws*, it is notable how often Caroline Norton refers to the question of protection. Because George Norton – 'her natural protector' – had failed to protect her, the law should step in and do so. 'Masculine superiority is incontestable, and with the superiority should come protection.' This distances her, she states clearly, from 'the wild and stupid theories advanced by a few women'. Her point is a different one: '*Power* is on the side of men . . . With it should come the *instinct* of protection.' This recalls the character based on Caroline Norton in an 1854 novel by Elizabeth Lynn Linton, herself a feminist: Charlotte Desborough 'had been taught to believe in men and honour them.'[4]

Caroline Norton ended *English Laws* by issuing a passionate appeal to the reader. 'Let that thought haunt you . . . and be with you in your readings of histories and romances, and your criticisms on the jurisprudence of countries less free than our own . . . I *really* suffered the extremity of earthly shame without deserving it (whatever chastisement my other faults may have deserved from heaven). I *really* lost my young children . . . and came too late to see one who had died a painful death, except in his coffin.'

It was perhaps just as well that, at this time of stress, Caroline entered the state which has brought happiness to so many down the ages: she became a grandmother. Whatever difficulties she encountered, the wise saying: 'Beware of what you wish for' was never appropriate to Caroline Norton and her grandchildren. One lady wrote to a friend that Caroline was 'nearly as beautiful as ever, under which brilliant circumstances it must be rather trying to be a grandmama'. This was Elizabeth Barrett Browning, with whom Caroline had struck up a friendship in Italy.[5] But the poet was wrong. Caroline Norton knew what she wished for. That was to have her own children back again, once more, young, lively, loving, in her care; the arrival of grandchildren, whatever the problems, went some way to remedy the tragic loss of those earlier childhoods. The sorrow of the mother could never be forgotten, but the pleasure of the grandmother could now be enjoyed.

Her younger son Brin, once described as kind, clever but wild, had ended up in Italy. Here the wildness appears to have prevailed, or perhaps it was the kindness. At any rate, while in Capri Brin became involved with a lovely peasant girl named Maria Elisa Chiara Federigo, known as Mariucca. Brin was twenty-two.

It was inevitable that Mariucca would be the target of snobbish comment. Caroline revealed to a friend that Lady Normanby had forwarded her a letter regarding Brin's wife, as Mariucca became: 'Poor Soul! It makes one sigh to think how little she understands, not only of her position, but of *all* our positions.' In Florence, Elizabeth Barrett Browning described Mariucca as uneducated and 'rather coarse in character'.[6]

Mariucca was certainly uneducated, being unable, it seems, to read and write, although that was not unusual for a girl in her circumstances. (Of her peasant family, her mother was said to be beautiful but her father rather deaf.) Caroline herself described Mariucca's sun-kissed Italian complexion and her freckled face, with its numerous moles, with something less than enthusiasm. However, William Le Fanu, a family friend, noted that she was rated the beauty of the island – this was for her fair hair, surprisingly blonde for an Italian – although he personally did not find her beautiful, just quiet and harmless.

Caroline saved her chief complaint for the fact that this uneducated girl was also an inadequate housekeeper with little idea of how to cook (at any rate by Caroline's standards).[7] The implication was that since Mariucca came from working peasant stock, she should at least have the virtues of her class. Mariucca continued to wear the clothes which, while beguiling, also stood out in company to mark her peasant status: white stockings, black velvet waistcoat, white blouse and skirt.

It is clear that Mariucca became pregnant very soon after the wedding, and was possibly already pregnant at the time if the baby came early. There was a secret Catholic ceremony in Salerno at the beginning of November 1853. On 14 August 1854, Caroline believed that Mariucca was unable to travel, being already 'in the eighth month'.[8] By this time Brin had discovered that by the relevant Italian law, secret weddings were not valid. There had therefore been another wedding on 1 August 1854 in an Anglican church in Florence. Carlotta Chiara Mary Norton was, in fact, born on 21 August. The first invalid marriage might have raised awkward questions had the baby been a boy. However, under the laws of male primogeniture which governed the English peerage, Carlotta was not in line for the Grantley title.

A second child followed almost at once. This proved to be the desired male heir. John Richard Brinsley Norton was born on 1 October 1855. It was this birth which was of significance in the world of aristocratic inheritance.[*] Norton's brother Lord Grantley, who was nearly sixty, remained childless, which meant that George was the heir to the title. This potential succession was something which had always been important to him (and some said it was important to Caroline too – the fact that she might one day be Lady Grantley). Now Richard represented the male line in the next generation.

In the meantime, Caroline embraced the new family and drew them into her own life. Her first encounter was in Florence. But while still in England, she continued to receive the sort of snippets of information calculated to delight a grandmother. Little Carlotta, for example, was said by Brin to resemble Caroline, for whom she had been named, in the Italian version; her grandmother wrote that it was 'very dutiful of Carlotta to be like me'.[9]

Then Carlotta was teething, while Mariucca was awaiting the birth of her second child. In return, Caroline supplied tips: Mariucca should endeavour to nurse (breast-feed) this second child. Caroline herself had, after all, nursed all her own children. There were suggestions like getting 'a good, sensible person as a nurse', not a fine lady and not the drunken nurse her own mother had had to put up with in South Africa.[10]

Caroline also worried about the lifestyle of her feckless son when Mariucca was occupied with the children: 'what's to

* The Grantley title has been borne by descendants of the marriage up to the present day.

become of Brin? He cannot live like a bird on a window sill.'[11] A tug of war gradually developed between Brin, who wanted his mother to leave her sisters and come and care for his family in Florence, and Caroline (and George Norton), who wanted him to bring them to England.

In the meantime, Caroline Norton's interest in social issues concerning women such as female emigration, previously mentioned, did not wane. The foundation of the Society of Female Artists immediately aroused her interest, on several levels. Caroline, as an amateur artist herself, whose sketches have much charm, was delighted to be included in the first exhibition of the Society held at a gallery in Oxford Street in the summer of 1857. She also liked the idea of this extension of the limits of the female world; the Royal Academy did not admit female artists, despite listing Angelica Kauffman and Mary Moser among its founders.*

After all, this represented another dimension in which women could do their own work to support themselves, the subject on which she felt so strongly. In writing to enlist another female artist, she added: 'There are so few employments for women, – and this is so clearly within the capacity of the capabilities of those who would fain earn their independence and cannot do it more laboriously.'[12]

Then there was her continuing engagement on a very different issue: the Divorce and Matrimonial Causes Bill, also known as the Marriage Bill. The Royal Commission on Divorce set up in 1850 had reported in 1853 and in 1854 that a Bill was introduced by the Lord Chancellor, Lord Cranworth, but did not survive the second reading in the House of Lords, on the grounds that there was no public desire for 'a cheap tribunal' for divorces.

It had begun with the aim of removing such legislation from the Ecclesiastical Courts but was gradually transformed so that it encompassed the ability of separated women to hold property in their own names and sign contracts.[13] Up until this point, the Ecclesiastical Courts had granted a divorce *a mensa et thoro* (from bed and board), which gave neither partner the right to

---

* Women were not admitted as Fellows of the Royal Academy until 1922.

remarry. An absolute dissolution of the marriage bond was only allowed when the marriage had been invalid in the first place, for a number of reasons including madness and impotence, and was therefore annulled.

Caroline Norton was quick to produce another campaigning work considering divorce from the woman's point of view. This was entitled *A Letter to the Queen on Lord Chancellor Cranworth's Marriage and Divorce Bill* and its main theme was protest against any legislation which gave one law for the men and the rich, and another for the women and the poor.[14]

The Queen, to whom it was ostensibly addressed, was no longer the vulnerable young girl who had appealed to her Prime Minister Melbourne. Victoria was now thirty-six, had been on the throne eighteen years and was already the mother of eight out of the nine children she would bear in total. The epigraph beneath the title, 'Only a woman's hair', referred to the famous expostulation of Thackeray concerning Jonathan Swift and the lock of his beloved Stella's hair: that theme of his writing which was found in his desk after his death.*

A Letter to the Queen began by outlining the various Bills so far, before proceeding to make it clear that this was not actually an appeal: 'The vague romance of "carrying my wrongs to the foot of the throne" forms no part of my intention: for I know the throne is powerless to redress them.' The days when oppressed subjects travelled to the presence of 'some glorious prince or princess' and had their wrongs instantly set right without reference to law are 'quaint old histories, or fairy fables, fit only for the amusement of children'.

Mrs Norton then offers three reasons for addressing the Queen. Firstly, there is the 'grotesque anomaly' of married women being 'non-existent' (the word which obsessed Caroline) in a country governed by a female Sovereign. Secondly, no reform can become law without the Queen's assent and 'sign manual'. Thirdly, she makes, once again, a reference to the Salic Law: if it existed here,

* The phrase (and its connotations) has inspired poets down the ages, including Lewis Carroll and T. S. Eliot.

'your Majesty would be by birth a subject, and Hanover and England would still be under one King.'* Caroline then recalled the scene at the opening of the new Hall of Lincoln's Inn: 'It was the very poetry of allegiance . . . the Treasurer knelt at a woman's feet and all the great Officers did obeisance in that Hall to their Queen.' She gave a chilling list of all the various legal disadvantages a married woman in England suffered, from appropriation of her earnings by her husband, 'whether she weed potatoes, or keep a school', down to the question of physical violence. Even here, 'her being of spotless character is of no advantage.'

After the divorce question, Caroline turned first to Royal history. It is, in fact, this use of history which subsequently caused the *Law Review* to describe *A Letter to the Queen* as one of the 'cleverest pamphlets that it has been our lot ever to read'.[15] She listed bygone Queens and their wrongs, such as Sophia Dorothea, the estranged wife of George I. When urged for reconciliation, Sophia Dorothea answered: 'No – if I am guilty, I am not worthy to be your Queen; if I am innocent, your King is not worthy to be my husband.' Caroline followed the Royal married women, the Queens, with a list of the Royal mistresses which naturally featured the unbridled and unpunished licentiousness of the monarchs concerned, such as Charles II, direct ancestor of a quiverful of Dukes. Roaming widely through history, and also countries, Caroline recounted the story of a heartbroken Creole woman, accompanied by a child, on a boat heading for her family in Martinique who turns out to be Joséphine de Beauharnais, future wife of Napoleon I. 'Your lot is grief . . . but you shall be Empress of France; the little girl at your side shall be Queen [of Holland] and her son an Emperor [Napoleon III].'

She also featured modern heroines such as Grace Darling, 'whose impulsive heroism saved wrecked sailors' lives', Mrs Fry and her 'gentle prison-visitings' and above all 'Miss Nightingale'.

---

* If the Salic Law had existed in England, the succession would have gone on the death of William IV to Ernest, Duke of Cumberland instead of Victoria, daughter of his older brother the Duke of Kent; as it was, Cumberland inherited Hanover, where the Salic Law did exist.

Florence Nightingale was at this point in the Crimea, but after her safe return – '(please God!)' throws in Caroline piously – the men of England might agree that the best testimonial to the worth of such women would be to give their sex a status and laws of protection afforded them in other European countries.

Throughout all this time Caroline Norton remained apart from the rising feminist movement, separated on the one hand by her own views on the subject and on the other by the feminists' view of her. The miasma of scandal which hung about her, although fading as Caroline grew older, was never quite absent: there was something morally undesirable about Mrs Norton, wasn't there? Of course, she suffered, but all the same . . .

Barbara Bodichon (her married name), a leading advocate of women's rights as well as a prominent supporter of women's education in particular, was nearly twenty years younger than Caroline Norton. It was her interest in women's education, among other elements, which would lead to the founding of the first women's college, Girton, at Cambridge in 1873. Their backgrounds were very different: Barbara Bodichon was the illegitimate child of a radical Whig politician, Benjamin Leigh Smith; his sister was the mother of Florence Nightingale, making the two women, radical in their different ways, first cousins.

From difficult beginnings – no Sheridan blood, no dark beauty – Barbara Bodichon emerged to help found the so-called Ladies of Langham Place, who met regularly to discuss and forward women's rights. Her own *A Brief Summary in Plain Language of the Most Important Laws concerning Women* (1854) was in fact inspired by the case of Mrs Norton, the ill-treated married woman, but also pointed to the fate of the unmarried girl, who had no remedy in law against seduction unless it be via her father, 'counted in law as being her master and she his servant, and the seducer having deprived him of her services' – in other words the grievance is once more that of the man.[16]

In 1856, Barbara Bodichon and her committee drew up a petition to be presented to Parliament on 14 March. Married women, it said, should have a right to their own earnings 'as a counteractive to wife-beating and other evils'. It also drew attention to the plight of the lower class, who couldn't afford to appeal for legal protection. The committee included Elizabeth Barrett Browning and the novelist Mrs Gaskell. Mrs Norton was not invited to join them. In 1858, Barbara Bodichon set up the *English Woman's Journal* to discuss all kinds of women's issues including employment as well as reform of the relevant laws.

In effect this was a different generation who would go forward to do great things in the next decades, culminating in the changes brought about after the maelstrom of the First World War. This was not Caroline Norton's fight. She was still occupied deftly acknowledging the divinely ordained inferiority of women in order to bring about practical results in their actual lives. Did she really believe in the inferiority of women and the superiority of men as being part of the divine order, as she sometimes declared – 'not a thing of man's devising, but of God's appointing'? Whatever lip service she paid to this idea, her own conduct showed no sense of her own inferiority.

A letter from her sister Georgia commenting on the birth of Carlotta – Brin's first child, but unable to inherit the Grantley title – highlights the difference: her sex is 'an unfortunate circumstance . . . as far as human judgement can foresee', but 'a girl will be a greater comfort and pleasure to him than a boy.' Caroline herself had written eloquently on the subject to Edward Trelawny at the height of her troubles over her sons in 1836: 'Thank God, let it end how it will, they are all boys – I leave no hereditary mortification to grind and grieve a daughter.' She was now glad that her 'earnest wish' to have a daughter had never been fulfilled: 'I remember the prayer of the Red Indian woman . . . "Let not my child be a girl for very sad is the lot of woman" and I think civilized or savage it is much the same.'[17]

Women were nicer than men, but they were not the same as men, and if the conventional way to express the difference was to invoke divinely ordained inferiority, so be it. The claim to equal rights between the sexes, what Caroline Norton called 'the wild views of women' in *A Letter to the Queen*, did not interest her: she was the representative of an earlier tradition. The practical details of women's lives and how to better them were her concern. She never took the next step to understanding that only the establishment of theoretical equality would bring the true protection which she craved for all women.

One thing is notable about *A Letter to the Queen*. That is Caroline Norton's feeling of mission: her ability to write, even her own personal sufferings (all fully recounted once more), have a purpose: 'Even now, friends say to me – "Why write? why struggle? it is the law! You will do no good." But if everyone lacked courage with that doubt, nothing would ever be achieved in this world.' Later: '*I* believe . . . that I am permitted to be the example on which a particular law shall be reformed.' And she exhorts the Queen once more: 'Not lone and vainglorious, like the Virgin Queen Elizabeth, – nor childless like the hypochondriac Mary, nor heirless like the feeble-minded Anne, – more of "the beauty of Womanhood" adorns the destiny of Queen Victoria, than has belonged to the barren reigns of former English Queens; and the link to all the interests of woman's life should be greater.'

Finally, Caroline Norton, as before, does not forget the plight of other women. She writes that she is aware how many women infinitely better than her, more pious, more patient and less rash under injury, 'have watered their bread with tears'. It is not her suffering which distinguishes her: 'it is the power to comment on and explain the cause of that wrong; which few women are able to do.' For *this*, I believe, God gave me the power of writing.' She ends on a note of defiance: 'Meanwhile, my husband has 'a legal lien (as he publicly proved) on the copyright of my works. Let him claim the copyright of THIS!'

In 1856, Lord Cranworth, as Lord Chancellor, brought back the Bill under the auspices of the Prime Minister, Lord Palmerston. Caroline Norton lobbied her political friends relentlessly with that artful mixture of artlessness and wisdom she thought best calculated to appeal to them. She also attended debates, such as the Committee stage of the Marriage Bill in the House of Lords on 28 May 1857. Caroline gave a vivid description of it in a letter: how the bishops with their white-lawn sleeves amid the dark coats and crimson benches of the House of Lords were like a garden plot of lilies, while 'old Lord Lyndhurst', her principal contact, spoke so eloquently.[18]

Lyndhurst, now eighty-five and still a brilliant orator, with the famous 'rich, melodious tones' of his voice coupled with his handsome 'Mephistophelean' appearance, had been Lord Chancellor under three Prime Ministers. Now he spoke three times on this issue. Lyndhurst certainly did not defend every reform: he had been opposed to Catholic Emancipation at one point and at the final debate on the Great Reform Bill he called it an attack on 'Monarchy and property itself'. But in this case he applied himself, in Caroline's words, to 'defending the bloom of future generations from bitter tears'. He drew attention to the fact that the Bill still put proceedings 'beyond the poorer classes of the community'.

Of the so-called lilies, five bishops spoke. The Bishop of Oxford sounded a familiar note of moral caution when he suggested that if they introduced, in any way, facilities for divorce, they should at the same time give 'a distinctly criminal character to the act of adultery'. The counter-argument to this was that sinful concubinage, perpetuating adultery, was actively encouraged under the present rules because there was no permitted alternative, such as divorce and remarriage. One authority has described the principal object of the Act as being 'to reduce the amount of unregulated adultery, and by improving the legal position of wives to shore up the family from the threats that surrounded it'.[19]

It was a raging-hot summer, the unusually high temperatures matched by the heat of the disputes in the two houses and elsewhere. Despite opposition from high-minded politicians such as Gladstone and Samuel Wilberforce, shocked by the diminution of the Church of England's influence, the Bill received Royal Assent on 27 August 1857.

Caroline Norton would reach her fiftieth birthday on 22 March 1858. In her own world, that world of shade and sun, the Matrimonial Causes Act was the second piece of legislation, following the Infant Custody Act, that had diminished the shade for women generally. She had the satisfaction of playing a part in both campaigns, principally by employing her talent as a writer. The arrival of her grandchildren brought her private sunshine. There was another human need which was unfulfilled; but perhaps Caroline was never destined to have the happy marriage which, as a young girl, she had hoped for with Ralph Leveson Smith, only to have her hopes cruelly dashed by his death. It remained to be seen what other consolations might be found.

PART FOUR

THE WINDS
OF CHANGE

'The winds of change afflict us. What to-day
We tether tight, to-morrow whirls away.'

Caroline Norton, epigraph to *Old Sir Douglas*, 1868

CHAPTER FOURTEEN

Reaping in Joy?

*'God giveth increase through all coming years
And lets us reap in joy, seed that was sown
in tears.'*

Caroline Norton, *The Lady of la Garaye*, 1862

THE FRIENDSHIP BETWEEN CAROLINE NORTON and William Stirling of Keir deepened in the years following their propitious encounter in Lisbon in 1848, at the time of Fletcher's illness. By June the following year, she was describing him warmly to her mother: 'I think the pleasantest letter-writer is Mr. Stirling.' Caroline explained that he was in Spain 'wallowing in pictures'. Stirling had, after all, shown himself to have that vital manly quality found in all her campaigning pamphlets: the instinct to come to the aid of the woman. Caroline ended the letter to her mother on a self-deprecating note: 'Mr. Stirling talks of coming [to Lisbon] when he has *done* Spain: but I think he will be bored here where there are no pictures – and only one tableau vivant by way of society.' Nevertheless: 'I hope he will come.'[1]

Stirling's own career flourished. Not for nothing was the Stirling family motto 'Gang Forward'. When he was young, he travelled daringly and extensively, not only in Spain but also in the Levant; this absence abroad included a spell living with monks on Mount Carmel in the Lebanon. He trod the route of private publication so familiar to Caroline for his collection of poems *Songs of the Holy Land*, dated Christmas 1845; forty copies were printed, with no author's name supplied, in Edinburgh.[2] These 'humble versions of several familiar passages of sacred song and story' were described as 'chiefly written in the lands to which they relate'. Poems included 'The Valley of the Bones', inspired by Ezekiel 37: 1–14:

Like some great den of lions old, or ancient field of fight,
But thicklier strew'd with bleachéd bones, all sere and snowy
    white . . .
'Oh, hear ye now, dry bones!' I cried ,'the bidding of the
    Lord . . .'
So life awoke in all the host, they rose up where they lay

It ended with the rousing climax to 'Judith':

But by the hand of woman
Our God hath foil'd the foeman . . .
Our gentle Judith smote
The faulchion through his throat.

It is, however, for William Stirling's next venture, his groundbreaking *Annals of the Artist in Spain*, that he is still respected today; this was published in 1848 in four volumes. After that a number of distinguished scholarly studies followed, including *The Cloister Life of the Emperor Charles V*, which ran into a second edition immediately.

William Stirling inherited Keir near Dunblane at his father's death in 1847; Archibald Stirling had been a liberal and charitable landlord who discovered iron, coal and firestone on his Scottish lands. Eighteen years later, William Stirling would also succeed through the female line to the estate of Sir John Maxwell, 8th Baronet, his mother's brother, as well as the baronetcy itself.

At this point, her friend became Sir William Stirling-Maxwell, 9th Baronet,[3] in both private and public life.*

Stirling was a Tory (like George Norton, but of a very different calibre in every other way); as such, he was elected MP for Perthshire in 1852. By nature more of a scholar than a politician, he was in demand for such roles as membership of the Universities Commission in 1859 and Rector of St Andrews University in 1862. There were many more distinguished appointments to come.

One of the marks of the friendship between Caroline and Stirling, as ever with her friendships, was a tireless correspondence. She envied him his travels with mock sorrow. As she told Abraham Hayward, 'I should so like to be a bachelor and do the same; but I am an encumbered female.'[4] Meanwhile she revelled in telling Stirling anecdotes of this encumbered life.

There was an alarming incident with her grandchildren in a hired brougham coming back from Highgate, which must have been terrifying at the time: the horse jolted and reared, refusing to go down the hill but flinging himself against the hedge. When Caroline tried to get herself and the children out, the horse sprang forward, throwing her to the ground. The 'accursed steel petticoat', her crinoline, got looped in the wheel and Caroline, expecting to be crushed at any minute, was left shrieking to some labourers nearby: 'Oh! drag me out [even] if you tear everything off me.' Richard and Carlotta were also crying with terror in chorus; altogether it was 'the most dreadful sensation of fright' she had ever felt. If it had not been for these labourers, 'I certainly should not be writing this note, nor you ever have to call in Chesterfield St again – unless on my heirs.' The ending of the letter was poignant: 'Make a little time to come & see how I am.'[5]

---

* Although according to Caroline he would have preferred Maxwell-Stirling. This inheritance through the female line was unusual. Legislation in 1707 allowed the so-called 'heir of entail' to succeed where there was no 'heir of the body', i.e. male heir.

Fortunately, not all her letters recounted such frightening mini-dramas. As ever with Caroline, there were jokes. Harriet Beecher Stowe was one of her heroines for her emancipated views on slavery. Nevertheless, she commended a joke on the subject of her saintliness to William Stirling. 'You will like this one,' she wrote. 'Why was Uncle Tom's Cabin written by no mortal hand? Answer: because it was written by Mrs. Beecher's Toe.' Stirling's travels began to include assignments with Caroline as she also travelled, if less hectically, from place to place. 'Patting your recalcitrant pate, with no undeserved blessing I remain / yours affectly C.N.' was how she ended one long description of her journeys. Once again, the real point of the letter was in the last few lines: 'sit down quickly . . . and write me a line saying what day you expect to be at Cowes – to Glen Isla . . . indeed, if you are very energetic you might telegraph it there.'[6]

At the same time, Caroline was able to bring Fletcher and Brin to Keir once contact was restored to her. Her grandchildren would be similarly welcomed there. William Stirling was the proud possessor of a beautiful garden at Keir to which he had added a gateway and an arcade, as well as terraces. He was also responsible for numerous alterations to the house itself, reversing the entrance from east to north and, appropriately enough for a scholar, adding a library.[7]

Scotland had long been part of Caroline's world of the romantic imagination. Now Keir and its surroundings were vividly in her thoughts – as well as engendering some quite proprietorial feelings. Caroline felt sufficiently entitled to write an introduction for Mr Gladstone to visit the garden, and request that he be shown round personally by the owner. One letter from Stirling, with flowers in it, allowed her 'to sniff the little roses from afar', and together with the foxglove, which presumably was also enclosed, 'gave me a wild shiver of desire to be walking in the wood myself instead of other co-mates who have no business there in comparison and they will pull up my foxgloves by the tree'.[8] Thus Stirling became part of Caroline's renewed family circle, someone to whom her sons also reported their mother's news. Fletcher, for example, writing as 'a Paris attaché', informed

Stirling about Brin's recent illness: 'My mother is going on well. Poor thing – it was a terrible shock for her nervous system not to speak of the real pain and irritation. Brin – is alive, and kicking – against the pricks.' Fletcher was also known to borrow money off Stirling.[9]

As to the exact nature of this relationship between William Stirling and Caroline Norton, it was suggested earlier that they were lovers. Helen reported to Georgia on a joint visit they paid to Clandeboye that Caroline was 'in high force and great beauty'. Indeed, after Stirling departed, Helen worried about her entertainment in wry sisterly fashion: 'I am rather nervous, if something flirtable is not thrown into the Lion's maw.' This happy affair, as it seems to have been, is in contrast to Caroline's relations with Melbourne, where the opposite assumption was made that Caroline and Melbourne were not actually lovers in the fullest physical sense, in spite of loving each other deeply. Stirling after all was a bachelor, with no commitments. He had an agreeable, scholarly appearance: a strong, even handsome face with a fine, slightly aquiline nose beneath a noble forehead, gradually revealed in all its intellectual splendour as his hair slipped back, tall if slightly stooped. Stirling was certainly not without humour: he once wrote himself a spoof epitaph commenting on his eccentricity:[10]

> Here lies Stirling of Keir,
> A very good man, but queer.
> If you want to find a queerer
> You must dig up Stirling of Keirer*

Above all, William Stirling combined kindness with intelligence and sensitivity.

Caroline at the age of fifty is revealed by the new art of the photograph – not quite so alluring as the majestic brushwork of Daniel Maclise and Benjamin Robert Haydon in her youth, and

---

* The word 'queer' simply meant odd at this date; it was first used as a derogatory term for homosexuals by the Marquess of Queensberry in 1894.

in a black and white photograph lacking the dramatic 'Babylon-ish' colouring that was an important part of her beauty. But one example, taken in 1863, still shows the charm of her face, those big beseeching eyes which had accrued so many compliments in their time, 'Satan's eyes' in Haydon's words, for their capacity to seduce. As for the rest of her face, there was an illuminating inci-dent at about the same time when Caroline was making herself 'very agreeable' to a group of young people on the Isle of Wight. There was some kind of conversation about age and appearance: 'Time cannot rob me of my beautiful nose,' said Caroline in her humorous way.[11]

So Caroline Norton was still playful as well as being both clever and cultured, a respected writer. It was no wonder the bachelor Stirling enjoyed her company. After all, she had been fully, if not legally, separated from her husband for many years. It was true that she was still a married woman, in the sense that she was not divorced from that husband. For better or for worse – possibly for the better from Stirling's point of view – any question of marriage to another man was out of the question.

The new Matrimonial Causes Act coming into force had not, in fact, produced total equality between the sexes. The double standard remained: a husband could sue his wife for adultery alone, whereas a wife needed to prove 'aggravated adultery', that is, the inclusion of some other offence such as cruelty, desertion, incest or bigamy.[12*] Undoubtedly, women now had legal pro-tection from economic exploitation by their husbands (such as Caroline had endured), and child custody, awarded to the mother only when the child was under seven by the Infant Custody Act, could now be awarded exclusively to either wife or husband by a judge. But a separated woman could only control her property if she was the innocent party, that is if deserted by her husband.

The issue of the paternity of children within marriage remained: the fact that adultery by a woman could result in the imposition of another man's child upon her husband – possibly as his heir – something which could not apply to a man, whose

---

* The double standard was not abolished until 1923.

bastards remained, by definition, outside his legal family circle. The dreaded concept of Crim. Con. under which George Norton had sued Melbourne for £10,000 was abolished. But it was replaced by another, more random method of seeking damages at the discretion of the judge. It would take some years and a lot more legislation before the whole question of married women's property was sorted out.

All this meant that the Nortons did not seek a divorce, not only because it was expensive but also because divorce did not really correspond to either of their needs. But they did continue their endless wrangling over finance, a wrangling that got more complicated as the boys turned into adults, and there was a new dependent family in the shape of Brin's children. It was in fact the fate of their children, once at the heart of the discord, which prompted an encounter between the unhappy pair which Caroline herself described as feeling 'like a dream'.[13]

The Nortons found themselves together in the same steam-packet office, where they had both gone separately to make arrangements for sending Brin and his family to Dinan in Brittany, a move which would take place 'by his Father's peremptory orders'. There 'a cheap retired place' awaited them. Caroline reported in September 1859 that there they were, 'all breakfasting together after Twenty years! . . . so ends the restless part of this life quarrel.' Nobody was sorry 'that our disputes are closed' but Norton's solicitor, said Caroline pointedly. She believed that he must have got little short of £4,000 (about £350,000 in modern values) out of Norton in twenty years of battle.

Brin's move meant that Caroline immediately set to work, in her familiar lobbying style, on her son's behalf. The Duke of Newcastle, the former MP Henry Pelham-Clinton, who had held various political appointments including Chief Secretary for Ireland and Secretary of State for the Colonies, was a supporter of hers. Caroline begged the Duke not to let 'this *really* clever and energetic son of mine *rot there,* doing nothing but pine'.[14] What about a vice-consulate in France and Italy? And what sort of things were candidates for that kind of office examined in? Brin spoke and wrote French and Italian perfectly after all these years abroad and, in his mother's opinion, would be 'useful and active'.

George Norton was now fifty-nine and was getting to the end of his own days of being useful and active. Much of his time was spent in Yorkshire at Kettlethorpe on the family lands (including those moors where poor Willie had died in 1842). His London life as a magistrate was moving to a close: that role in which Melbourne had helped him so long ago, at the request of Caroline, who had been ordered to do it by George himself. This was definitely the best part of Norton's public career. When the great Victorian biographer Thomas Carlyle was tackling one of his subjects in his classic study *On Heroes, Hero-Worship and the Heroic in History*, he wrote: 'I mean to say all the good of him I justly can'; it was the way of getting at his secret.[15] Certainly, on that basis, the genuinely high-minded side of George Norton's character should be stressed.

While he had not made much impact during the four years he had been the Tory MP for Guildford, he received warm tributes when he finally retired as a magistrate a few years later, as recent research has revealed. Henry Mayhew, in his study of 1861, *London Labour and the London Poor*, referred to the Hon. G. C. Norton as '"the beak", but good for all that'. A court guide based on the testimony of criminals mentioned him among persons 'known to be charitable'. At this retirement, after so many years of service, a senior magistrate declared that 'the poor would miss a true and valued friend . . . one who was ever ready to stretch forth a helping hand to those in distress.'[16]

It was scarcely surprising that over the years there were stories of George Norton and other women. Even at the time of the scandal in 1836, one of Caroline's admirers hastened to inform her that he had a mistress. Caroline responded: 'What you say of Mr. Norton, I know, that is I believe it; – there is a Mrs. Reed,' although she had forgotten where she lived. Caroline added that, given the situation, she was astonished by 'the insolence of a man forming an inquisition on his Wife's conduct'.[17]

As the years went by, Caroline, for one, remained convinced that Norton had a mistress (which does not seem unlikely under the circumstances). Later she named a certain Ellen Mathis, by whom he may have had children in the course of time, and there are various references to it in her correspondence. In October 1864, for example, she told Lady Holland that if she died, George Norton had promised Ellen Mathis, by whom he had two sons, to marry her.[18] Norton was said to parade her 'fearlessly' and Caroline commented snidely on the richness of Miss Mathis's clothes. (Nevertheless, Norton family records do not include references to these supposed offspring.)

Unfortunately, time had not mellowed Norton's explosive character, that streak of rage at any perceived frustration of his will which, directed towards his young wife, had taken the form of physical violence. Directing the lives of his surviving children, Fletcher and Brin, had not brought out the best in him, to say nothing of the unfortunate circumstances of Willie's death. Now the welfare of his grandchildren Carlotta and Richard provided a fresh challenge. And very shortly after the unlikely meeting in the steam-packet office, and hopefully the 'end of the restless part', tragedy struck the Norton family again. The new dream turned into the old nightmare which had haunted Caroline since 1842.

It concerned Fletcher, who had turned thirty in August 1859. At this point, Fletcher was not only his father's heir, but the ultimate heir to the Grantley title, currently borne by his childless uncle. This inheritance would presumably include whatever kind of financial benefit might be established as part of the family settlement.

Fletcher had always had excellent relations with his mother, something to which his persistent ill-health in youth had contributed, because it offered Caroline those valuable opportunities for care she craved. Fletcher himself, on the other hand, frequently felt unfairly blighted, as invalid children do. There was a point at which he lamented to his mother: 'What would I give to feel like any young man,' when by degrees dancing, riding, cricket and boating, and all the 'amusements of male youth', were forbidden him.[19]

As a result, he was quieter by nature than the ebullient Brin; Caroline treasured him. Fletcher, the diplomat, had been in Lisbon, where ill-health forced him to return to England, but he was then posted to Naples. He was currently an attaché in Paris, and had not married. But as events would show, he did have a relationship with an Italian widow Victoria Penelli, née Tombesi, although the exact nature of the relationship was not immediately clear.

Then began a fearful decline in his health: the consumption so cruelly endemic in the Sheridan family began to claim him. Caroline was able to be with him in Paris. Her series of letters to friends and family charting his decline are heart-rending. To her niece Ulrica – 'dearest Rica' – Georgia's daughter, she related his torments on 6 October. Even when he rallied a little from 'utter prostration' they were told to continue to expect the worst. In any case, Fletcher was so weak that they could hardly make out what he wrote on his slate. His extreme thinness was an additional cause of suffering. 'I can clasp his poor arm and meet my finger over it and below his shoulder,' in Caroline's words.[20]

Fletcher had shown a keen interest in religion, unlike either of his parents, from his teens. Once he was resident mainly abroad, he had become a Catholic. Now 'he took the sacrament and said he was prepared to die, and trustful in God's mercy.'*At the end, 'There he lay quite still on my bosom, breathing faster and faster till he died . . . I am thankful, when so many women have soldier sons dying far away from them, I was permitted to witness this blessed and gentle creature go from us in peace.'

Fletcher's very last word, spoken in a soft, sad tone, was 'Mother'. But shortly before he died, he was also able to say 'Father'. George Norton and Brin had both been sent for as Fletcher's condition turned critical. Norton was kneeling beside his son's bed, while Caroline cradled him. So this sad deathbed with both parents present was in solemn contrast, not only to

---

* Extreme Unction, administered by a priest to a Catholic who is believed to be dying.

soldiers dying alone on the field of battle, but also to the tragic end of Willie seventeen years earlier.

The Catholic religion which had been a consolation to the dying man proved a complication when it came to his funeral. Naturally Fletcher had desired a Catholic funeral. Equally under-standably, his father wanted him to be buried at Kettlethorpe in the churchyard where Willie lay. So the Catholic rite took place and all the Nortons then proceeded to Yorkshire. The house itself was let, so they stayed in two separate country inns, Caroline and Brin in one, George in the other. Caroline described the churchyard scene to her sister: 'This place is still as death, the hearse stopped at a gate in the ground, and the bearers took him round on the green walk of turf, round the little lake, like a dark vision.' She added that 'Brinny' was not at all well, but Mr Norton was being very kind to him. George was also anxious to be kind to her, 'but we feel so differently'.[21]

It remained for Victoria Penelli to demand the money which she believed to be due to her, with a muddle between various wills poor Fletcher had left. Caroline turned to the reliable William Stirling and suggested he might be a trustee of the new arrangement, which also involved possession of her own house at 3 Chesterfield Street.

The honour – or burden – of being the Grantley heir had now descended to Brin, and after him to his son Richard since Fletcher had left no children. The dream which had been hovering since Caroline's fiftieth birthday, of a settled, peaceful relationship with George Norton and a rich, meaningful friendship with William Stirling, had become a nightmare, or rather another example of the mother's greatest nightmare – the loss of a child.

In her grief about Fletcher, Caroline turned to poetry. 'In the Storm', written in Scotland, expresses her deepest desire:

> If, going forth in the snow and the hail
> In the wind and the rain,
> On the desolate hills, in the face of the gale
> I could meet thee again . . .

It ends on the comforting thought 'There is rest too in heaven', before wondering again: 'Is there rest? But the earth seems so near, as I swoon / And the heavens so far.'[22]

The Lady of la Garaye, a long, narrative book-length poem, was published in 1861.[23] At the end of the year, there was another sadly premature death, this time affecting not only a family but a whole nation. Queen Victoria's beloved husband, Prince Albert, died on 14 December 1861 at the age of forty-two. The Queen's own description of the deathbed was infinitely touching: like Caroline, she had witnessed her loved one go in peace. 'Two or three long but perfectly gentle breaths were drawn, the hand clasping mine and . . . All, all was over . . .'.[24]

Identifying with the Queen's grief, as once she had identified with her motherhood, when she addressed the Prince of Wales in *The Child of the Islands*, Caroline began by writing a memorial poem, 'Gone', for *Macmillan's Magazine*. She then despatched a copy of the new poem to the Queen. Caroline's nephew, Lord Dufferin, who was a lord-in-waiting, had already presented copies to the Queens of Prussia and Holland, who were 'very intellectual'. He would follow it up with the Queen 'when she is able, poor soul, to think of anything but the sudden and stunning loss'.[25]

The original edition of *The Lady of la Garaye* was ornamented by Caroline Norton's own sketches, including a portrait of the real-life Comtesse de la Garaye at the start, copied from a picture Caroline had seen in Brittany. *The Times* pointed to the contrast between the gay season of Christmas and the poem by the popular author Mrs Norton: it was a surprise to get tragedy 'when we had expected a pantomime', but the pleasure was equal to that of the pantomime, if of a very different sort.[26]

The poem was dedicated to one of Caroline Norton's long-term supporters, the eighty-two-year-old Whig politician and grandee, the Marquess of Lansdowne. Now described by the historian John Motley as 'a plain-looking benignant old gentleman in a white hat and a kind of old world look about him', he was generally praised for his liberalism in public, 'a sagacious counsellor . . . and a munificent patron'; in addition, he was a courteous host at Bowood in Wiltshire.[27]

Friend of old days, of suffering, storm and strife,
Patient and kind through many a wild appeal;
In the arena of thy brilliant life
Never too busy or too cold to feel.

In particular, Caroline touched on the comfort brought to her by the loyalty of those who, like Lansdowne, gave the same welcome to her 'saddened glance and withered cheek' as they had done to her when young.

In her Introduction, Caroline explained she had visited the Hospital for Incurables in Dinan in Brittany, founded by the Comte and Comtesse de la Garaye, the hero and heroine of her story. The château itself was crumbling, but the memory of the Comte and Comtesse was fresh in the memory of the people, while the couple themselves were buried 'among the poor' in the district of Taden. Caroline claimed to have invented nothing – and to have contributed only the language in which the story is told, that gift of writing on which she prided herself: 'The intangible gift of thought, whose silver thread / Heaven keeps untarnished despite our bitterest tears.'

This is the story of Gertrude de la Garaye, a beautiful young married woman who becomes crippled or 'crooked', in the language of the time 'Crooked and sick forever she must be / Her life of wild activity and glee / was with the past' – as a result of a hunting accident. Her husband desperately tries to rescue her as she lies trapped by her horse, having attempted to follow him jumping across a stream.

The poem moves to the development of their love from the passion of youth to this new, deeper feeling. There are moments of regret – 'O Claud – the old bright days!' – and Gertrude does undergo agonies of doubt for a while as to whether she can still be loved, only to be finally reassured by Comte Claud's devotion: 'Oh! Dearer now than when thy girlish tongue / Faltered consent to love while both were young.' The story then relates how, under the influence of a local prior of the Benedictines, the Comte and Comtesse begin to understand the plight of the poor and generously, compassionately, turn their castle into a refuge. Gertrude becomes 'the dear Lady of the liberal hand', while Claud develops a surgeon's touch: 'Long rows of simple beds the place proclaim / A hospital in all things but name.'

The Lady of la Garaye is fundamentally a tale of noble souls who conquer grief by compassion. It includes Caroline's laudable obsession with the poor, seen in so much of her work, during which she constantly questions what the poor have actually done to deserve their fate.

There was an additional sad coda to the poem when Sidney Herbert died. He was still only fifty. Caroline Norton referred not only to his work – 'HERBERT, not vainly thy career was run' – but also to his young widow and the 'children who boast thy good blood in their veins'. (The Herberts were fortunate enough to have had seven, in a fifteen-year-long marriage.) She had begun the poem with one friend's name in the shape of Lord Lansdowne; she ended with the name of another, Herbert: 'Names that shall sink not in oblivion's flood'. But in conclusion Caroline showed faith in the future: 'God giveth increase through all coming years – / And let us reap in joy, seed that was sown in tears.'

This, at least, was her hope. There had certainly been enough tears, with the death of a second child, to say nothing of a very different grief, the loss of old friends. It remained to be seen whether, and in what way, Caroline Norton might still reap in joy.

CHAPTER FIFTEEN

Nonna Wants the Pen

'I cannot write any more as Nonna wants the pen.'

Richard Norton to William Stirling, c.1866

THE MARRIAGE OF THE SURVIVING Norton son, Brin, and his Italian peasant wife Mariucca began to disintegrate. This was due not so much to her lack of conventional suitability as a wife as to Brin's increasingly erratic behaviour. If there was a silver lining to this new cloud in Caroline's life, it was the enhancement of her own role as grandmother.

Sometimes this behaviour of Brin's was positively abusive, although it seems that a kind of madness, rather than a terrible hereditary streak of cruelty, was responsible, but inevitably Caroline did compare the two: 'the causeless rages and contradictions are like a dreadful echo of my youth and the unhappy days at home.' In September 1862, for example, Brin was seen to pursue a young woman with his advances, whereupon she leapt into the sea. Brin then leapt after her and brought her back to shore safely, and without further assault on her virtue. In spite of such incidents, in Capri, according to Caroline, the people were kind and treated him as a sort of eccentric demi-god.[1]

Things were less easy in his home country. In Edinburgh, on a visit at the end of the year, he was said to have been 'tipsy and stupefied' and Caroline had to rescue the children. Not all the troubles were brought on by himself: Brin's health never seems to have been particularly good after he grew up. For example, at the age of twenty-five this 'last survivor of my lovely boys' was described by Caroline to William Stirling as having a small vascular tumour which plunged her into gloom and foreboding that a further death was imminent. At the age of thirty, Brin had a bad 'inflammatory attack' and, needing an operation, was brought to her house. He was put under chloroform because he was 'such a nervous, irritable subject'.[2] It had all begun with a hunting accident. Naturally, George Norton 'pooh-poohed' the whole thing.

But in March 1863, there was an incident which was embarrassing as well as frightening, because it took place within the family circle. The young Nortons, with 'Nonna' Caroline, were with the Dufferins at Clandeboye. Brin got out of control – among other things, he attacked his eight-year-old son Richard – and needed restraint. Future behaviour would include assaults on Mariucca, various kicks being exchanged, and Brin himself being stabbed by the husband of a woman he had attacked.

Under the circumstances it was perhaps not surprising that from time to time Caroline Norton took charge of the grandchildren, at the explicit request of their mother Mariucca, and with Brin's agreement. The surprising element for Caroline was Mariucca's subsequent behaviour: Caroline considered her 'pitiless' for not writing to her children. (Did it not occur to her that the pen was not necessarily the sort of instrument an 'uneducated' woman would use, unlike members of the Sheridan family?) Helen took a more tactful line about Mariucca and her apparent eccentricities: 'I shall talk of my niece as a princess in disguise.' Meanwhile, the lovely young woman put on weight, and became so fat that many thought she was expecting another baby.[3]

So there arose a situation with a certain grim irony about it: Caroline Norton tended her grandchildren, travelled with them, supervised their lives, watched over their respective schoolings, while all the time they had little or no contact with their actual mother. Caroline's grandmotherly role was in direct reverse to the agonizing years of her own children's upbringing, but once again the actual mother was out of touch.

Through all this time, Caroline pursued her chosen profession as a writer. She had once had witty observations to make on the subject of a working (that is, writing) mother. Now she was a working grandmother. Richard's letters contain frequent references to Nonna's work, going well, not going well, at all times a part of their lives. There is a touching sentence in his letter to William Stirling from Marseilles, where Caroline had taken the grandchildren: 'I cannot write any more as Nonna wants the pen.'[4]

Like many writers, Caroline occasionally indulged in wistful thoughts as to how much nicer it might be to write for pleasure, not for money. 'I wish – loving literary pursuits as I do – that a chain of evil circumstances, family disputes of my son's imprudent marriage, – did not make literature so much of a profession with me – & that I *could* be indifferent to all but the pleasure of success.'[5] She continued to take an acute interest in publishing details, matters such as binding and printing.

Above all, Caroline Norton was concerned about circulating copies of *The Lady of la Garaye* to the right people, which meant people of influence. 'Do you not think if you sent one to "the Editor" of the Times it would be well?' This would be in addition to the special copy she would despatch to Mr Delane personally at his house, she told Alexander Macmillan, of Macmillan publishers.[6]

But her literary preoccupations were not limited to her own works. Caroline Norton had always been quick to admire fellow women writers – Mary Shelley for example, way back, and George Eliot, whose *Middlemarch* deeply impressed her; then there was Mrs Gaskell, whose sympathetic study of a 'fallen woman', in other words an unmarried mother, *Ruth*, first published in 1853, had an enormous influence on her times.[7]

Caroline Norton corresponded with poets, such as Longfellow, to whom she wrote in July 1861, as a stranger 'according to the rules of worldly etiquette', but both familiar with his work and sympathizing with him for the recent death of his wife. She sent 'a brief little poem of my own', adding: 'I wish you could admire any one passage in it as I admire all of yours I ever read.'[8] Perhaps a whisper of that boldness which had caused her to write to Sir Robert Peel asking to be the first woman Poet Laureate was with her still. But it turned out that *The Lady of la Garaye* was her last book-length published poem, although she continued to write verse. Caroline's next major work was, in fact, a novel, *Lost and Saved*.

The travels, now with the grandchildren, were remorseless. And Caroline's own health was not of the best. A six-week journey to Germany, for example, in 1864 resulted in serious illness – at which point Brin came and took away his children. Although Brinsley Sheridan, her brother, reported: 'that archetype of devil her son' had seriously added to her illness by taking away her grandchildren, that may have been family prejudice against Brin for his tempestuous behaviour; such a move to aid her convalescence would seem sensible on the surface.[9]

There was increasing friction with her sisters, based partly on what they saw as Caroline's passion for publicity. Poor Helen had endured the grief of her first husband, Lord Dufferin, dying suddenly in 1841. Twenty-odd years later, she married a younger admirer, George, Earl of Gifford, only to have him die in turn two months. At which point, Caroline proposed to write a tribute to Lord Gifford in the press, only to be smartly rebuked. She accepted the rebuke.[10]

Another element in the friction was what the sisters saw as Caroline's refusal to accommodate herself to life's inevitable changes. The days when she was a focus of the scandalmongers were over, in the opinion of her sisters. Helen lectured her. 'Do Car open your eyes (and shut your mouth) and see that this is not our old world when we were all young handsome women, much observed and talked of, and that you are no longer an ideal of Vanity Fair surrounded by admirers and enviers.'[11]

Who cared nowadays about 'the trial'? A helpful reminder, perhaps, if not necessarily best given by a sister.

Lost and Saved was published in May 1863, as by 'The Hon. Mrs. Norton. Author of "Stuart of Dunleath"'.[12] Caroline waggishly wrote to her friend at *The Times*, John Delane, he who had been designated for two copies, that she hoped he would not bring her grey hair 'untimely to discredit', in the eyes of her grandson, by a bad review. Richard, now aged seven (who is revealed as already taking a keen interest in Nonna's literary career, presumably having grasped that was where the money came from), had 'gravely observed' that he hoped there would be 'a good fuss' about the book – as else it was no use to write one.[13]

In fact, by 23 June the publishers, Hurst and Blackett, were able to put an advertisement at the top of the front page of *The Times*, already referring to the third edition, and quoting from several excellent reviews. In *The Athenaeum*, *Lost and Saved* was described as a work of 'rare excellence', surpassing *Stuart of Dunleath*. It would have created a stir among novel-readers 'even if it had not had Mrs. Norton's name on the title page'. *The Morning Post* referred to 'true womanly tenderness', but it was *The Examiner*, with a reference to 'the brave soul' shining through the pages of the novel, which reminded readers of the author's dramatic personal history.[14] As an epigram, Caroline Norton took the lines from Goethe's *Faust*: 'Mephistopheles: *Sie ist rerichtet*! She is lost! / Chorus of Angels: *Ist gerettet!* Is saved!'

In her dedicatory letter to another supportive friend, the Earl of Essex, Caroline Norton herself did not hold back from making personal comparisons. She had spent much time in the past at his house, Cassiobury in Hertfordshire, with its beautiful park where he entertained generously: one of the first places where croquet became a popular game to beguile guests. Caroline reminded Essex of jesting together about his notions of charm and perfection in a woman, and how she had promised to create a heroine to his requirements, and then 'bring her to grief' in a novel. Finally, she hopes that there will be a home for Beatrice Brooke (her heroine) 'in his sunny library at Cassiobury, as near to a window as he can!'. She also wishes that frequent slips of paper will be found among the pages, 'to mark the young borrowing it'.

It is clear from the first that the character of Beatrice has an element of self-portrayal about it. She is introduced as a dashing and romantic young lady, who appears at a party with seaweed in her long hair: 'a mermaid toilette', she calls it, in honour of the birthday of a sailor brother. Captain Michael Treherne, 'handsome like Apollo', and Beatrice fall in love at first sight. It is made clear that Beatrice feels more than most people: 'she suffered more, she felt more' and at the same time 'life thrilled her'.

Various disasters follow, and the whole principle of matrimonial law is introduced into the plot. Although *Lost and Saved* is very far from being a pamphlet, it still has a campaigning tinge to it. Treherne and Beatrice elope to Alexandria, and go through what seems to Beatrice to be a marriage ceremony, performed by a consular 'chaplain'. The trouble is that the handsome Treherne is not only heir to a title, whose current holder has no son: unfortunately, he is also in line to inherit the vast estates as well as the title, according to a very complicated Treherne family settlement, if he marries one of five daughters within the prescribed female line. Thus, Beatrice discovers that her 'marriage' was actually a fake, the 'chaplain' a fraud: their little boy Frank is therefore illegitimate.

Caroline Norton comments on Beatrice's naïveté regarding the bogus ceremony: 'If my readers think it positively ridiculous to suppose that an educated girl of seventeen would be fooled by such a ceremony' – where were the witnesses? – 'let them remember that this was a country where Gretna Green had only just ceased to be a "Hymeneal temple".' This meant, of course, that little Frank could not inherit the family title because his parents had not been married at the time of his birth.*

So, the scandal emerges of two people who are not actually married according to the law, living together as husband and wife. This enables Caroline Norton to have a stab at the hypocrisy of the scandalmongers, people who go to church and make

---

* By the laws of the English peerage today, even a child whose parents marry subsequent to its birth still cannot inherit a family title.

pious promises, then return home 'to sit in judgment on their neighbours'. Thus they fiercely condemn Beatrice, whose history is to them 'a sealed book'. The unfortunate Frank is a sickly child; when he dies, the world shrugs its shoulders with the indifferent reaction: 'He's better off dead.'

Beatrice herself continues to believe that the marriage was in fact sanctified in the eyes of God, if not of man. And she does not remarry, in her own eyes, until after the death of Treherne. 'I believed I *was* his wife, as firmly as I believed in God!' Then she is rewarded with a happy marriage to Count Sforza, and 'a dark-eyed robust babe', as well as stepmotherhood, admirably carried out in her case, to his daughter.

If Beatrice is the mother as victim, Myra Grey and her niece, Milly Teasdale, Treherne's mistress, are seductive women as villains, or rather as villainesses; Myra is a 'Hindoo', full of Eastern wiles, and Milly has only one irreproachable thing about her, her perfect taste in clothes.

But the real message that Caroline Norton intended to convey in the three-volume novel (apart from telling a dramatic and hopefully bestselling story) comes at the end. 'The poaching of a hare or pheasant is still occasionally punished with far greater rigour than the ruin of some despairing girl, or a savage assault on some despairing woman.' So long as the true distinction between right and wrong is not upheld, in favour of appearances, other women will suffer as Beatrice Brooke suffered. Caroline's indignation over the sufferings of women, expressed in her pamphlets, is fully present too in this novel.

For all its popularity, there was one shocking element in *Lost and Saved* by contemporary standards: the fact that Beatrice continued to live with her husband after it turned out they were not legally married. Then, after many tribulations, she was no longer 'lost' but 'saved'. There was public criticism to this effect, including the disapproval of reviewers. In the words of a modern commentator: 'That Beatrice, an abandoned lover and mother of an illegitimate child, subsequently finds happiness in marriage and motherhood was too much for Mrs. Grundy to accept.'[15]

At this point, Caroline turned to that other pen of hers, the pen of protest. And she wrote a letter to *The Times* complaining that the book was meant for adults, not children.[16] What was more, operas were equally immoral: indignantly, she cited plots of operas that were enacted to a happy public two or three times a week: elopement, seduction and incest were regular subjects. There remained a theory that virginal daughters, great novel-readers, should not be allowed to read such a book.

Apart from writing to live, Caroline also taught her grandchildren. She took the whole subject of their education extremely seriously. In Bournemouth at one point, she decided to let Richard learn German for one and a half hours a day, and then teach him French herself. After all, the long, sandy walks of Bournemouth would benefit him far more than trailing through the London streets. From time to time, naturally, there were ructions: when Caroline accused her grandson of tyrannizing over her, he replied, according to her account, 'Ah, you hyperbolish, Granny!' Perhaps it was the ceaseless storm holding them indoors – 'it causes us to yowl and skirl like sea fowl' – which was the problem.[17]

This was a life which varied between seaside resorts – those healthy sands for the children to walk or play on – and convenient country houses and castles where friends and relations were prepared to entertain them. Sadly, as time passed, Richard Norton's letters to William Stirling began to include references to Nonna's health. In 1864, for example, he wrote: 'My dear Mr. Stirling . . . Nonna is as usual, tho' she can hardly move about and opposite our hotel a house being pulled down causes dust.'[18]

Caroline, throughout all this, found the prospect of her son Brin succeeding either to his childless uncle or his father as Lord Grantley a kind of symbolic compensation for everything she had suffered in the past. She wrote to her close friend Emma Munro Ferguson from Keir in October 1865 to that effect, at a time when her brother-in-law Grantley was investigating legal devices which might have depleted Brin's inheritance. 'The long weary struggle of life, & effort to "do the best" for my poor young ones – has always had one gleam in it (like the light at the end of an arched cavern) – that *in all human probability* some day my Son would inherit the Peerage & a settled home – & we should all spend the fading Sunset of my cloudy day *in comfort together*.'[19]

George Norton, however, showed no signs of dying. In August 1865, the whole family went to York to see a tree planted in memory of Fletcher. Richard was visibly 'slendering' like a drawn-out telescope, and Caroline feared that the heat of London in the summer was unhealthy – cholera was an ever-present contemporary threat. So they lived on eggs and fowls, fearing the dairies and the beef of the butcher.

In 1865, two things happened to William Stirling, one of which was to have an immediate impact on Caroline's life, but not, as might have been feared, a disastrous one. As arranged, William Stirling was transformed into Sir William Stirling-Maxwell, Bt by the death of his maternal uncle on 6 June. And on 26 April he had married his distant cousin, Lady Anna Melville, daughter of the Earl of Leven and Melville.

Neither one of the newly married couple was remotely young by the standards of the time. Stirling-Maxwell, as he will now be called, was forty-seven, and Lady Anna (who had never been married before) was thirty-nine. She was described by Caroline as decidedly handsome, with delicate regular features, fair hair and 'high-bred gentle manners'. Fortunately, since she had married a garden as well as a man, Lady Anna loved flowers. Altogether the bride was 'very cheery and very kind'. In another tribute to a friend, Caroline commented on her eyes 'that have all the good promises of home life tenderly shining out of them'.[20]

Jokingly, Caroline told William that she now hoped to give up hinting about young girls in her immediate circle 'who could be transplanted to Keir'. More seriously, there is every reason to believe in Caroline's sincerity when she wrote to William wishing that 'in this strange life of trouble both you and your wife may find the best lot that can be drawn there'. After all, William, unlike Caroline with her 'wretched experience', had not lost 'the belief that home-love is the only true happiness for either man or woman'.[21]

In so far as this was a marriage dictated by the need for an heir, it was immediately a great success. Lady Anna gave birth to

John Stirling-Maxwell in June 1866, and Archibald Stirling (as the younger son remained) the year after that.

From the point of view of Caroline Norton and her grandchildren, all of whom had come to depend on the thoughtful kindness and hospitality of William Stirling, the married Sir William Stirling-Maxwell did not let them down. And his bride followed suit. The Nortons were still included in the home life tenderly shining out of Lady Anna's eyes. A remarkable sign of this continuing intimacy was in fact contained in Caroline's invitation to William, while Lady Anna was in labour with her first child. 'I shall not go to bed till I know whether you have a son or a daughter,' she wrote, even if it was four in the morning *like the Reform Bill* (of 1832). She even suggested he should come round and see her at this point. 'You can do no good there.'[22]

Obviously, the credit for this admirable development must be shared between the three people involved, the two old friends and above all Lady Anna. But the generous side of Caroline's character in this kind of situation had already been displayed in her reaction to Sidney Herbert's marriage, with an especially poignant letter to his widow after his death. It is as though, in both cases, she felt she had given her blessing to the match.

Caroline soon began writing to 'Dearest Lady Anna'. There were reflections on the lighter side of electioneering, as when Lady Anna's brother-in-law was elected for South Lanarkshire, and a torchlight procession and bonfire in his honour followed at his home Dalziel House. Caroline hoped the conflagration was not really a punishment for his wife Lady Emily 'because she refused to kiss fairly "some exigeant and threatening elector"'.[23] This was in part an allusion to a Scottish folk song and partly to the celebrated occasion in the 1784 election when Georgiana, Duchess of Devonshire, kissed Whig supporters in exchange for votes, including a coal heaver, receiving the equivocal compliment that he 'would light a pipe at her eyes'.*

Another batch of correspondence concerned the draping or otherwise of naked statues of cupids and satyrs: Caroline

---

* The story is generally told about the Duchess kissing a butcher.

Norton's basic point being how ridiculous the order to drape naked statues was, 'a sort of ragged lump over the thighs and graceful limbs'. More practical was the request for Lady Anna to ask the gardener to enquire of the carpenter the exact proportions of tubs for orange trees.[24] Caroline Norton was also invited to be godmother to little John Stirling-Maxwell, whom she nicknamed 'Don John'.

During a spell of illness abroad, she reflected how glad, in contrast, she always was to be in Scotland, since she continued to maintain the inestimable value of 'Scotch air' as the only air in which anyone felt really well. As for Lady Anna, her attitude was summed up as follows: 'Nothing can be kinder than what the children call "Stirling's *new* wife" (as if he had had several).'[25]

The Stirling-Maxwells' generosity to her family was reciprocated. During a visit to Brighton in 1869, on which he had taken the boys, William had to go up to London on business. Caroline cared for the children and reported with satisfaction: 'Archy adores me and makes the drollest little caresses, holding my face with both hands in long strokings intermingled with kisses. Johnny is looking lovely, the deepest shade of rose colour in his cheeks, but neglects me for Carlotta.' It is easy to understand the satisfaction that this happy mixing of William's children and her grandchildren brought to her; as she admitted in a subsequent letter: 'I cannot conquer the dreadful instinctive yearning of my motherhood. I am always sighing for my vanished imaginary children.'[26]

William Stirling-Maxwell was still her court of appeal for help over the problems of her life, which, as a member of the Norton family, tended to be financial. This was notably over Fletcher's will and the complication of Victoria Penelli. Caroline did not hesitate to continue those demands for services on his part which would make her life more bearable. He was commissioned to buy her an oval clock. And, in another missive, to go into his library, 'where my valuable works repose', and calculate the number of words on a typical page of one of her novels. Both grandchildren also felt included, Carlotta recalling the 'special little caresses' which were her share of attention from Lady Anna, and Richard sending his 'topmost love'.[27]

This rotating life of hotels and castles and family houses and grandchildren was punctuated by great sadness when Helen, the charming middle sister of the Sheridan 'Three Graces', formerly Dufferin, now Countess of Gifford, fell ill. Although, in past years, the sisters might have disagreed, with Helen disapproving of Caroline's unhelpful passion for accosting the press, there was no doubt about the true grief of Caroline on her death – at the age of sixty, of breast cancer, having survived her second husband by five years. Relations with Georgia had soured too, although the death of Georgia's own son Edward St Maur in 1869 brought them closer.

Caroline dedicated the next product of Nonna's pen to Helen in honour of 'that unequalled companionship' broken by death. To her son, the present Lord Dufferin, she wrote: 'it is a melancholy pleasure to me to remember that she read and warmly praised some of it, during her last illness.' There was an appropriate epigraph from Robert Bulwer-Lytton, son of the celebrated Bulwer Lytton:

> The winds of change afflict us. What today
> We tether tight, tomorrow whirls away.

This novel was *Old Sir Douglas*, which was serialized in *Macmillan's Magazine*, a useful financial deal, and later also in an American magazine.[28] In book form it was published in three volumes in 1867 when Caroline Norton was fifty-nine.

The splendidly challenging opening lines of the book, however, appear to rejoice in the passing of the years: 'There is no example of human beauty more perfectly picturesque than a very handsome man of middle age.' Caroline goes on: 'No, smiling reader, not even a very handsome young man: not even that same man in his youth. The gain is in the expression, of which every age has its own; and perhaps there is more change in that than in the features, under the working hand of Time.' It is true that she is talking about the male sex, but Caroline Norton continues to expatiate on the charm of the middle-aged man: 'The smile of welcome in such a man's countenance is worth all the beauty of his adolescent years.' And if there should be any of her readers who refuse to become converts to 'such an unusual doctrine', that is because they never saw the man his tenants and relations familiarly called 'Old Sir Douglas'.

It turns out that Sir Douglas Ross of Glenrossie was called that even before the first silver thread appeared in his dark and thickly curled hair: 'chiefly, as it seemed, because everybody else was so young'. His mother had died young, leaving his father a widower at the age of twenty-five; he proceeded to wed 'the heiress of Toulmains, a very stiff and starched successor to the blooming and passionate girl he had laid in her grave'. The second Lady Ross, whose principal efforts are directed at repressing 'the sin of liveliness', clearly owes a lot to the character of Margaret Vaughan, George Norton's odious cousin who had been entrusted with the care of Caroline's sons during the dark years.

The 'kilted little lads', Douglas and Kenneth, are horribly punished, and even their terriers (described as 'four-footed plagues' by Lady Ross) are mistreated. Running away is the obvious reaction. Eventually Kenneth vanishes, is not seen in adulthood, but dies acknowledging a wife, Maggie, and little Kenneth as his son; making of course Douglas his uncle.

After that the plot is extremely complicated, at times positively grim, but the prevailing theme is the jealousy aroused by women who are beautiful and virtuous in other women who are neither. Gertrude is the beloved wife of Sir Douglas, but a wicked step sister-in-law Alice, daughter of the evil Lady Ross, manages to cast Gertrude's reputation in doubt for a terrible two-year span in the marriage. At least the book ends with Douglas and Gertrude happy in Glenrossie, in contrast to Alice, who ends up in a lonely garret in a stony house.

So good triumphs. As a result, when Queen Victoria had finished the book, she noted in her Journal that it was 'a most remarkable book, full of the most beautiful feelings, both religious and moral'. Her reaction, incidentally, has an unwittingly ironic element; Macmillan's and Caroline had clashed over the serialization, as to whether certain passages were actually offensive to the Crown.[29]

Only once more, at the end of the book, do the happy couple Sir Douglas and Gertrude glimpse Wicked Alice, on their way to some 'pleasant visit' near Inverness: 'There, in the grey evening, a spare figure stood motionless, gazing out on the dim colourless ocean: then waving its hands a moment as in some aching despair, it disappeared.'

It is as though Caroline Norton, in her last novel, managed to dismiss all those cruel, spare figures who had tortured her and her reputation for much of her adult life. Alice, daughter of the wicked stepmother, is 'Alone now. Alone forever.' Sir Douglas and Gertrude, on the contrary, are 'once again, in the glowing light of reconciled love, and the glorious autumn sunshine . . . talking of the past and future, with voices full of gladness and eyes serene with peace'. While it did not now seem likely that Caroline Norton's story would end with quite such gladness, it was to be hoped that at least her eyes would be serene with peace.

CHAPTER SIXTEEN

Floated Away from Shore

'My Ideal of death, probably what is really felt in conscious death, is very like being floated away from shore, in a dream.'

Caroline Norton to William Stirling, 30 December 1876

'I THINK IT WAS CLEVER of Disraeli to resign *now* and not after a little vain spirit of resistance to the present condition of parties.' That was Caroline Norton's verdict on the General Election of 1868, in a letter to Lady Anna Stirling-Maxwell, the Tories having been soundly defeated.[1] Over the years, Caroline did not lose that interest in politics which she had maintained throughout her adult life. It had reached one kind of peak at the time of her association with Lord Melbourne, and its political peak with the Infant Custody Bill. Her frequent travels broadened her horizon. Garibaldi, for example, elicited her admiration. Inspired no doubt by the Italian patriot's visit to Britain in 1864, she was moved to write verse celebrating his gallant campaign in the cause of his country's liberation.*

---

* Garibaldi was the subject of a Victorian cult, culminating in this visit, whose female members were particularly enthusiastic according to the Manchester *Guardian*.[2]

Garibaldi! Garibaldi!
Roused to just anger by his Country's wrong
In his own suffering, patient, brave and strong
Lovers of justice, make his welcome sure!
Deeds he hath done that keep his claim secure
In every heart that feels what's grand, and true, and
    pure . . .

In 1868, Caroline Norton could claim friendship with both leaders of the contending parties. There was William Gladstone for the Liberals: a merging of the old Whigs with more radical elements had led to this name replacing that of Whig as the alternative party.* The death of Lord Palmerston and retirement of Lord John Russell had led to Gladstone's emergence as leader.

As for Disraeli, that light-hearted prediction that Caroline had made when he was in his twenties – that he would turn into 'a *nasty* Tory' – had turned out to be accurate (if we leave out the pejorative adjective which came, after all, from a confirmed Whig). Benjamin Disraeli rose up among the Conservatives.† He became Prime Minister in February 1868, following the retirement of Lord Derby.

So the man who had once referred romantically to Caroline as 'Starry Night' was pitched against the man of whom she now said admiringly: 'Would that I could write as he speaks – and speak as he writes.' The election itself took place in the wake of a new campaign for parliamentary reform, leading to the 1867 Enfranchisement Act and a vast increase in middle-class voters. The effects were seen immediately. The result was a sweeping victory for the Liberals: 387 seats to 271 for the Conservatives.

Gladstone was cutting down a tree with an axe at Hawarden when the telegram came telling him to expect a messenger from Windsor. The Queen's letter was straightforward: 'Mr. Disraeli has tendered his resignation to the Queen. The result of the

---

* The traditional date of the change is June 1859.

† As the former Tory Party was known since the 1830s, although the word Tory persisted and persists in a way Whig did not.

appeal to the country is too evident to require its being by a vote in parliament . . . Under these circumstances, the Queen must ask Mr. Gladstone, as acknowledged leader of the liberal party, to undertake the formation of a new administration.'[3]

Caroline Norton's correspondence with Gladstone did not cease with his elevation. To his great credit – as she hastened to say – he replied to a request of hers three weeks later: 'I consider that in the midst of all your triumphant occupations, thinking of your promise . . . is only paralleled by the Emperor of the French writing me a note the morning of the Coup d'État about some papers I had asked for from the archives.'[4]*

There was another vigorous campaign for reform following the election. Unlike the previous reforming campaign for the 1867 Act, which was for male suffrage only – there had been, of course, no females voting in the 1868 election – in this campaign the plight of women was considered, specifically married women. The first of several Married Women's Property Acts was passed in 1870. Wages and property which a wife earned or inherited would now be regarded as her own. The new Act did not accomplish all that women might want: for example, it was not retroactive. But it did abolish the dreaded idea of couverture, which maintained that a married woman did not exist – only her husband existed – as Caroline Norton had pointed out indignantly so long ago.

This time, Caroline took no active part in the campaigning. Her part had already been played: she provided a glaring example of injustice which could always be quoted without fear of contradiction. Barbara Bodichon was the leading figure and she was already promoting the vital next step of female suffrage. Following previous publications on women's causes, her *Reasons for the Enfranchisement of Women* had been published in 1866. But Caroline was not quite done with public commentaries of a sort.

---

* Louis-Napoleon's coup on 2 December 1851 resulted in the destruction of the Second Republic and its replacement by a new regime.

There continued to be poems and other contributions to *Macmillan's Magazine*. She wrote songs – 'some succeed and some don't and no one can tell why' – of which an early one, 'Juanita', originally intended for Brinsley to sing to his guitar, was notably successful; Caroline got into the usual arguments with publishers, music publishers this time such as Chappell, over questions of payment, needing as ever to maximize her profits. In 1874, she would issue the privately printed pamphlet *Taxation by an Irresponsible Taxpayer*. As Caroline described it to Emma Munro Ferguson, it was 'a brochure written in my anger at tax gatherers in London – it is circulated but not published – a very slender difference'.[5]

The friendships which had been so important to her throughout her life continued. After all, even in her sixties Caroline Norton was 'indomitably handsome and witty', as reported to her old friend Fanny Kemble by someone who had recently met her. It was this combination of qualities which continued to make her remarkable: the striking looks with the 'deep lustrous eyes', her reputation as a survivor – and her jokes.[6]

One such friend was Robert Bulwer-Lytton, son of Bulwer Lytton and his wife Rosina, whose own marriage had ended disastrously; Robert succeeded his father as Lord Lytton in 1873. As with William Stirling-Maxwell, there are frequent references to Lytton's wife and children: 'I was glad to see your handwriting again!' Caroline wrote in November 1874, '& the only disappointment was your next speaking of yourself – the children & the sweet Wife!'[7] (Lytton had married Lady Edith Villiers and they proceeded to have seven children.) Lytton was a diplomat who had already served, among other places, in Florence, Vienna, Paris and Lisbon.

Two years later, when he was appointed Viceroy of India, Disraeli observed: 'We wanted a man of ambition, imagination, some vanity and much will and we have got him.' Lytton also wrote poetry under the name of Owen Meredith. Caroline further consulted Lytton about Richard's education and whether Dresden would be a good place to wind up with a year in Germany. He reminded her of the happy early times with Fletcher, to whom he had been a friend.

She now consulted him about her pamphlet on taxation. In doing so, she encapsulated her own position about campaigning – or not campaigning. 'I know Lord Napier thought as you do – that private and public grievances should be kept separate – but other friends thought with me, that this chance of being *read* was increased by the connection of my points with the public grievance.' Referring to his own family scandal, she admitted: 'It is very difficult for you, dear Lytton, who were yourself the child of a broken home, to judge much, or in what way these miseries should be alluded to.'[8]

She admitted that she would rather talk to him than discuss it on paper, and where the dredging up of her past was concerned, she had her grandchildren to consider. All the same, Caroline remained defiant in her belief in the need to speak up: sometimes 'the larger view' had to be considered, 'not so much because these things have happened to *me*' but so that 'they may never happen again to other women!'.

Caroline Norton's life in her sixties was marred by rapidly declining health. In the past, there had been pains in the head, and rheumatic pains. Now everything got worse. There were collapses, periods of illness, often abroad, and often resulting in family difficulties if she was in charge of youngsters. The 'detestable headaches' which had plagued her since her thirties increased and were bad enough to cause real difficulties when reading or writing. There had also been episodes of spitting blood, which, with the hovering shadow of consumption, led to natural anxiety.

She was therefore feeling weak, if still spirited, when the curtain went up on the last act of her life. The grandchildren were basically a pleasure for all the inevitable problems. But lurking in the wings, as ever, was the villain of the piece, George Norton, still after all these years her legal husband. Her surviving son Brin was the rogue element. His own health was not good, whether due to hereditary illness or an unsatisfactory way of life or a combination of the two. The marriage to Mariucca waxed and waned, unlike the charming Mariucca herself, who waxed in every sense of the word, not only enlarging physically but prospering in her beloved native Capri.

Brin's own relationship with his father, of whom he was the destined heir (as neither side ever forgot), was also troubled. In January 1868, Caroline received from him, then in Capri, a registered envelope tied with green ribbon. She had hoped for a will, in view of the complicated family situation, with Brin's own health, the future of his son Richard, and George's expectations from Grantley all involved. It was '*not* what I hoped', as she told Stirling-Maxwell, but seventeen sheets of writing, covering 'his own fancies' including the politics of Europe. Later in the year, he had a row with his father about signing the custody of his children to him and flounced off to Capri.

All of this concentrated Caroline's mind on the fact that she had come to a crisis about 'my dear soft cubs'. Richard needed to go to school as his father, his grandfather and his ancestors had done. As might be expected, George Norton created as much trouble as he could, telling Caroline by letter that he had Brin's authority to send Richard to Eton, and that both children were now to stay with him. Caroline simply ignored his letter.

She told Stirling-Maxwell that George Norton's whole plan was to vex her. Caroline, personally, was *not* against Eton (remember the fresh air on the banks of the river, which she had extolled at the time Brin went there), but she knew that if she had suggested Eton, Norton would have chosen Harrow; if she had then agreed to Harrow, he would have chosen Rugby.[9] So Richard Norton went to Harrow in 1870, when he was fourteen.

He was a clever boy and his odd, fragmented upbringing helped in some respects. For example, by the age of seven he had been able to find out the direction of the wind from a newspaper, with William Stirling's sailing in mind, as his mother proudly told her friend. By 1871, he was top of his form at Harrow. Nowadays, his troubles with his grandmother were not about work but about smoking. This timeless dispute was complicated by the fact that there was no specific law against smoking at Harrow; boys caught drinking were punished more severely.[10]

It was in vain that Caroline pointed out two things in her most reasonable mode. On the one hand, if it was a small thing to ask, then it was a small thing to give up. On the other hand, if it was a great thing to give up, then surely no sacrifice was too great for him to make – considering how much she herself had sacrificed for his education. But at the end of it all, Richard simply refused to give up smoking. Caroline confided to Stirling-Maxwell that 'a certain taint of Nortonism' made Richard think that what she, 'only a woman', said was 'of not so much importance'.[11] (Although here Caroline's own prejudices about George Norton were surely responsible for elevating the natural irritation of a teenager into something of more consequence.)

In due course, Richard Norton left Harrow and enjoyed a succession of tutors for a period. Despite promises, bills for tobacco continued to come in with remarkable frequency. Then, in 1874, he went on a tour of Europe. Carlotta, in the meantime, was accorded the traditional girl's education of lessons via various governesses, music lessons and so forth, in her case backed up by lessons from her grandmother. Caroline herself, of course, had been sent away to school; it is probable, however, that she remembered that period of schooling as a kind of rejection, quite apart from the part it played in bringing about her disastrous marriage.

Carlotta at this point, in the frank estimation of her grandmother, had no ear for music, no grace for dancing and no skills for working, although work she would inevitably have to do. She would have to seek 'a situation', as a companion to a gentlewoman perhaps, such as 'the lady who lives with Baroness Rothschild'. In appearance, Carlotta was short and her feet were said to be rather clumsy – but then Newfoundland puppies had clumsy paws which became shapely and proportionate once they were dogs. In accordance with her Italian blood, her complexion was quite dark: when she was eleven, she was reported to be blooming and darkening daily 'like a hedge blackberry'. A more imaginative comparison was made about the same time by a friend of Caroline who said that Carlotta looked like a child of St John Baptist, during the period he lived on locusts and wild honey.[12]

To make up for it all, Carlotta was good as gold and both sensible and helpful. When she was twelve years old she had chosen a thimble with 'Constancy' engraved on it, and asked her brother to read 'an extract about *Love*' after tea, thinking it must be time for her to be thinking about such things, 'and I rather like stories about Lovers'.[13] In fact, she would choose constancy in life, as time would show, if not exactly the constancy she had envisaged when she was a child.

It was an earlier perception that Carlotta had when she was six, as reported by her grandmother to William Stirling, which would prove the significant one. 'Carlotta suddenly addressed me yesterday thus: "it has come into my mind that we think we are sitting still and walking flat – but in reality we are all going *up* to Heaven or *down* to hell.' Caroline for her part regretted that as little Carlotta had so little to attract the love of men in general, it was sad she didn't have that of her father.[14]

Then Death struck. But this time it was not one of Caroline's children. Nor indeed her own death, which in view of the perilous state of her health must always have been a possibility. It was Lady Anna Stirling-Maxwell, who was the victim of an appalling accident. An epileptic fit caused her to fall into the fireplace at Keir. She suffered hideous burns. A few days later, on 8 December 1874, she died. The ideal marriage of Sir William and Lady Anna had lasted less than ten years; their boys Johnny and Archy were seven and six respectively.

Caroline's letter to the bereaved husband came from the heart: 'I do not try to comfort, but I do give as deep a sympathy as one human being ever felt for another.' She stressed how the boys would help him bear it. Then she reflected: 'How the *earthly* storm of grey snow and cloud has melted with peace today. It is so with her – believe it.' Caroline looked at the clock that the Stirling-Maxwells had given her: 'and often and often shall I look at its dumb face, and think, how far better *she* spent her hours'.[15]

Two more deaths followed, neither of which, in contrast, Caroline mourned in any way. Furthermore, from her point of view the deceased died in the wrong order. George Norton died on 1 March 1875. He had recently been in correspondence with Caroline over a monument to their dead son Willie, evoking memories of that saddest time. The last vindictive thing that

George Norton did to Caroline Norton, as she might have put it, was to die shortly before his elder brother. Certainly, her reaction expressed to William Stirling-Maxwell was bitter enough: 'He dies in that cruel brother's house, pre-deceasing him and I am here with my forlorn wreck, his last surviving son of those quarrelled over children and next heir to the title.'[16] As might have been expected, arrangements over his will and Brin's inheritance were complicated and not necessarily beneficial to his heir. Six months later, Lord Grantley himself died at Wonersh in Surrey, where Caroline had first encountered George Norton. Thus, the Grantley title, to which George had looked forward for many years, passed directly to her son Brinsley Norton, who became the 4th Lord Grantley on 28 August 1875.

Caroline's state of health did not improve. In all this time, her whole correspondence was dotted with reports on its decline, especially that 'churchyard' rheumatic gout plaguing her, so that she found it difficult to get out of a bath, and had to slide out of bed by hauling on a cloth tied to the bedpost.[17] In May 1876, she was confined to bed for eight weeks; and in August that year 'mown down' once again by rheumatic gout. On this occasion she added a cheerful note: 'but they swear I shall skip like a ram by Monday'.[17] The cheerfulness did not last. In the autumn, Carlotta described 'poor Granny's' need for a professional nurse. Caroline was enduring such terrible pain in her spine and the left side of her heart that she told William: 'I really was inclined to howl like a dog with pain.' Carlotta continued her gloomy reports. Her grandmother's hands were crippled so that she could not write, and when they recovered, the ailment went to her 'great joints', so that she could neither get out of bed nor stand. By December 1876, Caroline was telling William that her ideal of death was probably what is really felt in conscious death, 'very like being floated away from shore, in a dream'.[18]

At some point it all became too much. Not too much for Caroline Norton, even if she was beginning to long for the dream of floating away. But too much for William, the generous-hearted, protective, kindly man who had been her benefactor for so long.

On 19 February 1877, Caroline Norton wrote a letter to her cousin William Le Fanu, the great Irish railway engineer. It began once again with a recital of her sufferings, how, after six months of 'grunting and groaning' with rheumatism, she could not even sign her name – although Carlotta made an excellent secretary. It appeared to be yet another health report, and a grim one at that. The next paragraph changed the tone utterly: 'You will be surprised in this doleful account of my Condition, to hear that I have promised to marry Sir William Stirling on the 1st March.'[19]

It was true. Let Caroline Norton tell the story in her own words: 'We have been friends since *1848(!)* and never has he swerved from good & gracious acts to me and mine & now he has wished, for the sake of his boys – (& our own sakes) – to make one home for such brief time as God may see fit to accord me, of peace and happiness, – and after my long life of struggle and torment!' She added: 'We were long wavering – discussing, – but it is quite fixed now.' It might seem '*supernaturally*' late in life to her, who was still in her teens when she got married to George Norton, 'still if it adds to *his* happiness the opinion of others ought not to touch me, more than "the wind that bloweth where it listeth"' (she quoted St John's Gospel).

Although this marriage between a widow and a widower, evidently long debated, owed a great deal to the perilous state of Caroline's health, it was still a generous and romantic gesture on William's side, and on her side the grateful, even ecstatic acceptance of that protection she had always sought, always felt denied. In spite of, or perhaps because of the difference in their ages, this was a romantic match in a way that her first youthful marriage had never been.

She now refused to worry about '*settlements*' and how she might be left, after all his kindness to her. She needed nothing but 'the *hope of contenting you hereafter*'. The pain did not go away – how could it? But she was able to address 'Beloved Husband' and bless him for '*the past* and the hope that rose for a *future* however brief'. Significantly, she added: 'I bless your children.'[20] Caroline Stirling-Maxwell intended to be the very reverse of the wicked stepmother.

The actual ceremony was evidently a problem given Caroline's bedridden state, and the medical men feared for the effects of a cold church on the frail bride. The solution was a ceremony by special licence in Caroline's house, after a certain amount of fuss from the local rector of St James's, Piccadilly: 'I cannot say what is usual in such cases, for I have only had one in the whole of my incumbency.' He stressed the need for an authorized official to attend with the register to make it legal. Caroline herself was 'mortified in the extreme at not being able to go down stairs or walk'. Under the circumstances, it was agreed that there should be no lavish party, but that 'my husband' should receive the two clergymen and she should do nothing but 'rest and order 5 o'clock tea for my ladies'. Among the tea things was a set of Irish china which was the Le Fanus' wedding present: 'greatly was the delicate ware from Erin admired!'[21]

Caroline now moved to William's house at 10 Upper Grosvenor Street, not far from her previous home in Chesterfield Street: 'my new address', as she proudly told Henrietta Le Fanu.[22] She also told Henrietta that the fact that all this happiness and peace was coming 'very, *very* late in life' increased, rather than diminished, her gratitude. She spoke of being ashamed of 'one's name, for *years, and years, and years*, of cruel alienation!'. Now she had suddenly changed to 'real "*Home*", real love': Henrietta would hardly wonder that 'I have accepted my good lot and *cling to the Giver.*'[23]

To William on his birthday on 8 March, Caroline wrote a poem which made a pleasingly open reference to the difference in their ages:[24]

> Let me live on – to hear thee call me wife
> But I say, blest be every fleeting morn
> Since first Fate welcomed thee to cradled life
> And taking note of me – though earlier born –
> Let me live on, to hear thee call me wife.

Caroline Stirling-Maxwell did live on; for a short while. Even now, there were some traces of the unhappy past, and that scandal-mongering which had caused her such pain. To William, she complained of being treated as if she had caused him to elope with her from his marital home. She had thought that '*all insult was over* when you gave me your honoured name (which has only respect and distinction attached to it) in lieu of the one that I bore as a clouded burden linked with bitterness, alienation by *a mockery of fame*'. She concluded: 'I am under *your protection* now. Let me lean on that. I will deserve it. God bless you.' There was just a little hint of the old Caroline when she promised not to write to the papers if he did not wish it: the least she could do was acknowledge his 'headship'. But she pointed out that she hadn't written to *The Times*, or anywhere else, since Brin became Lord Grantley.[25]

On 11 March she wrote to William as 'Beloved Husband', giving details of a will she had drawn up: 'Do see to my Carlotta's interests.' But the important section came at the end: her gratitude: 'I have my heart so full of your generosity and goodness – your tender comforting words since I came – (crawling, an infirm creature!) to this home of peace & rest – are such a balm to me even in this dark hour of expectation and sinking down from it into death – that I do not know in what words to put my gratitude.' She concluded: 'O my dear, farewell. Your poor unfit but most loving wife.'[26]

Arrangements were duly made. Her will, which Caroline specifically wanted to be under her new name, made 'my beloved Husband' and Carlotta her executors. Everything was left to Carlotta, as she had always intended. She had specified that she wanted to be buried at Frampton, home of the Brinsley Sheridans, where she had found refuge so often. That was crossed out and in a frail hand the word 'Keir' was inserted.

Caroline, now Lady Stirling-Maxwell, lived for three months after the wedding. The death certificate would give the cause of her decease as 'catarrh, a weak jaundice and five days local peritonitis'. Sir William annotated a letter of 10 June 1877: 'The last lines I ever received from my beloved Caroline . . . the Sunday before she died. It is characteristic of her in every way – of her thoughts for others & her feelings-failings.' She referred tenderly to his boys as 'demi-godlings', the nickname she had given them long ago, and declared her intention of getting up 'out of the way of my maid's Sunday'.[27]

In his own Diary Sir William wrote a touching account of her death: 'And so it went on through the night, the dear small face more and more drawn and hollow.' It ended with serenity: 'Her last expressed thoughts were those of care for us. "Kiss me dear and go to bed." were the last words I could recognise.' To satisfy Caroline, he went briefly out of the room, before returning silently to sit with her and watch as the daylight softly dawned; and about the same time her breathing ceased.[28]

Caroline Stirling-Maxwell, once more the married woman, died at the age of sixty-nine on 15 June 1877. But her married state was different. She was now what she had never been, a happily married woman, loved and honoured. She died with these words as her motto: 'I am under *your protection* now. Let me lean on that. I will deserve it. God bless you.'

In Caroline's family, the melancholy toll of deaths continued. On 24 July 1877, her surviving son Brinsley died of consumption. At least Caroline had the dubious consolation of dying before the last of her three children. Thus, her grandson Richard Norton became, in turn, the 5th Lord Grantley.

Nor did Sir William Stirling-Maxwell long survive his wife. In January 1878, he took his stepdaughter Carlotta back to Capri to see if they could assist her mother Mariucca, now a widow. On his way home, in Venice, Sir William contracted typhoid fever. He died on 15 January at the age of fifty-nine. It was discovered in the last century that, far from being buried abroad, as once thought, his body had been returned to Scotland. Caroline's body had also been taken to Scotland – the land where she felt at peace. Sir William had described her funeral on 21 June in his Diary as 'a bright and lovely longest day, the rhododendrons and redthorns out in all their first pinkness, the place looking just as my dear Caroline always desired to see it and for often as she had been here, she had never seen Keir in all its summer glory.'[29] Sir William is buried in the crypt of the Stirling family church at

Lecropt, alongside Lady Anna – and Caroline, born Sheridan, Norton for most of her life and, at the very end of it, contentedly Stirling-Maxwell.

The grandchildren of Caroline, in contrast to their father Brin, had long lives. Richard, who did receive the Grantley inheritance, including five houses, in 1877, died in 1943; at times his was a raffish existence, beginning with an affair with his own cousin's American wife, and the birth of a son to them, very shortly after they succeeded in getting married. His second marriage began with an elopement – in true Sheridan style – while his first wife was still alive. He was cited in a divorce case in the year of his death, aged eighty-seven, some hundred years after Lord Melbourne underwent the same experience.[30]

Carlotta, on the other hand, who died at the age of seventy-eight in 1931, discovered that constancy which she had seen engraved on a thimble as a child. Her nephew, who wrote his Memoirs, remembered her well as 'a saint on earth, and the least worldly woman in its truest sense that I have ever known'.[31] The granddaughter of Caroline Norton spent nearly all her life as a deaconess, devoting fourteen or fifteen hours a day to visiting those in trouble in her district, and giving all her money to the poor. When Carlotta died, for fifty-one years she had never worn any dress other than her simple deaconess's uniform.

One of the Little Hinges

*'From time immemorial, changes in the laws of nations have
been brought about by individual examples of oppression.
Such examples cannot be unimportant, for they are, and ever
will be, the little hinges on which the great doors of justice
are made to turn.'*

Caroline Norton, *Letter to the Queen*, 1855

CAROLINE NORTON'S DEATH EVOKED A generous letter
of condolence from Queen Victoria: she was writing to Helen's
son Lord Dufferin, a distinguished public servant who was
currently Governor-General of Canada. The Queen described
Caroline as 'one of the most gifted as well as the handsomest of
women and who had many fine qualities'. She died 'just when
her troubled and stormy life seemed to have entered a safe
haven'.[1] Lady Stirling-Maxwell, as Caroline Norton had become
in the last months of her life, was evidently far removed from
that other married woman, forty years earlier, whose citation for
adultery with the Queen's beloved Prime Minister Melbourne
had scandalized all London, including the youthful Queen
herself.

It was her nephew Lord Dufferin who would speak up for
Caroline after her death when George Meredith published his

novel *Diana of the Crossways*. This was based on the premise that Caroline Norton had sold information derived from Sidney Herbert to John Delane, editor of *The Times*. When the novel was published eight years after Caroline's death in 1885, Dufferin issued a strong statement in the *St James's Gazette* blaming Lord Aberdeen, not Caroline Norton, for the leak, and persuading Aberdeen's private secretary to confirm this information in the *Edinburgh Review*.[2] There was further trouble a few years later when the Anglo-Irish politician Sir William Gregory repeated the scandal in his Memoirs, edited after his death by his widow Augusta, Lady Gregory. But Dufferin did manage to secure a retraction by Meredith in future editions of *Diana of the Crossways*, to the effect that the Corn Laws slur was 'a fiction'.

Although the novel continued to preserve the image of a beautiful, wilful woman, one who aroused much jealousy in her peers, Meredith's Diana was not a mother. It is impossible to consider the life – and career – of Caroline Norton without taking the issue of motherhood into consideration. Thus, motherhood and loss permeate her work.

She was destined to undergo this loss in two quite different ways. The first was when she was legally deprived of access to her three children after the failed case against Melbourne. Caroline, the married woman who was their mother, understood that this would not have happened if the children had been illegitimate: the custody of bastards lay with their mothers, an anomaly which showed up the full hypocrisy as well injustice of the law. The second loss was the tragic death of Willie Norton aged nine as a result of an accident when under his father's care; it was said he died calling for his mother.

'Fame is the spur', in the words of Milton.[3] But with Caroline Norton, fame was not the spur, although she was by no means averse to it: it was loss which spurred her on, and loss in these two separate, these two cruel ways. Loss turned her into a campaigner, and one who was prepared to use her personal circumstances in any way she could, particularly her gift of writing, to protest against injustice and press for reform.

None of this prevented her from having a rich, private life and enjoying to the full the advantages of wit and beauty, a combination which, as George Meredith said, gave a woman power. Flirtatiousness – or at any rate a strong wish to please men – was part of her stock in trade as everyone agreed, whether in praise or blame. It is, however, noticeable that Caroline showed herself attracted to men of idealism, or at any rate men of political ideas and energy, beginning with Lord Melbourne. Two romances, with Sidney Herbert and the young William Stirling, showed that a clever man could entrance her – particularly a handsome, clever, young man.

Nor should her extremely active life as a writer be forgotten: articles for magazines, some of which she edited, poems, novels, streamed forth as well as her campaigning pamphlets. Many of them were written not so much for money as an end in itself as to support herself and her family; the flirtatious Caroline Norton, with her seductive eyelids and curvaceous lips, her magical low voice, was also a hard-working writer who bargained with publishers because the nature of the sum made a real difference to her.

Towards the end of her life, the sheer charm of Caroline Norton had not withered, but altered. Something more distanced, more dignified, the result of life's tragedies, had taken its place. The obituary in *The Athenaeum* singled out for praise *Stuart of Dunleath* (1851) and *Old Sir Douglas* (1867) as 'incomparably the best fruits of her inventive genius', together with 'her eloquent pleadings for that is weak in right and unacknowledged in good'. But the obituary then drew attention to the fact that although 'nothing could be simpler or more direct, nothing more tender and noble than her ordinary conversation', 'as a result of her sufferings the iron had entered her soul, and every now and then there was a spice of mockery or scorn bitter as wormwood.'[4]

The indulgent words of Mary Shelley when Caroline was in her twenties, that it was impossible not to go '*tousy-mousy*' for Mrs Norton, were no longer applicable. Now someone nobler and more serious had emerged. This was someone it was possible to love and honour, as William Stirling established so romantically at the very end to the woman who replied simply: Let me hear you call me wife.

Where her political campaigning was concerned, she summed up her feelings in *English Laws for Women in the Nineteenth Century*: 'I desire to prove, not my own suffering or his injustice, but that the present law of England cannot prevent any such suffering or control any such injustice.' The position of the husband at the time of Caroline's marriage was well expressed in *Stuart of Dunleath*: 'Everything that's yours is mine. The law doesn't admit a married woman to a farthing's worth of property.' This was what she believed must change.

As for the contempt that certain men would feel for Caroline Norton (to which she might have added – certain women also), it was of more importance that the law should be altered than that she should be approved. 'Many a woman may live to thank Heaven that I had the courage and energy left to attempt the task.'

As a result, Caroline Norton made a real contribution to two causes that subsequent generations have come to take for granted: infant custody rights for the mother, and property rights for the married woman. The one has been described as the first piece of feminist legislation, and the other is symbolized by Caroline's inability to sign a lease for Chesterfield Street, while in fact she was quite as able to support herself as a man in a similar profession. Campaigners are not necessarily seen as saintly people to their contemporaries who disagree with them. As Caroline told Lord Lytton, sometimes painful events had to be aired, not so much because these things had happened to *her* but so that they might never happen again to other women.

This is where Caroline's courage comes in. Given that the verdict in the case was innocent, whereupon George Norton behaved as if she had been found guilty, it would have been easy for her to accept her fate. A period of submission would have followed, endurance of a bout of physical violence perhaps, and continuance as they were before, an unhappy married couple with three children. Domestic violence, incidentally, meant that she could identify with all women, including working-class women.

Although her sisters and others disapproved of some of her actions – in the modern phrase, they believed that she sought the oxygen of publicity – Caroline Norton refused to be typecast. She was not to be defined as the Girl of the Period: a frivolous creature 'whose sole idea of life is plenty of fun and luxury', having done away with such 'moral muffishness' as consideration for others. These were the words of Elizabeth Lynn Linton, the novelist and feminist, in the *Saturday Review* of 1868.[5] As for the question of publicity, she was not afraid to confront it. Women who had the 'true woman's lot' of being unknown out of their home circle might thank God for that blessing: 'But for me publicity is no longer a matter of choice.' It was indeed this fearlessness in speaking up and speaking out from youth onwards which led to the accusation that Caroline Norton was 'mannish', despite her obvious enjoyment of her own femininity.

Not only did she not submit in private: she also made public her anger. She used all her political contacts, and above all her agile pen, to tread boldly forward in protest. Caroline found early on that she had the gift of writing in a cause. She looked on her pen, as she once said, as a soldier looked on his sword, and to the end prided herself on using it: not for herself alone, as she made clear again and again, but for all women. After all, the injustice was towards all women. And she never forgot the women of the poor, who were frequently blamed for faults which were in fact the result of lack of education or material advantage generally. Several of her works make that clear: *The Lady of la Garaye* and *A Voice from the Factories*, for example. In the same way, her stories feature characters who would now be called disabled, then 'crippled', and mixed-race when the word 'brown' was used. She sympathized with the movement against slavery – that 'accursed thing' – as several of her pamphlets make clear. *English Laws for Women*, for example, stresses the hideous treatment of slave women and children. In short, along with courage, Caroline Norton had compassion, arguably the two most important human qualities.

Above all Caroline Norton sought justice. This was where the mixture of courage and compassion led her. It began with justice for herself, and moved towards justice for women, and a demand for their 'protection' in the future. Daniel Maclise chose to paint her as the figure of Justice, a dominating female with huge dark eyes cast upwards, holding a pair of scales. On either side of her are angels; one of the figures below is an emancipated slave and another is a symbolic child. Although at the time when no justice had been done to her Maclise's use of her figure was seen as a fearful irony, it now seems appropriate.

Caroline Norton would have been happy to personify Justice. As it was, she described her own significance in her *Letter to the Queen* of 1855. It is a verdict we can accept: 'From time immemorial, changes in the laws of nations have been brought about by individual examples of oppression. Such examples *cannot* be unimportant, for they are, and ever will be, the little hinges on which the great doors of justice are made to turn.'

REFERENCES

House of Commons and House of Lords plus date refer to Hansard entry.

Newspapers are accessible online under date of entry.

The Works of Caroline Norton: details of editions used are given in the Sources on p. 255.

PROLOGUE

1. Norton, *English Laws*, p. 157
2. Caine, *English Feminism*, p. 67
3. Hilton, p. 354
4. Ibid., pp. 357–8
5. Norton, *Stuart of Dunleath*, p. 26
6. B & M, Vol. II, p. 267

CHAPTER ONE

1. Sadleir, *Blessington*, p. 258; (Trelawny) *Letters*, p. 199 note 1
2. Norton, *Undying One*, p. 304
3. Fitzgerald, Vol. I, pp. 2–3
4. GRO T-SK 29/23/387, 29/14/1864
5. Fitzgerald, Vol. I, p. 334
6. Disraeli, *Letters*, Vol. I, p. 334
7. Kemble, Vol. I, p. 282
8. Norton, *Undying One*, pp. 247–9
9. Haydon, Vol. IV, p. 96
10. Hoge & Olney, p. 3
11. Hobhouse, Vol. VI, p. 114
12. *Brownings*, Vol. VI, pp. 347 et seq.
13. PRONI D 1071 BE 3/2; Perkins, p. 155
14. Kelly, *Sheridan*, p. 189, p. 9; Fitzgerald, Vol. I, p. 26
15. Perkins, p. 2
16. Bradford, *Disraeli*, p. 60
17. Kelly, *Sheridan*, pp. 264–5 et seq.
18. Fitzgerald, Vol. I, p. 9
19. Perkins, p. 3
20. Nicolson, p. 20
21. Worsley & Souden, pp. 7 et seq.
22. Atkinson, p. 39
23. History of Parliament, Hon. G. C. Norton
24. GEC, Vol. VI, Grantley, note c
25. Ellis, p. 222

26. B & M, Vol. I, p. 95 and note 8
27. B & M, Vol. II, p. 256
28. Atkinson, p. 49
29. Norton, *English Laws*, p. 27
30. Perkins, p. 15

CHAPTER TWO
1. Airlie, Vol. II, p. 181
2. Perkins, p. 222
3. O'Keeffe, p. 325; Haydon, Vol. IV, p. 449
4. Fitzgerald, Vol. II, pp. 354–5; Adburgham, pp. 192–3, 198; Hobhouse, Vol. IV, p. 27
5. Hardy, *Far from the Madding Crowd*, Ch. 30; PRONI D 3319/8/10
6. Holland, *Journal*, p. 292; Pope-Hennessy, Vol. I, p. 90
7. GRO T-SK 29/20/294; Haydon, Vol. IV, p. 10l
8. *Miss Eden's Letters*, p. 112; Anderson & Zinsser, Vol. II, pp. 124 et seq.; Flanders, p. 50
9. Bradford, p. 61
10. Trollope, Ch. LVII
11. GRO T-SK 29/25/337
12. Forster, p. 27
13. Mitchell, *Bulwer Lytton*, p. 62; Scott, pp. 66–7
14. Hammerton, pp. 120–21
15. Ibid., p. 81; Craig, p. 109 et seq.
16. Tomalin, pp. 58–9
17. Perkins, p. 113
18. Lytton, *Life*, p. 380; Norton, *Sorrows of Rosalie* (Sources)
19. Russell, p. 23; Adburgham, p. 196
20. Atkinson, pp. 63–4
21. *The Times*, 26 December 1828; Chedzoy, p. 65
22. Norton, *The Undying One* (Sources)

23. (NLS) Murray Archives, 7 October 1836
24. Stewart, pp. 31 et seq.; Sadleir, *Blessington*, pp. 210–11; Trollope, *Phineas Finn*, Ch. I.
25. *Fraserian Papers*, pp. lxxxi et seq.
26. Miller, p. 196
27. Molloy, Vol. II, pp. 1–4; pp. 30, 95, 302
28. History of Parliament, Hon. G. C. Norton
29. Byron, *Don Juan*, Canto XI

CHAPTER THREE
1. Haydon, Vol. IV, p. 111; Kemble, Vol. I, pp. 66–7
2. Mitchell, *Melbourne*, p. 56
3. Ibid., p. 6
4. *Holland House Diaries*, p. 300; Kemble, Vol. I, pp. 76–7
5. *Miss Eden's Letters*, p. 258
6. Mitchell, *Melbourne*, pp. 83–5; Brown, p. 112; Ziegler, *Melbourne*, p. 108
7. Mitchell, *Melbourne*, p. 85
8. HALS D/ E L b F 14; Blake, p. 143
9. Hoge & Olney, p. 30
10. B & M, Vol. I, p. 46
11. Ibid., p. 47 and note 6
12. Hoge & Olney, p.25, p.27
13. Craig, p. 17; Pope-Hennessy (I), p. 88
14. Holland, *Journal*, p. 292; GRE C/81/251, 252
15. Blake, p. 114; Belson, Vol. I, p. 118; *Lord Beaconsfield's, Letters*, p. 82
16. Blake, p. 81
17. Adburgham, p. 198
18. Belson, Vol. I, pp. 87–8, p. 110
19. Cecil, pp. 310–14
20. B & M, Vol. II, p. 122

21. Cecil, pp. 362–3; Haydon, Vol. IV, p. 287
22. Wroath, p. 83
23. History of Parliament, Hon. G.C. Norton; Belson, Vol. I, p. 46
24. Belson, Vol. I, p. 121
25. B & M, Vol. I, p. 72; Norton, *English Laws* (Sources), p. 26
26. Forster, *Significant Sisters*, p. 27; Sadleir, *Blessington*, p. 231
27. Norton, *The Wife* (Sources)
28. Haydon, Vol. IV, pp. 184, p. 284
29. Norton, *The Dream* (Sources)
30. Norton, *[The Wife and] Woman's Reward* (Sources)
31. Perkins, p. 71

CHAPTER FOUR
1. B & M, Vol. I, p. 166
2. Adburgham, p. 268
3. Trelawny, *Adventures*, Intro. p. ix
4. Kemble, Vol. III, p. 309
5. Marshall, Vol. I, p. 9
6. Ibid., Vol. II, p. 110
7. (Trelawny) *Letters*, p. 192 note 1
8. PRONI D 1071-F-E-2-7
9. Seymour, *Shelley*, pp. 247–9
10. Ibid., pp. 448, 449; B & M, Vol. I, p. 137 note 1
11. B & M, Vol. I, p. 137
12. Perkins, pp. 67–8
13. Chedzoy, p. 101
14. Atkinson, p. 124
15. Norton, *The Dream*, (Sources) pp. 212–15
16. B & M, Vol. I, p. 139
17. Ibid., pp. 142–3
18. Ibid., p. 143
19. Norton, *The Coquette* (Sources)

20. Mitchell, *Melbourne*, p. 222
21. Acland, p. 65
22. Ellis, p. 25; Chedzoy, p. 154
23. B & M, Vol. I, p. 41
24. Fitzgerald, Vol. II, pp. 404–5
25. Hoge & Olney, pp. 64–5
26. B & M, Vol. I, pp. 173–4
27. Hoge & Olney, pp. 72 et seq.
28. Cecil, p. 36

CHAPTER FIVE
1. B & M, Vol. I, p. 206
2. Stone, p. 5
3. Ibid., pp. 4 et seq.
4. Ibid., pp. 231–2
5. Ibid., pp. 281–2
6. Perkins, p. 85
7. Atkinson, p. 114
8. Ibid., pp. 115–16
9. Wroath, p. 96; Chessell, pp. 9 et seq.; pp. 82–3, p. 99
10. Hoge & Olney, p. 7; Perkins, p. 85
11. Hoge & Olney, pp. 71–2
12. (Trelawny) *Letters*, p. 201
13. Mitchell, *Melbourne*, p. 222
14. Hoge & Olney, p. 73
15. Ibid., pp. 75–6
16. Perkins, p. 92
17. *Holland House Diaries*, p. 345
18. Mitchell, *Melbourne*, p. 214; Hoge & Olney, p. 56
19. Brown, p. 121
20. Hoge & Olney, p. 157
21. Riddell, pp. 13, 21, 234
22. Hoge & Olney, p. 107
23. Perkins, p. 93
24. Ibid., p. 91
25. History of Parliament, Sir John Campbell
26. Wroath, p. 85
27. Haydon, Vol. IV, pp. 352 et seq.
28. Greville, Vol. III , pp. 349–51;

Haydon, Vol. IV, p. 353
29. B & M, Vol. I, p. 200
30. Norton, *The Coquette*, pp. 69–71

CHAPTER SIX
1. Unless otherwise stated, reference is to (TRIAL. *Norton v. Viscount Melbourne*)
2. Dickens, *Pickwick Papers*, Intro., pp. xx–xxi, pp. 454–5
3. Slater, p. 73
4. Marshall, Vol. I, p. 153

CHAPTER SEVEN
1. BL Add MSS 4267 fol. 5; B & M, Vol. I, pp. 204–5
2. Greville, Vol. III, p. 351
3. *The Times*, 23 June and 24 June 1836
4. Greville, Vol. III, p. 351
5. Hickman, p. 153; Austen, *Mansfield Park*, p. 579
6. (NLS) Murray Archives, MS 42507 fol. 5, MS 4088 fols 12–13
7. (NLS) Murray Archives, MS 42507 fols 7–12
8. Norton, A V*oice from the Factories* (Sources)
9. Belson, Vol. I, p. 145
10. Perkins, p. 206
11. Hoge & Olney, p. 107
12. Perkins, p. 101
13. Norton, *Observations on the Natural Claim of the Mother* (Sources)
14. Seymour, *Shelley*, p. 448
15. Belson, Part 2, p.32, p. 38
16. Chedzoy, p. 158
17. Perkins, p. 114
18. Ziegler, *Melbourne*, p. 228
19. Hoge & Olney, p. 11
20. Perkins, p. 112

21. Wright, pp. 175 et seq.
22. Ibid., p. 202
23. House of Commons, 25 April 1857
24. Lytton, *Life*, p. 516
25. Wroath, p. 94
26. Longford, p. 58

CHAPTER EIGHT
1. B & M, Vol. I, p. 313
2. Hoge & Olney, p. 142
3. Wroath, p. 101
4. Craig, pp. 111 et seq.
5. Ibid., p. 114
6. Wroath, p. 102
7. Bod MS Abinger c.49. fol. 100
8. *The Times*, 5 September 1837
9. Ibid., 12 September 1837
10. Hoge & Olney, p. 143
11. Worsley, p. 86
12. Hobhouse, Vol. V, pp. 80 et seq.
13. B & M, Vol. I, p. 299; Hoge & Olney, pp. 148–9
14. B & M, Vol. II, p. 142
15. Cecil, p. 514
16. Norton, *Separation of Mother and Child* (Sources)
17. History of Parliament, Sir Edward Sugden; House of Commons, 21 December 1837 et seq.
18. Wroath, p. 99
19. House of Commons, 14 February 1838
20. House of Commons, 9 May 1838
21. House of Lords, 30 July 1838 et seq.
22. *Creevey*, Vol. I, p. 223
23. Perkins, p. 142
24. House of Lords, 30 July 1838
25. Norton, *Plain Letter to the Lord Chancellor*, p. 70

26. Wroath, p. 93
27. Holcombe, pp. 55 et seq.
28. Wroath, p. 110; Perkins, p. 126
29. Hoge & Olney, p. 97

CHAPTER NINE
1. Caine, p. 57 et seq.
2. *British and Foreign Review*, p. 371
3. B & M, Vol. II, pp. 41–2
4. Ibid., pp. 42–4
5. Norton, *Plain Letter to the Lord Chancellor* (Sources)
6. B & M, Vol. II, p. 57
7. House of Commons, 25 April 1839
8. House of Lords, 18 July 1839 et seq.
9. QVJ, 17 August 1839
10. Wroath, p. 112
11. Linton, 'One of our Legal Fictions', pp. 259–60
12. Stone, p. 158
13. PRONI D 1071/F/A/3/4/1-27
14. B & M, Vol. II, pp. 60–61
15. Hoge & Olney, p. 157
16. QVJ, 4 May 1837, 2 August 1837
17. GEC, Dufferin, Vol. V, pp. 86–7 note g; Haydon, Vol. VI, p. 356
18. Fitzgerald, Vol. II, pp. 55 et seq.
19. Chedzoy, p. 169
20. Perkins, p. 178
21. Hobhouse, Vol. V, p. 280; Longford, p. 151
22. RA RC IN/1085304
23. Horne, Vol. 2, pp. 130 et seq.; Norton, *The Dream* (Sources); Longford, p. 151
24. Perkins, pp. 175 et seq.
25. B & M, Vol. II, pp. 67–8
26. Perkins, p. 162

27. Stone, p. 178
28. Hoge & Olney, p. 107
29. B & M, Vol. II, p. 108
30. Perkins, p. 166
31. Perkins, p. 166; B & M, Vol. II, p. 111
32. GRO T-SK 29/23/40l & 401a

CHAPTER TEN
1. Atkinson, p. 309; Latané, pp. 67–8
2. Belson, Vol. I, pp. 155–6
3. B & M, Vol. II, p. 150
4. Ibid., pp. 156–7
5. Ibid., p. 152
6. Ibid., p. 152
7. Stanmore, Vol. II, p. 399
8. Malmesbury, p. 173
9. Craig, p. 136
10. Haydon, Vol. IV, pp. 13 et seq.
11. Ibid., p. 107
12. Ibid., p. 226
13. Dickens, *Letters*, Vol. II, p. 73 note 3
14. B & M, Vol. II, p. 96
15. Boase, pp. 319–58
16. BL Add MSS 402526 fol. 3122
17. Norton, *The Child of the Islands* (Sources)
18. Moore, *The Summer Fete*, dedication
19. Atkinson, pp. 321–3; Perkins, p. 184
20. B & M, Vol. II, p. 154
21. Perkins, p. 195
22. B & M, Vol. II, p. 195
23. Brontë, *The Tenant of Wildfell Hall*, pp. 14, 371; Merchant, Brontë, p. xvii

CHAPTER ELEVEN
1. *The Times*, 4 December 1845
2. Pope-Hennessy (1), pp. 243–4

3. Hoge & Olney, p. 3
4. Meredith, *Diana of the Crossways*, p. 403
5. Foster, pp.144 et seq.
6. Ibid., pp. 170–71
7. Ibid., p. 114
8. Latané, p. 178
9. Pope-Hennessy (1), pp. 110–11
10. B & M, Vol. II, pp. 178–9
11. Ibid.
12. Cecil, pp. 525–6 et seq.; Ziegler, *Melbourne*, p. 360; Cecil, p. 531
13. B & M, Vol. II, p. 148
14. Hoge & Olney, p. 165
15. B & M, Vol. II, p. 212
16. Ibid., pp. 210–11
17. Ibid., p. 210
18. Perkins, p. 213
19. Ibid.
20. B & M, Vol. II, p. 212
21. Chessell, p. 102
22. Ibid., p. 101
23. Norton, *Letters to the Mob* (Sources)
24. B & M, Vol. II, p. 183
25. Perkins, p. 203
26. DHC D/SHE /11
27. Atkinson, p. 344

CHAPTER TWELVE
1. Bod MS Abinger 49 fol. 100
2. Holcombe, p. 55 et seq.
3. Norton, *Stuart of Dunleath* (Sources)
4. B & M, Vol. II, p. 266
5. Ibid., p. 259
6. Atkinson, p. 359; *Brownings' Correspondence*, Vol. IX, pp. 311–13
7. B & M, Vol. III, p. 306; Foster, pp. 170–8
8. Clough, p. 11
9. B & M, Vol. II, p. 256

10. Perkins, p. 256
11. Holcombe pp. 55 et seq.; Chessell, p. 104
12. Perkins, p. 227
13. GRO T-SK 29/5/108
14. Acland, pp. 209–10
15. Perkins, pp. 229 et seq.
16. Chessell, p. 104
17. *The Times*, 20 August 1853; 24 August 1853; 2 September 1853

CHAPTER THIRTEEN
1. Norton, *English Laws* (Sources)
2. PRONI D 1071-F-A-3-4
3. B & M, Vol. III, pp. 310 et seq.
4. Linton, 'One of our Legal Fictions', p. 257
5. *Brownings' Correspondence*, Vol. IX, pp. 311–13
6. Macnaghten, p. 7
7. B & M, Vol. II, p. 350
8. Ibid., p. 343
9. Ibid., p. 338
10. Rauchbauer, pp. 335–9
11. Macnaghten, p. 9
12. B & M, Vol. II, p. 358
13. Shanley, pp. 355–76
14. Norton, A *Letter to the Queen* (Sources); Chedzoy, pp. 246–7
15. *Law Review*, 23, p. 181
16. Bodichon, *American Diary*, p. 47
17. GRO T-SK 29/6/310; B & M, Vol. I, p. 184 and note
18. House of Lords, 28 May 1857
19. Stone, p. 383

CHAPTER FOURTEEN
1. Bucks D/RA/A2c/11/7/1
2. *Songs of the Holy Land* (Sources)
3. Belson, Vol. II, p. 344; *Burke's*

Peerage, Stirling-Maxwell
4. Belson, Vol. II, p. 290
5. B & M, Vol. III, p. 82; GRO T-SK 29/13/233
6. GRO T-SK 28/12/1862
7. *Stirlings of Keir*, pp. 82 et seq.
8. B & M, Vol. III, p. 61
9. GRO T-SK 29/6/21
10. PRONI D 1071-F-AS-3-4; Perkins, p. 216
11. Bod MS 17906 Hungerford Pollen
12. Hammerton, p. 119
13. Belson, Vol. II, p. 318
14. B & M, Vol. III, pp. 18–19
15. Carlyle, Lecture II, 'The Hero as Prophet', p. xix
16. Mayhew, p. 314; Belson, Vol. II, p. 45
17. BM Add MS 52126 fol. 159
18. BM Add MS 52126 fol. 59 note 4
19. GRO T-SK 15/210
20. B & M, Vol. III, pp. 34–5
21. Fitzgerald, Vol. II, p. 444; Perkins, p. 365
22. Norton, Perkins, pp. 268–70
23. Norton, *The Lady of la Garaye* (Sources)
24. Wilson, *Prince Albert*, p. 384
25. B & M, Vol. III, p. 61
26. Atkinson, pp. 408–9
27. GEC, Lansdowne, Vol. VII, pp. 439–40

CHAPTER FIFTEEN
1. Belson, Vol. II, p. 292
2. GRO T-SK 29/28/64; B & M, Vol. III, p. 57
3. PRONI D 1071- F-A-3-4; Belson, Vol. II, p. 387; GRO T-SK 29/12/20
4. GRO T-SK 29/15/253
5. B & M, Vol. III, p. 58

6. Ibid., p. 59
7. Belson, p. 360
8. B & M, Vol. III, p. 53
9. GRO T-SK 29/14/255
10. B & M, Vol. III, p. 77
11. Gailey, p. 118
12. Norton, *Lost and Saved* (Sources)
13. B & M, Vol. III, pp. 85–6
14. *The Times*, 23 June 1863; Atkinson, p. 410; Chedzoy, p. 275
15. Craig, p. 55; Belson, Vol. II, p. 339
16. *The Times*, 22 May 1863
17. GRO T-SK 29/28/165, 29/15/20
18. GRO T-SK 29/14/2220
19. B & M, Vol. III, p. 107
20. Belson, Vol. II, p. 53
21. GRO T-SK 29/66/105
22. GRO T-SK 29/68/55
23. Belson, Vol. II, p. 347
24. GRO T-SK 29/17/20
25. GRO T-SK 29/19/256
26. GRO T-SK 29/19/ 256a, 270
27. GRO T-SK 29/15/206, 225
28. Norton, *Old Sir Douglas* (Sources)
29. QVJ, 25 May 1975; B & M, Vol. III, pp. 124–5

CHAPTER SIXTEEN
1. B & M, Vol. III, p. 176
2. Olusoga, p. 16; GRO T-SK MM 219/14/215
3. Morley, Vol. II, pp. 252–3
4. B & M, Vol. III, p. 179
5. Ibid., p. 278
6. Kemble, Vol. I, p. 289
7. B & M, Vol. III, p. 274
8. GRO T-SK 29/18/93
9. GRO T-SK 29/18/94
10. GRO T-SK /29/28/12; Harrow

Archives
11. GRO T-SK 29/22/377
12. Belson, Vol. II, p. 403; GRO
    T-SK 29/25/331, GRO T-SK
    29/17/136
13. GRO T-SK 29/25/331
14. B & M, Vol. III, p. 130
15. GRO T-SK 29/25/339, 310
16. GRO T-SK 29/25/316
17. GRO T-SK 29/26/234; 248;
    Belson, Vol. II, p. 414
18. GRO T-SK 29/26/218; 234;
    Belson, Vol I, p.357
19. B & M, Vol. III, pp. 292–3
20. Ibid., p. 296
21. Ibid., p. 293; GRO T-SK
    29/27/106, 110
22. GRO T-SK 21/14/215; Perkins,
    p. 296
23. B & M, Vol. III, p. 293

24. GRO T-SK 29/71/B/Q
25. GRO T-SK 29/71/B9
26. B & M, Vol. III, p. 295
27. Ibid., p. 298 and note
28. Stirling Diary, 14 June 1877,
    GRO T-SK 28/16/i–xiv
29. Stirling Diary, 21 June; GRO
    T-SK 28/16/i–xiv
30. See Grantley, *Silver Spoon*,
    passim
31. Ibid., p. 16

EPILOGUE
1. Gailey, p. 388
2. Ibid., pp. 316–17
3. Milton, *Lycidas*, I. 64
4. *Athenaeum*, 23 June 1877, p.
   797
5. Linton, *Rebel of the Family*, p.
   413

SOURCES

NOTE: Hardback edition and place of publication London, unless otherwise stated.

Acland, Alice, *Caroline Norton*, 1948

Adburgham, Alison, *Silver Fork. Society, Fashionable Life and Literature from 1814 to 1848*, 1983

Airlie, Mabell, Countess of, *Lady Palmerston and her Times*, 2 vols, 1922

Anderson, Bonnie S. and Zinsser, Judith P., *A History of Their Own. Women in Europe from Prehistory to the Present*, Vol. II, pbk, 1990

Arnold, Arthur, *The Hon. Mrs. Norton and Married Women. The Married Women's Property Committee*, Manchester 1878, reprint 1987 *The Athenaeum*, no. 2591, 23 June 1877

Atkinson, Diane, *The Criminal Conversation of Mrs. Norton*, pbk, 2013

Austen, Jane, *Mansfield Park*, Ultratype edns, 1971

(B & M) Belson, Ross and Mulvey-Roberts, Marie, *The Selected Letters of Caroline Norton*, 3 vols, 2020

Lord Beaconsfield's Letters, New Edn. Edited by his Brother, 1887

Bell v. Murray Case. 'Issue, in Which the Case in which Alexander Bell, Teacher in Dundee in Pursuit, and William Murray, now or lately Rector of the Dundee Academy is Defender', 16 December 1833, Edinburgh

Belson, Ross, *A Rediscovered Life: A Selective Annotated Edition of the Letters of Caroline Elizabeth Norton, 1828–1877*, 2 vols, Faculty of Arts and Cultural Industries, University of the West of England, Bristol, 2016

(BL) British Library, London

Blake, Robert, *Disraeli*, New York, 1967

Boase, T. S. R., 'Decoration of the New Palace of Westminster 1841–1863', *Journal of the Warburg and Courtauld Institutes*, Vol. 17, Nos 3/4, 1954

Bodichon, Barbara Leigh Smith, *An American Diary 1857–1858*, ed. Joseph W. Read Jr, 1972

(Bod) Bodleian Library, Oxford

Bodichon, Barbara Leigh Smith, *Women at Work*, New York, 1859

Bostridge, Mark, *Florence Nightingale. The Woman and her Legend*, pbk, 2009

Bradford, Sarah, *Disraeli*, pbk, 1996

The British and Foreign Review, or European Quarterly Journal, Vol. VII, July–October 1838

Brontë, Anne, *The Tenant of Wildfell Hall*, Introduction and Notes by Peter Merchant, pbk, Ware, Herts, 2001

Broomfield, Andrea L., 'Much more than an Antifeminist: Elizabeth Lynn Linton's Contribution to the Rise of Victorian Popular Journalism', *Victorian Literature and Culture*, Vol. 29, No. 2 (2001)

Brophy, Julia and Smart, Carol, 'From Disregard to Disrepute: The Position of Women in Family Law', *Feminist Review*, No. 9, 1981

Brown, Colin, *Lady M. The Life and Loves of Elizabeth Lamb, Viscountess Melbourne, 1751–1818*, 2018

The Brownings' Correspondence, Vols IV–XIII, ed. Philip Kelley and Scott Lewis, 1986–95

(Bucks) Centre for Buckinghamshire Studies, Aylesbury, Bucks

Burke's Genealogical and Heraldic History of the Peerage, Baronetage and Knightage, ed. Peter Townend, 1970

Burton, Hester, *Barbara Bodichon 1827–1891*, 1949

Caine, Barbara, *English Feminism 1780–1980*, Oxford 1997

Carlyle, Thomas, *On Heroes, Hero-Worship, and the Heroic in History*, pbk, Amazon, n.d.

Cecil, Lord David, *The Young Melbourne & Lord M.*, pbk, 2001

Chedzoy, Alan, *A Scandalous Woman. The Story of Caroline Norton*, pbk, 1992

Chessell, Antony, *The Life and Times of Abraham Hayward Q.C., Victorian Essayist*, rev. edn, 2009

Clough, Arthur Hugh, *Mari Magno, Dipsychus and other Poems*, ed. Anthony Kenny, Manchester, 2014

Craig, Randall, *The Narratives of Caroline Norton*, New York, 2009

The Creevey Papers, ed. Sir Herbert Maxwell, 2 vols, 1904

(DHC) Dorset History Centre, Dorchester

Dickens, Charles, *Hard Times. For These Times*, ed. and with an Introduction and Notes by Kate Flint, pbk, 2003

Dickens, Charles, *The Posthumous Papers of the Pickwick Club*, ed. and with an Introduction and Notes by Mark Wormald, pbk, 2003

Dickens, Charles, *The Letters of Charles Dickens*, ed. Madeline House and Graham Storey, Vol. II, Oxford, 1969

Disraeli, Benjamin, *Letters*, Vol. I, *1815–1834*, ed. J. A. W. Gunn, John Matthews, Donald M. Schurman and M. G. Wiebe, Toronto, 1982

Dolin, Kieran, 'The Transfigurations of Caroline Norton', *Victorian Literature and Culture*, Vol. 30, No. 2, Cambridge, 2002

Miss Eden's Letters, ed. by her great-niece, Violet Dickinson, 1919

Mrs Ellis, *The Women of England. Their Social Duties and Domestic Habit*, pbk reprint, New York, 2012

Finch, Marianne, *The Englishwoman in America*, 1853

Fitzgerald, Percy, *Lives of the Sheridans*, 2 vols, 1886

Flanders, Judith, *Inside the Victorian Home. A Portrait of Domestic Life in Victorian England*, pbk, New York, 2006

Forster, Margaret, *Significant Sisters. The Grassroots of Active Feminism 1839–1939*, pbk, 1986

Foster, R. E., *Sidney Herbert. Too Short A Life*, pbk, Gloucester, 2019

Fraser, Antonia, *The King and the Catholics. The Fight for Rights 1829*, 2018

The Fraserian Papers of the late William Maginn, L.L.D. Annotated with a Life of the Author, ed. R. Shelton Mackenzie, New York, 1857, reprint

Gailey, Andrew, *The Lost Imperialist. Lord Dufferin, Memory and Mythmaking in an Age of Celebrity*, 2015

(GEC) G. E. Cockayne, *The Complete Peerage of England, Scotland, Ireland, Great Britain and the United Kingdom*, 13 vols, reprint, 1982

Graner, Elisabeth Rose, 'Plotting the Mother: Caroline Norton, Helen Huntingdon, and Isabel Vane', *Tulsa Studies in Women's Literature*, Vol. 16, No. 2, 1997, University of Tulsa

(Grantley) *Silver Spoon. Being Extracts from the Random Reminiscences of Lord Grantley*, ed. Mary and Alan Wood, 1954

(Grantley) *Silver Teaspoon. The Colourful Early Life and Times of the 6th Lord Grantley (1892–1954)*, Aspects of Markenfield 9, the Friends of Markenfield, 2019

Granville, Harriet, Countess, *Letters 1810–1845*, ed. her son The Hon. F. Leveson Gower, 2 vols, 2nd edn, 1894

(GRE) Grey MSS, Durham University Library, Durham

The Greville Memoirs: A Journal of the Reign of King George IV and King William IV, ed. Henry Reeve, 3 vols 2nd edn, 1974

The Greville Memoirs 1814–1860, ed. Lytton Strachey and Roger Fulford, Vol. IV, 1938

(GRO) Glasgow Record Office, Glasgow City Archives, Glasgow

Hammerton, A. James, *Cruelty and Companionship. Conflict in 19th Century Married Life*, pbk, 1995

(HALS) Hertfordshire Archive and Local Studies, Hertford

(Hansard) http:/ / hansard.millbanksystems.com/commons; http://millbanksystems.com/lords

Hardy, Thomas, *Far from the Madding Crowd*, Ware, Herts, pbk, 1993

Harrow Archives, Harrow School, Middlesex

(Haydon) *The Diary of Benjamin Robert Haydon*, Vols IV and V, ed. Willard Bissell Pope, Cambridge, Mass., 1963

Hickman, Katie, *Courtesans*, pbk, 2004

Hilton, Boyd, *A Mad, Bad and Dangerous People? England 1783–1846*, pbk, 2006

Hirsch, Pam, *Barbara Leigh Smith Bodichon, 1827–1891: Feminist, Artist and Rebel*, 1998

History of Parliament. http//www.historyofparliamentonline.org

(Hobhouse) Lord Broughton (John Cam Hobhouse), *Recollections of a Long Life*, ed. Lady Dorchester, Vols IV, V and VI, 1910–11

Hoge, James O. and Olney, Clarke, *The Letters of Caroline Norton to Melbourne*, Columbus, Ohio, 1974

Holcombe, Lee, *Wives and Property. Reform of the Married Woman's Property Law in 19th Century England*, Toronto, pbk, 1983

Holdsworth, Sir William, *A History of English Law*, Vol. XIV, 1903

The Holland House Diaries, 1831–1840, ed. with an Introductory Essay and Notes by Abraham D. Kriegel, 1977

(Holland, *Journal*) *The Journal of the Hon. Henry Edward Fox (afterwards 4th and last Lord Holland)*, ed. Earl of Ilchester, 1923

Horne, R. H., *A New Spirit of the Age*, 2 vols, 1844

House of Commons – see (Hansard)

House of Lords – see (Hansard)

Kaye, J. W., 'The "Non-Existence" of Women', *The North British Review*, August 1855, Vol. XXIII, Edinburgh, 1885

Kelly, Linda, *Richard Brinsley Sheridan. A Life*, 1997
Kelly, Ronan, *Bard of Erin. The Life of Thomas Moore*, Dublin, 2008
Kemble, Frances Ann, *Record of a Girlhood*, 3 vols, 1878

Lacey, Candida (ed.), *Barbara Leigh Smith Bodichon and the Langham Place Circle*, 1987
Lamb, A. R., *Can Woman Regenerate Society?*, 1844
Langland, Elizabeth, *Nobody's Angels: Middle-Class Women and Domestic Ideology in Victorian Culture*, Ithaca, NY, 1995
Latané, David E., Jr, 'Two Letters from Caroline Norton to Charles Westmacott', *Notes and Queries*, March 2005
The Law Review, 23, 1855–6, Article XIV, 'Hon. Mrs. Norton's Letter to the Queen'
Leigh-Smith, Barbara (Mme Bodichon), *A Brief Summary in Plain Language of the Most Important Laws of England Concerning Women*, 1854
Lewis, Sarah, *Woman's Mission*, 7th edn, 1840
Linton, Elizabeth Lynn, 'One of our Legal Fictions', *Household Words*, Vol. IX, No. 214
Linton, Elizabeth Lynn, *The Rebel of the Family*, ed. Deborah H. Meen, Peterborough, Ontario, 2002
Longford, Elizabeth, *Victoria R.I.*, 1964
Lyall, Sir Alfred, *The Life of the Marquess of Dufferin and Ava*, 2 vols, 1905
Lytton, Victor Bulwer, Earl of, *The Life of Edward Bulwer, First Lord Lytton*, 1913

Daniel Maclise, 1806–1870, with an Introduction by Richard Ormond, National Portrait Gallery, London/Arts Council of Great Britain, 1972
Macnaghten, A. I., 'Some Letters of Caroline Norton', *Notes and Queries*, January 1949
Malmesbury, Rt. Hon. The Earl of, *Memoirs of an Ex-Minister. An Autobiography*, new edn, 1885
Markenfield Hall Caroline Norton Exhibition and Guide, with

an Introduction by Diane Atkinson, Markenfield Hall, 2018

Marshall, Mrs Julian, *The Life and Letters of Mary Wollstonecraft Shelley*, 2 vols, 1889

Matoff, Susan, *Marguerite, Countess of Blessington. The Turbulent Life of a Salonnière and Author*, Newark, Delaware, 2016

Meredith, George, *Diana of the Crossways*, with a new Introduction by Lorna Sage, pbk, 1985

Miller, Lucasta, *L.E.L. The Lost Life and Scandalous Death of Letitia Elizabeth Landon, the celebrated 'Female Byron'*, New York, 2019

Mitchell, Leslie, *Bulwer Lytton. The Rise and Fall of a Victorian Man of Letters*, 2003

Mitchell, L. G., *Lord Melbourne 1779–1848*, Oxford, 1997

Molloy, J. Fitzgerald, *The Most Gorgeous Lady Blessington*, 2 vols, 1896

Moore, Thomas, *The Summer Fete*, 1831

Morley, John, *The Life of William Ewart Gladstone*, 3 vols, 1903

Murray Archives – see (NLS)

Nicolson, Harold, *Helen's Tower*, 1937

(NLS) National Library of Scotland, Edinburgh, Works of Caroline Norton

The Child of the Islands. A Poem. By the Hon. Mrs Norton, 2nd edn, 1846

The Coquette, and Other Tales and Sketches. In Prose and Verse, 2 vols, 1835, reprint

The Dream and Other Poems, 1840, reprint Washington D.C., 2001

English Laws for Women in the Nineteenth Century, 1854, reprint, with an Introduction by Joan Huddleston, Chicago, Illinois, 1982

'The Invalid's Mother, to the Sun, at Lisbon', Dorset Archives

The Lady of la Garaye. By the Hon. Mrs Norton, 1862

A Letter to the Queen on Lord Chancellor Cranworth's Marriage and Divorce Bill, 1855, reprint, Dodo Press

Letters to the Mob by Libertas, 1848, reprint, Victorian
  Women Writers' Project
Lost and Saved, 2 vols, 1862, reprint
*Observations on the Natural Claim of the Mother to
  the Custody of her Infant Children, as affected by the
  Common Law Right of the Father*, 1837
Old Sir Douglas, 2 vols, 1867, reprint
*A Plain Letter to the Lord Chancellor on the Infant Custody
  Bill* by Pearce Stevenson, Esq., 1839 reprint
*The Separation of Mother and Child by the Law of 'Custody
  of Infants', Considered*, 1838
The Sorrows of Rosalie: with Other Poems, 1829, reprint
Stuart of Dunleath. A Story of Modern Times, 3 vols, 1851,
  reprint
The Undying One; Sorrows of Rosalie And Other Poems,
  New York, 1854, reprint
A Voice from the Factories, 1836, reprint
The Wife and Woman's Reward, 3 vols, 1835, reprint

O'Keeffe, Paul, *A Genius for Failure. The Life of Benjamin
  Robert Haydon*, 2009
Olney, Clarke, 'Caroline Norton and Lord Melbourne',
  Victorian Studies, Vol. 8, No. 3, 1965
Olusoga, David, 'Hidden Histories', *BBC History Magazine*,
  July 2020
Onslow, Barbara, *Women of the Press in Nineteenth-Century
  Britain*, 2000

Parker, Sarah E. et al., *The Hampton Court Palace Community
  1750–1950*, pbk, 2005
Perkins, Jane Gray, *The Life of the Honourable Mrs. Norton*,
  pbk, New York, 1909
Poovey, Mary, *Unseen Developments. The Ideological Work of
  Gender in Mid-Victorian England*, pbk, 1989
Pope-Hennessy, James (I), *Monckton Milnes. The Years of
  Promise 1809–1851*, 1949
Pope, Willard Wissell, *Invisible Friends. The Correspondence of*

Elizabeth Barrett Browning and Benjamin Robert Haydon, Cambridge, Mass., 1972

Pope-Hennessy, James (II), *Monckton Milnes. The Flight of Youth 1851–1885*, 1955

(PRONI) Public Record Office, Northern Ireland, Belfast

(QVJ) Queen Victoria's Journals, http://www/queenvictorias journals

(RA) Royal Archives, Windsor Castle

Rauchbauer, Hans Otto, 'Some Unrecorded Letters of Caroline Norton', *Notes and Queries*, Vol. 17, No. 9, 1970

Riddell, John M., *Eve's Herbs. A History of Contraception and Abortion in the West*, Cambridge, Mass., 1997

Ridley, Jane, *Victoria. Queen, Matriarch, Empress*, 2015

Rover, Constance, *Love, Morals and the Feminists*, 1970

Russell, G. R., *Collections and Recollections*, 1898

Letters of Runnymede. Series of Nineteen Open Letters, 18 January 1836–15 May 1836, Anon.

Sadleir, Michael, *Bulwer: Panorama. Edward and Rosina 1803–1836*, 1936

Sadleir, Michael, *Blessington-D'Orsay. A Masquerade*, new edn, New York, 1947

Scott, Jeremy, *Women Who Dared to Break All the Rules*, 2019

Seymour, Miranda, *In Byron's Wake. The Turbulent Lives of Lord Byron's Wife and Daughter: Annabella Milbanke and Ada Lovelace*, 2018

Seymour, Miranda, *Mary Shelley*, pbk, 2000

Shanley, Mary Lyndon, '"One Must Ride behind": Married Women's Rights and the Divorce Act of 1857', *Victorian Studies*, Vol. 25, No. 3, Spring 1982

Shattock, Joanne (ed.), *Journalism and the Periodical Press in Nineteenth-Century Britain*, Cambridge, 2017

Slater, Michael, *Charles Dickens*, 2009

Songs of the Holy Land, Edinburgh, 1846 (Sir William Stirling-Maxwell, 1818–1878)

Stanmore, Lord, *Sidney Herbert. Lord Herbert of Lea. A Memoir*, 2 vols, 1906

Stewart, David, 'The Magazine and Literary Culture', in Joanne Shattock (ed.), *Journalism and the Periodical Press in Nineteenth-Century Britain*, Cambridge, 2017

St Clair, William, *Trelawny. The Incurable Romancer*, 1977

Stirling Papers (Maxwell Muniments) – see (GRO)

The Stirlings of Keir, and their Family Papers, William Fraser, privately printed, Edinburgh, 1858

Stone, Lawrence, *Road to Divorce. England 1530–1987*, Oxford, reprint 2003

Tomalin, Claire, *The Life and Death of Mary Wollstonecraft*, rev. pbk edn, 1992

Trelawny, Edward John, *Letters of Edward John Trelawny*, ed. with a brief Introduction and Notes by H. Buxton Forman, C.B., 1910

Trelawny, Edward John, *Adventures of a Younger Son*, ed. and with an Introduction by William St Clair, reprint 1974

(TRIAL. *Norton* v. *Viscount Melbourne*) *Extraordinary Trial!* Fifth edition, 1836. Price Sixpence.

Norton v. *Viscount Melbourne*, for CRIM.CON. Damages laid at £10,000! A full and accurate report of this remarkable Trial taken in short hand by an eminent Reporter expressly for this edition, containing the Attorney General's reply, – the Letters-Examination of Witnesses, etc. Embellished with a PORTRAIT AND MEMOIR. London; W. Marshall, 1 Holborn Bars

Trollope, Anthony, *Can You Forgive Her?*, pbk, 2012

Van Thal, Herbert, *Eliza Lynn Linton. The Girl of the Period, A Biography*, 1979

Victoria, Queen *The Letters of Queen Victoria*, ed. Arthur Christopher Benson and Viscount Esher, 3 vols, 1908

Walkowitz, Judith, *Prostitution and Victorian Society: Women, Class and the State*, Cambridge, 1980

Warner, Marina, *Monuments and Maidens. The Allegory of the Female Form*, pbk, 1996

Wilson, A. N., *Prince Albert. The Man who Saved the Monarchy*, 2019

Wilson, A. N., *The Victorians*, pbk, 2002

Wise, Sarah, *Inconvenient People. Lunacy, Liberty and the Mad-Doctors in Victorian England*, pbk, 2013

Wollstonecraft, Mary, *A Vindication of the Rights of Woman*, Seven Treasures Publications, US reprint, 2010

Worsley, Lucy and Souden, David, *Hampton Court Palace. The Official Illustrated History*, 2005

Worsley, Lucy, *Queen Victoria. Daughter, Wife, Mother, Widow*, 2018

Wright, Danaya C., 'The Crisis of Child Custody: A History of the Birth of Family Law in England', *Columbia Journal of Gender and Law*, Vol. 11, No. 2, 2002

Wroath, John, *Until They Are Seven. The Origins of Women's Legal Rights*, Winchester, 1998

Ziegler, Philip, *King William IV*, Newton Abbot, 1973

Ziegler, Philip, *Melbourne. A Biography of William Lamb, 2nd Viscount Melbourne*, pbk, 2013

ACKNOWLEDGEMENTS

I wish to thank Her Majesty the Queen for permission to reproduce a poem from the Royal Archives. I am most grateful to Archibald Stirling of Keir and William Stirling of Keir for advice on the Maxwell Muniments (Stirling Papers) in the Glasgow Record Office, as also to Barbara Neilson, Archivist; and to Angus Lyon for his invaluable research there on my behalf. Lord Grantley and Lady Deirdre Curteis of Markenfield Hall were kind and supportive; as was Sarah Robson, the Archivist and Administrator; and I am grateful to Lord Grantley for advice on George Norton's portrait. Jamie Andrews of the British Library was as usual extremely helpful.

I am grateful to Sir Mark Hendrick MP, who enabled me to inspect the portrait of Caroline Norton as Justice in the House of Lords; and to Rupert Gavin, Chairman, Historic Palaces, who arranged an expedition to Hampton Court Palace, together with Polly Putnam.

I thank the following in particular for help over documents: the late Marchioness of Dufferin and Ava and Lola Armstrong, Curator of the Clandeboye Estate, Bangor, Co. Down; Gillian Hunt, Ulster Historical Foundation, Public Record Office of Northern Ireland, Belfast; Lisa Dotzauer, Bodleian Library, Oxford; Ann Dinsdale, Principal Curator, Brontë Parsonage Museum; Mrs June Wailling, Archivist, Centre for Buckingham Studies, Aylesbury; Emelia Clark, Dorset History Centre, Dorchester; Mike Harkness, Senior Search Room Assistant, Durham University Library Archives and Special Collections, Durham; Joshua Insley, Interim Archivist, Eton College; Miss Tace Fox, Archivist,

Harrow School; Lynne Burton, Hertfordshire Archives and Local Studies, Hertford; Kirsty McHugh and Malcolm Anderson, John Murray Archives, National Library of Scotland, Edinburgh.

There have been several previous biographies of Caroline Norton; chronologically they range from that of Emily Perkins, a special source because it was first published in 1909 in the lifetime of Caroline Norton's grandchildren, and Diane Atkinson in 2012; from all of these I have derived benefit, gratefully acknowledged in the References. During the writing of this book, Ross Belson and Marie Mulvey-Roberts also published their peerless *The Selected Letters of Caroline Norton*, of enormous benefit to scholars.

I am grateful to the following in many different ways: Lord (Kenneth) Baker of Dorking; the Duchess of Beaufort; Mark Bostridge; Dr Ambrogio Caiani; Sarah Bradford; Eliza Chisholm; Honor Fitzgerald for legal research into the trial at an early stage; Dr R. E. Foster; Richard Gaunt; Dr Andrew Gailey; the late Linda Kelly for expertise on the subject of the Sheridans; Sir Anthony Kenny, especially for the reference to Arthur Hugh Clough; Alan Mallinson; Lucasta Miller; Dr Leslie Mitchell for helpful criticism; Valerie Pakenham; Professor Munro Price; Rozzy Wyatt Puttnam; Julian Sands for advice over portraits of Caroline Norton; Dr Ruth Scurr; Emma Sergeant; Miranda Seymour; Nan Steele; Hugo Vickers; A. N. Wilson.

The team at Weidenfeld & Nicolson were encouraging and helpful at all times, led by Alan Samson and Lucinda McNeile; I am most grateful to them, including Linden Lawson as copy-editor, Sue Phillpott as proofreader, Christopher Phipps as indexer and Cathy Dunn as picture researcher. Lastly, I wish to acknowledge the many people who encouraged and helped me during the writing of this book, much of which took place during the recent lockdown. These include my agent, Jonathan Lloyd, and, at home, the late Linda Peskin, followed by Pascale Clark. My family, many of them writers, were always a support, with special thanks to Atalanta Fitzgerald and Damian Fraser, who read the book at different stages and responded with enthusiasm.

LIST OF ILLUSTRATIONS

15 Lord Melbourne, Prime Minister of Great Britain, by Sir George Hayter (World History Archive/Alamy Stock Photo)

16 Sir William Stirling-Maxwell (Chronicle/Alamy Stock Photo)

17 Sidney Herbert, later Lord Herbert of Lea (National Portrait Gallery, London)

18 Edward John Trelawny (Picture Art Collection/Alamy Stock)

19 Caricature of Caroline with Lord Melbourne (Hamza Khan/Alamy Stock Photo)

20 Bust of Caroline by Francis John Williamson, 1873 (National Portrait Gallery, London)

21 Bust of Sir William Stirling-Maxwell by Francis John Williamson, 1873 (National Portrait Gallery, London)

22 'Farewell' from *The Sorrows of Rosalie: with Other Poems* by Caroline Norton published in 1829 (courtesy of Lady Deirdre and Ian Curteis, Markenfield Hall)

23 Mariucca Federigo (courtesy of Lady Deirdre and Ian Curteis, Markenfield Hall)

24 Albumen *carte de visite* by John and Charles Watkins, 1863 (Pictorial Press/Alamy)

25 Caroline with her grandchildren, Carlotta and Richard (courtesy of Lady Deirdre and Ian Curteis, Markenfield Hall)

26 *The Spirit of Justice*, tempura mural painting by Daniel Maclise, 1847-9 (Parliamentary Art Collection/www.parliament.uk/art)

INDEX

72

INDEX

Branden, William Crosbie, 4th Baron, 36–7

Brighton, 14, 54, 223

Brin/Brinny *see* Norton, (Thomas) Brinsley (later 4th Baron Grantley; CN's son)

British and Foreign Review (journal), 125–6, 127

Brocket Hall (Hertfordshire), 39, 159–60

Brodie, Sir Benjamin, 108

Brontë, Anne, *The Tenant of Wildfell Hall*, 153

Brontë, Charlotte, *Jane Eyre*, 153

Brookfield, Revd William, 102

Brougham and Vaux, Henry Brougham, 1st Baron, 119–20, 127–8, 145

Brown, Hannah, murder victim, 109–10

Browning, Elizabeth Barrett, 15, 135, 173, 185, 186, 192

Brummel, Beau, 143

Bulleman, Thomas, 86

Bulwer Lytton, Edward (*later* 1st Baron Lytton), 45, 244; marriage and children, 26, 105, 224, 230; on the Irish, 4; on Lady Caroline Lamb, 37; on reign of William IV, 39–40; on William Maginn, 32; *England and the English*, 39–40

Bulwer-Lytton, Robert *see* Lytton, Robert Bulwer-Lytton, 1st Earl of

Bulwer Lytton, Rosina (*later* Lady Lytton), 230

Burke, Edmund: on domestic servants, 89; on feminine delicacy, xvi–xvii, 123

Bury, Lady Charlotte, 45

Bushy Park (Middlesex), 30, 54

Byron, George Gordon, 6th Baron, 30, 36, 50, 52–3, 102; CN compared to, 135; *Don Juan*, 33

Callander, Henrietta Caroline *see* Sheridan, Henrietta

Campbell, Sir John (*later* 1st Baron Campbell), Attorney General: background, character and early

career, 75–6; counsel in *Norton* v. *Melbourne* Crim. Con. trial, 80, 84–90, 93, 161; on Infant Custody Bill, 106

Canning, George, 5

Capri, 186, 213, 231, 232, 239

Carlisle, George Howard, 6th Earl of, 174

Carlyle, Thomas, 32; *On Heroes and Hero-Worship*, 206

Caroline *see* Norton, Caroline (*née* Sheridan)

Caroline, Queen Consort of George IV, trial, 80, 119

Carroll, Lewis, 189

Cassiobury House (Hertfordshire), 217

Catholic Emancipation, xv, 17, 118, 154, 183, 194

Chamberlaine, Frances (*later* Sheridan), 8, 9

Chapel Thorpe Hall (Yorkshire), 137

Chappell (music publishers), 230

Charles II, King, 190

Charlotte, Princess of Wales, 151

Chartists, 163–5

child custody laws *see* Guardianship of Infants Act; Infant Custody Acts

Clandeboye (Co. Down), 182, 203, 214

Clarence, Adelaide, Duchess of *see* Adelaide, Queen Consort

Clarence, Prince William, Duke of *see* William IV, King

Clarke, Mary Cowden, 51

Clifford, Sir Augustus, 143

Clough, Arthur Hugh, *Dipsychus*, 174

Cobden, Richard, 154

Colburn and Bentley (publishers), 31

Coleridge, Hartley, 135

Coleridge, Samuel Taylor, 32

Conroy, Sir John, 106

consumption, 9, 99, 166, 208, 231, 239

Conyngham, Francis Conyngham, 2nd Marquess, 126

Copley, John Singleton, 118

copyright, for married women writers, xvi, 44, 193